MW01134934

SOVIET POLICY TOWARD EAST GERMANY RECONSIDERED

RECENT TITLES IN
CONTRIBUTIONS IN POLITICAL SCIENCE
SERIES EDITOR: BERNARD K. JOHNPOLL

SOVIET POLICY TOWARD EAST GERMANY RECONSIDERED

The Postwar Decade

Ann L. Phillips

Contributions in Political Science, Number 142

GREENWOOD PRESS
New York • Westport, Connecticut • London

LIBRARY OF CONGRESS CATALOGING-IN-PUBLICATION DATA

Phillips, Ann L.
  Soviet policy toward East Germany reconsidered.

  (Contributions in political science, ISSN 0147-1066 ;
no. 142)
  Bibliography: p.
  Includes index.
  1. Germany (East)—Foreign relations—Soviet Union.
2. Soviet Union—Foreign relations—Germany (East)
3. Soviet Union—Foreign relations—1945-
I. Title. II. Series.
DD284.5.S65P55 1986   327.470431   85-17729
ISBN 0-313-24671-8 (lib. bdg. : alk. paper)

Copyright © 1986 by Ann L. Phillips

All rights reserved. No portion of this book may be
reproduced, by any process or technique, without the
express written consent of the publisher.

Library of Congress Catalog Card Number: 85-17729
ISBN: 0-313-24671-8
ISSN: 0147-1066

First published in 1986

Greenwood Press, Inc.
88 Post Road West, Westport, Connecticut 06881

Printed in the United States of America

The paper used in this book complies with the
Permanent Paper Standard issued by the National
Information Standards Organization (Z39.48-1984).

10 9 8 7 6 5 4 3 2 1

COPYRIGHT ACKNOWLEDGMENTS

Tables 1, 2, 6, 9, 10, 13 are reprinted from Wolfgang F. Stolper, *The Structure of the East German Economy* (Cambridge, Mass.: Harvard University Press, 1960); reprinted by permission of Harvard University Press. Tables 3, 5, 11 are reprinted from J. P. Nettl's *The Eastern Zone and Soviet Policy in Germany, 1945-1950* (London: Oxford University Press, 1951). Tables 17, 22 and material in Appendix D are taken from United Nations, Economic Commission for Europe, *Economic Survey of Europe, 1957* (Geneva: Economic Commission for Europe, 1958); reprinted with permission of the United Nations Publicaton Board. Material in Appendices C and D, taken from Heinz Köhler's *Economic Integration in the Soviet Bloc with an East German Case Study* (New York: Frederick A. Praeger, 1965), is reprinted with permission. Table 18 is taken from Frederic L. Pryor's *The Communist Foreign Trade System* (Cambridge, Mass.: MIT Press, 1963); reprinted with permission of MIT Press and Allen & Unwin, Ltd.

"Ethical notions are very seldom a cause, but almost always an effect, a means of claiming universal legislative authority for our own preferences, not, as we fondly imagine, the actual ground of those preferences."

Bertrand Russell
Proceedings of the Aristotelian Society, 1915-16
p. 302

"Theories of international morality are . . . the product of dominant nations or groups of nations. For the past hundred years, and more especially since 1918, the English-speaking peoples have formed the dominant group in the world; and current theories of international morality have been designed to perpetuate their supremacy."

Edward Hallett Carr
The Twenty Years Crisis, 1919-1939
pp. 79-80

Contents

Tables

Abbreviations

CDU	Christian Democratic Union
CMEA	Council for Mutual Economic Assistance
CPSU	Communist Party of the Soviet Union
DKP	German Communist Party
DM	deutsche Mark
DWK	German Economic Commission
EDC	European Defense Community
EEC	European Economic Community
KPD	Communist Party of Germany – successor to the DKP)
LPD	Liberal Party of Germany
SAGs	Sowjetische Aktiengesellschaften – German corporations expropriated by the Soviet temporarily as part of the Soviets' reparations claims, run as joint stock companies
SBZ	Soviet Occupation Zone
SED	Socialist Unity Party
SMAD	Soviet Military Administration of Germany
SPD	Social Democratic Party of Germany

VEBs   Volkseigene Betriebe - publicly owned
            enterprises

VVBs   Vereinigungen Volkseigener Betriebe -
            association of publicly owned enterprises

WTO   Warsaw Treaty Organization

WTZ   Wissenschaftlich-technische Zusammenarbeit -
            economic-technical cooperation

SOVIET POLICY TOWARD EAST GERMANY RECONSIDERED

1
Introduction

This study analyzes Soviet political and economic policies toward East Germany from 1945 to 1955, focusing on
the transition in Soviet policy from ambivalence to
support. Soviet policy toward East Germany was inti-
mately intertwined with the evolution of Soviet goals
in Germany as a whole within the postwar international
environment. The main hypothesis of this work is that
the Soviet Union pursued an ambivalent policy toward
East Germany between 1945 and 1955 because of the
unclear relationship among the World War II Allies
sharing the joint occupation of Germany and because of
competing and often contradictory goals pursued by the
Soviet Union in Germany. The Kremlin did not settle on
a policy of commitment to the continued existence of
the German Democratic Republic (GDR) until 1955, fully
a decade after the end of the war and almost six years
after the official establishment of the two German
states. The ambivalence of Soviet policy during that
period was apparent in the contrasting policies of
economic extraction on the one hand and the moderation
in socialist transformation on the other, which served
a mix of political and economic goals that were often
incompatible. The dynamic interaction of the burgeoning conflict between the Soviet Union and the West,
Soviet national security requirements, and opportunities for expanding Soviet influence in Germany produced
the experimental policies which set East Germany apart
from the East bloc during the postwar decade. The
study will focus on the shift in Soviet policy and the
complex of political and economic factors contributing
to the change.

The time period 1945-1955 was chosen because it encompasses the Allied agreement which tried to formulate the postwar status of Germany and the acceptance in Soviet policy of the existence of two German states. The intervening period provided the context within which Soviet policy toward East Germany developed and changed.

The time from which the division of Germany became final is still subject to debate and is one of those issues which depend largely on the perspective from which they are examined. From an international legal perspective, the division became final in 1972, when the two German states signed the Grundvertrag (Basic Treaty) of mutual recognition and normalization of relations. From a more general international perspective, it can be said the the future of East Germany as well as the status of East Europe remained in doubt until 1975, when the Helsinki Accords provided implicit Western recognition of the geopolitical results of World War II. The de facto division of Germany, on the other hand, is placed much earlier. One authority contends that Germany's fate was sealed by the joint occupation agreement and the decision to extract reparations on a predominantly zonal basis.[1] Other sources mark 1946 or 1947 as the critical year, but 1948 is the most frequently cited as the year during which the division of Germany became final.[2] The case for 1948 is based on the end of a common German currency, the Berlin blockade and, more broadly, on the East-West tension generated by the Prague coup and the sovietization of East Europe. The establishment of two German states in 1949 and the inclusion of the GDR into the Council for Mutual Economic Assistance (CMEA) in 1950 are considered by others critical events which ended the possibility for German reunification.[3]

The perspective appropriate to this work is neither legal nor de facto status but rather the Soviet policy perspective, i.e., when the Soviet Union began to treat the existence of two German states as an established fact and develop its policy accordingly. This did not take place until 1955, although the shift in policy toward East Germany began in the the summer of 1953. A significant number of scholars concur with this time frame for differing reasons.[4]

The actual events of the decade stir little debate, but the interpretation of those events and the implications for Soviet policy generate strong controversy to this day. The literature can be divided according to broad lines of interpretation of Soviet goals in Germany. There are overlapping elements in each of the interpretations, but distinctions are, nonetheless, possible and helpful. One interpretation concludes that the primary objective of Soviet policy in Germany was economic exploitation of the area for reconstruction of the Soviet Union.(5) Adherents point to the harsh occupation policy--extensive dismantling, claims on current production, appropriation of the most important industries--as evidence that the Soviets had no intention or hope of retaining control of the territory or extending the socialist revolution to Germany. Further evidence of the lack of Soviet political ambitions in Germany is cited in the determination of the Oder and Neisse rivers as the Polish-German border. The expansion of Polish territory westward at the expense of Germany was unpopular with all elements of the German population including German communists. As early as 1946, Soviet Foreign Minister Vyacheslav Molotov presented the Oder and Western Neisse as the final border. The Socialist Unity Party (SED), at the same time, openly and officially opposed any reduction in German territory. The German Party had to change its position and, less than one year after the founding of the GDR, officially sanctioned the loss of territory in an agreement signed with Poland. Such action, proponents contend, demonstrates Soviet preference for securing Poland's dependence over political ambitions in Germany.

An opposing interpretation of Soviet goals is grounded in theoretical arguments rather than specific policy.(6) The general argument contends that Germany represented an advanced industrialized society ripe for socialism according to Marx. Winning Germany meant winning the key to Europe, which would shift the balance of forces in favor of socialism as well as provide a model for other advanced capitalist countries. The importance of Germany for the socialist cause was recognized very early. At the time of the Russian revolution, Bolshevik leaders considered the chances for success minimal unless the revolutionary wave spread to Germany. Because of Germany's strategic and ideological significance, it is argued, Joseph Stalin followed a blueprint for a new order in Germany, the elements of which could be tactically changed. Shifts in Soviet policy toward Germany, therefore, should not be misconstrued as improvisation or spontaneity.

The latter interpretation lends itself to delinea-
tion of maximum and minimum goals: maximum being incorporation of all Germany within the Soviet orbit;
minimum, retention of the Eastern Zone.(7) This approach can be argued from the defensive perspective of
national security requirements as well as the offensive
one of exporting revolution. Regardless of the imputed
motivation, the general approach rejects the possibility of the Kremlin giving up all control in Germany,
whereas those interpretations which accord primacy to
Soviet economic requirements in formulating policy
toward Germany minimize the political prospects and
intentions of the Soviet leadership in Germany.

Variations on the two major opposing viewpoints
focus on a qualitative shift in Soviet policy. One
interpretation contends that Soviet policy shifted from
one of short-term economic exploitation to one of anticipated long-term association characterized by re-
organizing, rebuilding, and socializing social and
economic life.(8) This marked a change from primarily
economic to political goals. Another agrees with the
qualitative shift concept but in terms contained within
the political sphere. According to this interpretation, the Soviets discarded the maximal goal for consolidation of East Germany after failing to gain influence in the Western Zones.(9)

The inadequacy of these interpretations stems
primarily from the approach or method of analysis employed and/or from the time period examined. Virtually
all of the literature focuses on either political or
economic aspects of Soviet policy toward Germany. There
are two exceptions to this general pattern, both of
which, however, are primarily descriptive. Neither
articulates or follows an analytical framework. First,
J.P. Nettl's The Eastern Zone and Soviet Policy in
Germany, 1945-1950, published in 1951, discusses both
political and economic facets of Soviet policy.   Its
inadequacy for purposes of this study lies in the time
frame as well as the lack of documents and resources
then available.(10) The book, nontheless, remains one
of the best on this subject. The second source which
integrates political and economic policy is Konstantin
Pritzel's Die wirtschaftliche Integration der sowjetischen Besatzungszone Deutschlands in den Ostblock und
ihre politischen Aspekte. This work focuses primarily
on the GDR's role in the CMEA after 1955, the economic
ramifications of that integration, and the political
and ideological aspects of economic integration.

Discussion of the postwar decade is, by comparison, rather brief. This study includes political and economic policy in an effort to overcome the predominant omission of the literature on the subject. The perspective adopted here is closedly attuned to the writings of Robert Gilpin and Edward Hallett Carr.(11) Gilpin and Carr posit the inseparability of politics and economics instead of the dominance of one sphere over the other. Carr looks into history for support for this contention, citing late-nineteenth-century imperialism and World War I as illuminating examples. Gilpin, in a more theoretical elaboration of his approach, defines the relationship between economics and politics as "reciprocal."(12) He identifies two stages of influence: In the short run, politics determines the economic structure to serve the interests of the dominant groups; in the long run, however, the economic process distributes wealth and power, transforming power relationships among groups, which in turn, leads to a new political system and ultimately to a new economic structure.(13) This ongoing dynamic interaction blurs the distinction between politics and economics. In international relations, Gilpin concludes that nations of all ideological persuasions "compete over the territorial division and exploitation of the world in pursuit of wealth and power."(14) This study accepts the premise of the dynamic interaction of economics and politics which renders clear distinctions between the two artificial and misleading. While a given historical situation may engender conflicting economic and political goals, the pursuit of wealth and power are, ultimately, mutually supporting and indistinguishable.

This perspective applied to the study of Soviet policy toward East Germany during the postwar decade illuminates the complexity and interdependence of political and economic goals. The time period illustrates the conflicts in policy which cut across political and economic lines generated by the uncertain environment and the final resolution of those conflicts in favor of consolidation of the GDR. This study benefits from the wealth of information presented in the many scholarly works which touch upon this subject and, at the same time, overcomes the pervasive weakness of approach. The primary contribution this study makes to scholarship in the field lies in the integration of politics and economics which lends a new, more comprehensive understanding of Soviet policy toward East Germany during that critical period.

In addition to the many and varied secondary sources, this research draws on several collections of documents, the most important being _Dokumente der deutschen Politik und Geschichte_, edited by Johannes Hohlfeld, published in West Germany, and _Dokumente zur Deutschlandpolitik der Sowjetunion_, by the Deutsches Institut für Zeitgeschichte, published in East Germany. These complementary sources are supplemented by _Documents on Germany under Occupation, 1945-1954_, edited by Beate Ruhm von Oppen; _Dokumente zur Aussenpolitik der Regierung der Deutschen Demokratischen Republik; Beziehungen DDR-UdSSR: 1949 bis 1955_; and _A Decade of American Foreign Policy, Basic Documents 1941-1949_, as well as other, more specific, document collections. Economic statistics are taken primarily from the East German statistical yearbook, _Statistisches Jahrbuch der Deutschen Demokratischen Republik_; the United Nations' series, _Economic Survey of Europe_; Paul Marer's statistical compendium, _Soviet and East European Foreign Trade_; and Wolfgang Stolper's _The Structure of the East German Economy_. The Western sources cited based their computations on official East German statistics. The shortcomings and weaknesses of official statistics of Soviet type economies for purposes of analysis and understanding in the West are well known.(15) Therefore, economic data compiled by Western economists skilled at compensating and adjusting for inadequacies or inaccuracies in East European accounting practices are heavily relied upon. The earliest postwar data is the most sketchy in the case of East Germany because of the sensitive reparations issue. The Soviets had political and economic interests in undervaluing reparations payments. As a result, estimates of this critical element of East German economic activity vary widely. Nonetheless, the significance of reparations in Soviet policy toward Germany is readily discernible. In general, the economic picture of East Germany is sufficiently complete and accurate to identify trends within the economy which reflect Soviet policy and to make general comparisons with other Soviet type economies.

This study develops Soviet political and economic policy toward East Germany thematically as well as chronologically. Although at times it is necessary to address political and economic policies separately, the underlying interdependence of the two is always assumed. Chapter 2 examines the economic and political issues of the postwar settlement which fostered disagreements among the Allies and traces the development of mutual misunderstanding and antagonism between the superpowers--a condition arising from competing and incompatible goals which came to be symbolized in the creation of two German states in 1949. This provides the international context within which Soviet policy toward East Germany evolved. The element of conflict within the Soviet leadership over German policy is introduced as a key to inconsistent policies pursued in the Eastern Zone and remains a constant theme until the summer of 1953. Discussion of the restoration and development of political life in the zone provides concrete evidence of Soviet goals.

Chapter 3 complements Chapter 2 by exploring the many facets of Soviet economic policy toward East Germany. The question of exploitation which must be addressed in light of the Potsdam Agreements is the focal point. The juxtaposition of political and economic policy demonstrates the interdependence of the two and, at the same time, points up the pervasive inconsistencies of Soviet policy at the time.

Chapter 4 examines radicalization of the SED under the influence of Walter Ulbricht and the accompanying Construction of Socialism Program adopted in the summer of 1952 against the background of deteriorating East-West relations over Korea and the stalemate on German reunification, a situation further aggravated by the progressive integration of West Germany into the Western alliance. This chapter's focal point is the June 1953 uprising which was the culmination of a combination of political and economic factors within East Germany and the USSR which had undermined the stability of the SED regime.

The uprising initiated a new, uniform Soviet policy of support for East Germany and consolidation of the Ulbricht regime. The political and economic aspects of the shift in policy comprise the heart of Chapter 5.

Chapter 6 presents a comparison of Soviet policy toward East Germany and the East European countries of the Soviet bloc. The comparison provides further evidence to support the hypothesis that Moscow did not settle on a policy of incorporating the GDR into the East bloc until long after that had ceased to be a question in the rest of East Europe.

NOTES

1.   John Backer, The Decision to Divide Germany
(Durham,   N.C.:   Duke University Press, 1978), pp. 171-
78.   Backer does not attribute the division to a grand
design on either side.

2.   Die   sowjetische Hand in der deutschen   Wirtschaft (Bonn: Bonner Berichte,   1952) makes a case for
1946.   Vladimir Rudolph, "The Administrative Organization of Soviet Control," in Soviet Economic Policy   in
Postwar Germany, ed. by Robert M. Slusser (New York:
Research Program on the USSR, 1953), considers 1947 the
critical year.   The following sources consider 1948 the
decisive year: Manuel Gottlieb,   The German Peace Settlement and the Berlin Crisis (New York: Paine-Whitman,
1960); Jonathan Steele,   Socialism with a German Face
(London: Johathan Cape,   1970); Carola Stern, Porträt
einer bolschewistischen   Partei (Cologne: Verlag für
Politik und Wirtschaft,   1957); David   Dallin,   Soviet
Foreign Policy after Stalin (New York: J.B. Lippincott
Co.,   1961); Viktor N. Beletskii, Die Politik der Sow-
jetunion in den deutschen Angelegenheiten in der Nach-
kriegszeit,   1945-1976   (Berlin: Staatsverlag   der
Deutschen Demokratischen   Republik,   1977);   Walter
Laqueur, Russia and Germany: A Century of Conflict
(Boston: Little, Brown and Co. 1965); Karl C. Thalheim,
"Die sowjetische Besatzungszone Deutschlands," in Die
Sowjetisierung Ost-Mitteleuropa, ed. by Ernst Birke
(Frankfurt am Main: Alfred Metzner Verlag, 1959).

3.   Konstantin Pritzel, Die wirtschaftliche Integration der sowjetischen Besatzungszone Deutschlands in
den Ostblock und ihre politischen Aspekte   (Bonn:
Deutscher Bundes-Verlag,   1962); Boris Meissner, Russland, die Westmächte und Deutschland: Die sowjetische
Deutschlandpolitik,   1943-1953 (Hamburg: H.H.   Nölke
Verlag, 1953).

4.   Victor Baras, "Stalin's German Policy after
Stalin," Slavic Review (June 1978); Peter Bender, "The
Special Case of East Germany," Studies in Comparative
Communism (April 1969); Melvin Croan, "Reality and
Illusion in Soviet-German Relations," Survey (October
1962); Eberhard Schulz, "Die DDR als Element der sow-
jetischen Westeuropa-Politik," Europa Archiv 27 (25
December 1972); Gerhard Wettig, Die Parole der nation-
alen Einheit in der sowjetischen Deutschlandpolitik,
1942-1967 (Cologne: Berichte des Bundesinstituts für

Ostwissenschaftliche und Internationale Studien, 1967);
Paul R. Willging, "Soviet Foreign Policy in the German
Question: 1950-1955" (Ph.D. diss. Columbia University,
1973). Beletskii and Pritzel are hard to pin down.
Beletskii cites 1955 as "cementing" the division of
Germany after judging the 1948 Berlin crisis as the
culmination of the division of Germany. Pritzel also
notes two critical dates: in 1949 the Soviets realized
that they could not sovietize all of Germany, and in
1954-55 they would not give up the Soviet Zone. Both
works cited above.

    5. Werner Bröll, Die Wirtschaft der DDR: Lage und
Aussichten (Munich: Günter Olzog Verlag, 1974); Erich
Klinkmüller and Maria Elisabeth Ruban, Die Wirtschaft-
liche Zusammenarbeit der Ostblockstaaten (Berlin: Dunc-
ker & Humblot, 1960); Heinz Köhler, Economic Inte-
gration in the Soviet Bloc with an East German Case
Study (New York: Frederick A. Praeger, 1965); Meissner,
Russland, die Westmächte und Deutschland; J.P. Nettl,
The Eastern Zone and Soviet Policy in Germany, 1945-
1950 (London: Oxford University Press, 1951); Die sow-
jetische Hand; Harry Schwartz, Eastern Europe in the
Soviet Shadow (New York: The John Day Co., 1973); Adam
Ulam, Expansion and Coexistence (New York: Praeger,
1974). Ulam says exploitation was the main theme of
Soviet policy in Germany at least through 1949.

    6. Werner Erfurt, Die sowjetrussische Deutsch-
land-Politik (Esslingen: Bechtel Verlag, 1959); J. Kurt
Klein, Die Bedeutung der DDR für die Sowjetunion (Hildesheim: Gebrüder Gerstenberg, 1969); Stern, Porträt;
Thalheim, "Die sowjetische Besatzungszone." Robert
Slusser, ed., Soviet Economic Policy in Postwar Germany
(New York: Research Program on the USSR, 1953).
Slusser cannot decide: He contends that economic needs
overrode political goals in Germany at one time and
then declares sovietization of all Germany was the
primary goal from the start.

    7. Studiengesellschaft für Zeitprobleme, Die
sowjetische Deutschlandpolitik, 4 parts (Duisdorf bei
Bonn: Studiengesellschaft für Zeitprobleme, 1962) parts
2-4; Croan, "Reality and Illusion."

    8. Köhler, Economic Integration. Köhler cites
1953 as the year marking the shift from short term to
long term objectives. His work is included under the
first interpretation as well. According to Meissner,
Russland, die Westmächte und Deutschland, the shift

dates   from 1952.   His work is also cited in the first
category.   And according to Pritzel, _Die wirtschaft-_
liche Integration, the shift dates from 1953.

    9.   Croan, "Reality and Illusion"; Wettig, _Die_
Parole.

    10.   Nettl did not have access to any of the
document collections used in this study or to works by
former SED and/or Soviet personnel directly involved in
Soviet-GDR relations who later defected, such as
Gregorii Klimov, Erich Gniffke and Fritz Schenk.

    11.   Robert Gilpin, "The Nature of Political Econ-
omy," in _U.S. Power and the Multinational Corporation_
(New York: Basic Books, 1975), pp. 21-24, 33-43; Edward
Hallett Carr, _The Twenty Years' Crisis, 1919-1939_ (New
York: Harper & Row, 1964), pp. 114-20.

    12.   Gilpin, "The Nature of Political Economy,"
p. 21.

    13.   Ibid., pp. 21-22, 43.

    14.   Ibid., p. 38.

    15.   Nicolas Spulber, _The Economics of Communist_
Eastern Europe (New York: John Wiley & Sons, 1957),
pp. xxi-xxv; Thad P. Alton, "Economic Structure and
Growth in Eastern Europe," in _Economic Developments in_
Countries of Eastern Europe (Washington, D.C.: Government Printing Office, 1970), pp. 42-43; Alton, "Economic Growth and Resource Allocation in Eastern Europe,"
in _Reorientation and Commercial Relations of the Econ-_
omies of Eastern Europe (Washington, D.C.: Government
Printing Office, 1974), pp 252-54; Paul Marer, "Soviet
Economic Policy in Eastern Europe," in _Reorientation_,
pp. 143-50.

2
Germany, 1945–1949

DIVISION OF THE PRIZE

Soviet policy toward the Soviet Occupation Zone (SBZ) in Germany evolved in accordance with Soviet domestic policy needs and in response to the dynamic of growing Soviet-Allied conflict in the international arena in general and over Germany in particular. Germany, a unifying factor in the alliance initially, became a core element in its disintegration, a focus of the incompatibility of U.S. and Soviet long-term interests. A brief review of the breakdown of the alliance leading to the de jure division of Germany in 1949 is necessary to understand Soviet actions in the Eastern Zone.(1)

The trauma of the German invasion and deep penetration into Soviet territory accompanied by terrible losses of life and materiel was indelibly imprinted in the Soviet memory. Despite the total defeat of Germany, signalled by its unconditional surrender, the Soviet sense of insecurity seems to have remained overpowering. This marked the second time within the span of a few decades that Russia had been at war with Germany; therefore, a primary Soviet goal in the aftermath of World War II was to ensure that Germany would never again be in a position to attack the Soviet Union. Stalin also pressed for substantial reparations from Germany as partial compensation for the tremendous losses suffered by the Soviet Union in World War II. The tension within the alliance arose not from these goals per se but rather from differing, albeit ambiguous, notions as to how these goals might best be achieved.

During the course of the war, consultations had been held at the highest levels to coordinate Allied efforts against the Axis powers as well as to plan for peace. The first such meeting, the Moscow Conference of Foreign Ministers in October 1943, established the European Advisory Commission to "study and make recommendations to the three governments on European questions arising as the war develops."(2)   U.S. policy checked all efforts to use this forum to negotiate postwar settlement plans during the war, when, in retrospect, the conditions for agreement seemed most propitious.(3)   Even at that time several significant incidences fueled mutual suspicions within the alliance. For the Soviets, the most convincing evidence of bad faith was provided by the Western delay in launching the Second Front and the negotiation of an armistice with Italy without Soviet participation.(4)   The West, for its part, was outraged by the Soviet failure to aid the Warsaw uprising.(5)   Nor was mistrust limited to East-West differences. U.S. President Franklin Roosevelt and British Prime Minister Winston Churchill had differing appreciations of the role of <u>Realpolitik</u> in international affairs which created incompatible visions of the postwar world.   The most famous example was the Churchill-Stalin division of Europe into spheres of influence at their meeting in Moscow in October 1944, which raised the ire of the Americans.(6) Some U.S. government officials had been sufficiently pessimistic to warn against the illusion of cooperation with the Soviet Union.   Both W. Averell Harriman, U.S. Ambassador to Moscow, and George F. Kennan, a member of the embassy staff at the time, felt that the relatively friendly relations with the Soviet Union would not survive peacetime.(7)   It is evident, however, that the people who ultimately counted in policy formulation during the war years, i.e., President Roosevelt and Secretary of State Cordell Hull, were fascinated, charmed, and somewhat awed by Marshal Stalin.(8)

The Soviets appear to have been equally unsure about the prospects for cooperation with the West after the war.   The Soviets did publicly praise the Western Allies when they launched the Second Front.   D-day was given great attention and was cause for celebration in the USSR.   Only days after the invasion, the Soviet press detailed deliveries of military supplies received from the West since October 1941.   This positive presentation of Allied aid and war effort indicate that Stalin may have believed for a time that a joint postwar policy was possible.(9)

     The   Yalta   Conference proved to be pivotal   in
fashioning   the   postwar   environment by defining the
issues which would become the focus of enduring Allied
disagreement.(10)   The atmosphere of conviviality which
softened disagreements at the conference only served to
heighten feelings of betrayal on both sides as conflicts began to fester under the   scrutiny of more
skeptical participants at Potsdam.   The Yalta Conference, 4-11 February 1945, produced general agreement on
the joint Allied occupation of Germany.   In the final
communique it was announced that the forces of the
three powers would each occupy a zone and that the
French would be invited to occupy a zone.(11)   The
central Control Council was provided to coordinate
administration and control throughout Germany.   (12)
Berlin was to be under joint occupation.

     The effort to establish unified administration and
control   was in apparent contradiction to   the   secret
agreement reached at Yalta for dismemberment which was
to be added to the surrender terms.(13)   Ironically,
the Americans and British most strongly favored dismemberment, while Stalin publicly refuted the policy immediately following the German surrender.(14)   The French
would prove to be the strongest opponents to the establishment of a central German government in the coming
years.

     Key areas of disagreement at Yalta, for purposes
of this study, centered on the issues of reparations
and Poland.   Only the Soviet Union had prepared a plan
for reparations, which was presented to the Allied
leaders by Ivan Maisky, Deputy People's Commissar for
Foreign Affairs.   The plan called for Germany to pay
reparations in kind amounting to $20 billion, one-half
of which would be allotted to the Soviet Union in
recognition of her unequal burden in the war effort.
Half of the value of reparations was to be derived from
property removal immediately following the end of the
war.   German heavy industry, i.e., iron, steel, electrical power, and chemical industries, was to be reduced 80 percent. Specialized industry useful only for
military purposes, such as aviation factories and synthetic oil refineries, was to be totally removed.   The
additional $10 billion in reparations was to be paid in
kind over a period of ten years.(15) A special reparations committee was to be established with its seat in
Moscow to work out a final program.

In the discussion which followed the initial presentation of the proposal, President Roosevelt commen-
ted that he would willingly support any claims of the
Soviet Union for reparations. Furthermore, he felt
that the German standard of living should not be higher
than that of the USSR.(16) The British Prime Minister
disagreed with the possibility and advisability of
trying to extract such large reparations from Germany,
based on the experience following World War I. It
should be noted, however, that the reparations proposed
by the Soviets amounted to approximately one-third the
level imposed on Germany after World War I.(17)
Churchill also objected to the mention of any monetary
figure for reparations in the protocol. Stalin replied
that no commitment was involved but that the $20 bil-
lion figure should be taken up by the committee as a
basis for discussion.(18) In the final Protocol on
German Reparations, the British officially excluded
themselves from the mention of $20 billion in repara-
tions to be referred to the Moscow Reparations Commission.(19) The protocol did specify three categories of
reparations: removals for demilitarizing Germany,
reparations from current production, and use of German
labor, to which all three parties agreed. Reparations
from current production and the Soviet claim to $10
billion in reparations were to become major areas of
contention at Potsdam and afterward.

The Polish questions were cited by Winston
Churchill as the "most urgent reason for the Yalta
Conference . . . and the first of the great causes
which led to the breakdown of the Grand Alliance."(20)
Disagreements focused on the formation of a Polish
provisional government and determination of Poland's
western border. The Soviets pressed for recognition of
the Lublin government at the expense of the London
government-in-exile. The London Poles would not negotiate with Stalin and refused to recognize the Curzon
Line as the border between Poland and the USSR despite
British prodding. Churchill and Roosevelt had accepted
that boundary in principle in 1943.(21) The Lublin
Committee, by contrast, accepted the border in 1944.
The intransigence of the London Poles, while understandable given the age-old animosity between Russians
and Poles and the recent Soviet occupation of Polish
territory in conjunction with Nazi Germany in 1939, did
not serve the long-term interests of the government-in-
exile.

While not enamored with the London Poles because they were perceived to be too uncompromising and unrealistic, Roosevelt and Churchill refused to recognize the Lublin government because of its undemocratic composition. Molotov then argued for reorganization of the Polish government, maintaining the Lublin government as the core and adding democratic elements from the Poles both at home and in exile. He stressed that elections were to be held in one or two months, minimizing the importance of any provisional decision made by the Allies, and, that in the meantime, stability in Poland, which could only be provided by a government friendly to the USSR, was important to the progress of the Red Army. The British and Americans countered that elections held under the auspices of the Lublin government would not be free.(22) The final communique recorded a victory for the Soviet position on this issue, although the West was not ready to concede Poland.(23)

Poland's western border also became a thorny issue among the Allies, although substantial agreement had been reached in Moscow in October 1944 between Churchill and Stalin. The Oder River and either the Neisse or Western Neisse were to form the western boundary, while the Curzon Line was recognized as Poland's eastern border.(24) Roosevelt appeared to defer to the other two when he avoided the issue at Tehran and, at Yalta, said he was less concerned about the borders than the problems of the Polish government.(25) Nonetheless, final determination of the western border was deferred to the peace conference, while the Curzon Line, with some variations in favor of Poland, was recognized at the eastern frontier.(26)

By the time the Potsdam Conference convened (16 July 1945), the mutual confidence of the Allies had been further eroded by intervening events which affected the quality of cooperation and willingness to compromise. Roosevelt had died in April and was succeeded by Harry S. Truman, who came to Potsdam without benefit of prior experience in foreign affairs or personal rapport with either Churchill or Stalin. He also was much less sympathetic toward the Soviet Union than Roosevelt had been. Truman's first meeting with Molotov had been a heated one in which Truman gave the Soviet Foreign Minister a severe dressing down. Truman also had abruptly terminated Lend Lease aid to the USSR in May of 1945, a matter of considerable concern to the Soviets.(27)

The British also chose a new Prime Minister.   As a result of general elections which occurred during the conference, Churchill was replaced by Clement Attlee. Attlee pursued Churchill's foreign policies generally but was a much weaker presence in the negotiations.

In the meantime, the Moscow Reparations Commission, which had been meeting during the interim between the Yalta and Potsdam Conferences, reached an impasse on the issue of reparations from current production. U.S. policy insisted that there could be no reparations from current production until Germany had exported enough goods to pay for necessary imports.(28)   This was referred to as the First Charge Principle, developed by the State Department in economic briefing papers for Yalta.   The commitment was based on the judgment that the United States had financed virtually all reparations payments after World War I.   The State Department position discounted the Office of Strategic Services study which demonstrated German ability to pay reparations.(29) The Soviets saw this as a major turnabout from Roosevelt's expressed support for the Soviet reparations plan at Yalta.

Wrangling over reparations continued throughout the Potsdam Conference.   The Soviets accused the United States of reneging on their agreement that the Soviet Union should receive $10 billion in reparations from Germany, while the Americans insisted that they had agreed to the figure only as a basis for discussion. The U.S. position at the time of the conference was that the figure was no longer realistic due to the destruction caused by occupying armies and the removal of large quantities of materiel and equipment from the Soviet Zone.   Stalin countered the implied accusation against Soviet practices with a report from Marshal Georgii Zhukov, Supreme Commander and Military Governor of the SBZ, that American and British soldiers had removed more than ten thousand loaded railroad cars prior to their withdrawal from the Soviet zone.(30) While not denying the charge of Soviet dismantling, Stalin wanted it on record that all sides were doing the same.   The United States added that consideration of the $10 billion figure had been based on the ability of the whole of Germany to pay and, since that time, the Soviets had turned over much of Silesia to Poland.(31) The new Secretary of State, Frank Byrnes, proposed that each country exact reparations from its own zone of occupation and then exchange goods as needed between the zones.(32) Molotov prophetically

pointed   out that if reparations were not treated as   a
whole,   the overall economic administration of   Germany
would be affected.(33)

The   issue was temporarily dispensed with by the
following formula in the Potsdam Protocol: Each victor
was to extract reparations from his designated occupation zone.   In addition, the Soviet Union was to receive a total of 25 percent of the industrial equipment
removed from the zones: 15 percent would be exchanged
for food and raw materials, and 10 percent would be
free.   Removal of industrial capital equipment was to
be completed within two years; the amount of equipment
to be removed from the Western Zones for the Soviet
Union was to be determined within six months of the
Potsdam Conference.   The Control Council was to determine the amount and kind of industrial capital equipment not needed by the German peace economy which
would, therefore, be available for reparations, subject
to the final approval of the zone commander where the
equipment was to be removed.(34) Thus, the Potsdam
reparations agreement was an interim one, purposefully
vague, which led to differing interpretations.

The general terms of exchange of reparations represented a significant concession on the part of the
Soviets.   No fixed amount of reparations was established, for which the Soviets began pressing at Yalta;
rather, only percentages for exchange were agreed to,
which the Soviets rightly contended were meaningless.(35) Furthermore, there was no guarantee of reparations from current production, although this had been
agreed to at Yalta, because of the recognition of the
First   Charge   Principle demanded by   the   United
States.(36)

The Polish issues, by contrast, were resolved to
the advantage of the USSR, despite the fury aroused by
the Kremlin's unilateral recognition of the Lublin
government   prior to the   Potsdam   Conference.(37)
President Truman dispatched Harry Hopkins, President
Roosevelt's Special Assistant, to Moscow in May to try
to salvage the unacceptable situation. He succeeded in
negotiating for a conference of Poles, including the
Lublin group, who, in conjunction with a Commission of
Three composed of Molotov, Averell Harriman, and Clark
Kerr, would work out the composition of an acceptable
Polish government.(38) By 21 June 1945 this task was
accomplished, although only six cabinet posts out of
twenty were to be held by "independent" Poles.(39)

Neither Kerr nor Harriman were very optimistic about
the   results,   but on 5 July the British and American
governments simultaneously announced recognition of the
new   Polish   Provisional   Government   of   National
Unity.(40)

Having succeeded in obtaining Western recognition
of the Polish Provisional Government, Stalin pursued an
effort at Potsdam to eliminate any shred of influence
or legitimacy that the London government-in-exile might
retain. At the second plenary meeting he proposed that
all ties with the London Poles be severed. He further
recommended that all Polish property and other assets
at the disposal of the London Poles be turned over to
the new Polish government and that all members of the
Polish armed forces serving the London group be subor-
dinated to the Provisional Government.(41) The Soviet
position was in essence adopted and included in the
Conference Protocol of Proceedings.(42) The commitment
of the Polish Provisional Government to hold free and
unfettered elections was duly noted, but there was only
fragile hope in the West that it would be honored.

The Soviets also acted unilaterally on the Polish
border question and presented the Western Allies with a
fait accomplis at Potsdam. German territory east of
the Oder River and the Western Neisse had been transferred to Polish administration.(43) Stalin explained
that the Germans had fled before the advancing Red
Army, leaving no alternative, and, that in any case, it
was preferable to have stability and a friendly administration to aid the war effort.(44) President Truman
complained that this amounted to the Soviet government
giving the Poles a German occupation zone.   Despite
protests, the Soviet position prevailed. The protocol
recognized the transfer of territory while at the same
time reiterating that the final determination of the
western frontier would await the peace settlement.(45)
The three powers also agreed to the orderly transfer of
German populations from Poland, Hungary, and Czechoslovakia, an act which later undermined Western protests
concerning the provisional nature of the transfer of
German territory.(46)

Despite the gravity of the issues dividing the
Allies, it was felt at the time that the Potsdam Conference, nonetheless, held the promise of a unified
Germany. In the principles adopted to govern the
treatment of Germany, supreme authority was to be exercised by the Commanders-in-Chief in their respective

zones and "also jointly, in matters affecting Germany
as a whole, in their capacity as members of the Control
Council."(47)   Although no central German government
was to be established for the time being, central
German administrative departments were called for,
particularly in the fields of finance, transportation,
communications, foreign trade, and industry. The departments, to be headed by State Secretaries, were to
function under the direction of the Control Council.(48) Further, under the Economic Principles adopted, it was agreed that "during the period of occupation Germany shall be treated as a single economic
unit."(49)   Common policies were to be developed on
reparations and removal of industrial war potential,
import and export programs, industrial production and
its allocation, etc. Allied controls on the German
economy were to be limited to those necessary to carry
out industrial disarmament, demilitarization, reparations, and approved trade, to assure that the needs of
the occupying forces and displaced persons would be
met, and to ensure the just distribution of essential
commodities among zones to produce a balanced economy.(50)

    In sharp contrast to these efforts to provide a
basis for unified policy in Germany stood the division
of the country into separate zones of occupation, reinforced by a zonal reparations plan. The ambiguity
toward Germany's future evidenced at Yalta in the juxtaposition of the secret agreement for dismemberment
with the machinery for joint administration of Germany
was not resolved at Potsdam, as is apparent in the
conflicting decisions in the protocol. Nevertheless,
there was a common spirit of celebration of the great
victory won over a deadly enemy which overshadowed the
specific areas of conflict among the Allies. Potsdam,
however, proved to be the last meeting of the three
heads of state, and the spirit of harmony, however
illusory, could not be recaptured.

    Disagreements became more bitter and positions
less flexible as the medium for Allied cooperation
shifted to the Council of Foreign Ministers.(51)   The
first meeting of the council was held in London from 11
September to 2 October 1945. Virtually no progress was
made on the many substantive issues facing the body as
the members became bogged down in disputes over organization of the council and the agenda for the conference.(52)   The two issues which brought the conference

to an impasse, according to Secretary Byrnes, were the refusal of the United States and Great Britain to recognize the governments of Rumania and Bulgaria, and the Soviet request to discuss the control of Japan, which had not been on the agenda.

The failure of the London Conference did not bode well for future Allied cooperation, although Soviet policy remained flexible. During what Erich Gniffke called the half-open door policy, Austrian elections took place, the Soviet army withdrew from Czecho- slovakia and from parts of Poland, and U.S. and British journalists were admitted to Rumania and Bulgaria.(53) The reparations issue continued to plague the Allied relationship. The Control Council was able to estab- lish a common level of industry for all of Germany as required by the Potsdam Protocol, but the purpose was undermined by Soviet refusal to account for capital equipment removal and by continued exactions of repara- tions from current production. The Soviets were acting to circumvent an unfavorable reparations formula which to them amounted to the SBZ subsidizing the Western Zones. Reparations from the Western Zones for the Soviet Union were only expressed in percentages, while the West asked for uniform food ration levels and import of coal from the Soviet Zone. This meant that the Soviets would be dependent upon Western lar- gesse.(54) At the same time, the United States and Great Britain were supplying their zones with food. As a result, the West felt that it was indirectly subsi- dizing reparations payments to the Soviet Union.(55) This was precisely the position that the United States was determined to avoid and which Britain was unable to sustain. As a consequence, General Lucius Clay, Mili- tary Governor of the American Zone, stopped all deliv- eries to the Soviets prescribed by the Potsdam repara- tions formula in May 1946. Clay was reportedly influ- enced by George Kennan's analysis of Soviet intentions in the Long Telegram and by Kennan's recommendation to partition Germany in order to check the expansion of Soviet influence.(56) The significance of this act toward undermining the possibility for unified Allied policy toward Germany is difficult to gauge, but it was the first overtly hostile act within the alliance.(57)

The Soviets responded to the cutoff in deliveries by printing money to purchase goods needed from the Western Zones. All zones shared a common currency. This strategy served to circumvent American policy for a time but ultimately led to the separate currency

reform   in the Western Zones.   In addition,   inflation
became a serious economic problem in the SBZ.(58)

In the meantime,   the Council of Foreign Ministers
convened   in   Paris   from   15 June   to   12   July   1946.
Molotov   pushed   for   the creation of a   single   German
government   able to fulfill obligations to the   Allies,
especially   reparations deliveries,   and   "sufficiently
democratic   to   be able to extirpate   all   vestiges   of
fascism."   Molotov declared that a central German government   had   to be established before a   peace   treaty
could be signed.   Citing discrepancies in the administration   of basic policy agreed to at Potsdam in   individual zones,   the Soviet Foreign Minister renewed   the
call   for inter-Allied control over German industry   in
general and over the Ruhr industries in particular.(59)
Secretary Byrnes, agreeing that four-power control over
Germany   was   not working well and that the zones   were
being administered as closed compartments in contradiction   to   the Potsdam   Agreements,   proposed   that   the
United   States would administer its zone in conjunction
with   any and all other zones.   Only the   British   expressed interest.(60)   The meeting ended without general agreement.

A   decisive change in American foreign policy   was
signalled in the autumn of 1946 in Secretary Byrnes's
"Restatement   of Policy on Germany," a speech delivered
in Stuttgart.   Byrnes declared U.S.   determination   to
remain involved in Germany and Europe.

Security forces will   probably have to remain
in Germany for a long period.   I want no misunderstanding.   We   will not shirk our duty.
We are not withdrawing....As long as there is
an occupation   army in   Germany, the American
armed   forces will be part of that occupation
army.(61)

Until this time, American policy was assumed to be that
expressed   by Roosevelt at Yalta,   which favored   early
withdrawal of American forces.   Roosevelt had indicated
a   presence   of   no more than two   years   following   an
armistice.

In addition,   Byrnes reiterated his remarks at the
Paris Council of Foreign Ministers,   drawing broad public   attention to the difficulties in four-power administration of Germany and the American proposal to unify
zones.

The British accepted the American proposal, and an agreement on the economic fusion of the two zones into Bizonia was signed 2 December 1946. It was stated that the aim of the two governments was to achieve the economic unity of Germany as a whole.(62) The Soviets responded that the fusion of the zones was in violation of the Potsdam Agreements and would have serious consequences for Germany's political future.(63)

Meanwhile, in the Soviet Union, Andrei Zhdanov ascended to prominence in the Kremlin leadership. (64) He was associated with an aggressive anti-Western domestic and foreign policy. Within the Soviet Union, a zealous campaign against all Western influences was launched, especially in the arts and sciences, which went so far as to intern soldiers who had served in the West. It was called the Zhdanovshchina, after its author. His period of influence, from 1946 to 1948, was marked by deepening conflict between the Western powers and the Soviet Union due not only to differences over Germany and East Europe but also to confrontation worldwide.(65)

The overwhelming impression and fear in the West of Soviet expansion led to the Truman Doctrine and the Marshall Plan. At the same time, in response to the perceived threat from the United States' newly active engagement in world affairs and U.S. political and economic efforts to pressure the USSR, the Soviet Union established the Cominform to coordinate Communist Party activities and moved to consolidate its position in East Europe.(66) The U.S. policy of containment looked like encirclement in Moscow.(67) These actions served to consolidate opposing camps in Europe as well as to underline growing mutual hostility. Ironically, the Council of Foreign Ministers was meeting in Moscow when President Truman delivered a policy statement to Congress which became known as the Truman Doctrine. Molotov was, nonetheless, surprisingly conciliatory. In remarks on Germany he stated that all matters concerning reunification could be resolved if a solution to the reparations problem could be found. Further, the Soviet government was prepared to provide a full accounting of everything that had been done concerning reparations in the Soviet Zone at the proper time.(68) Disagreement on the reparations issue continued to focus on reparations from current production. The Soviets asserted that the Yalta Protocol which approved such reparations was still valid, while the West contended that the Potsdam Agreement made no provision for

such payments,   thus voiding the initial agreement.(69)
The   Soviets   did not regard the Potsdam Agreements   as
superseding   or obviating the Yalta Protocol but as   an
elaboration   of the decisions reached   at   Yalta.   The
critical   difference between the two interpretations is
obvious.

Control of the Ruhr remained an issue of disagreement,   and the Allied split over a German central   government   persisted.   The Soviets favored a strong central government,   while the British, the Americans, and
especially the French wanted a federal system.(70)   The
Council of Foreign Ministers failed to reach any general agreement on Germany.   During a private meeting with
Stalin   at   the end of the   conference,   the   new   U.S.
Secretary of State,   George Marshall,   became convinced
that   the   Soviets   saw it as in   their   interest   that
matters   be allowed to drift.   Stalin appeared to   the
American   Secretary to be undisturbed by the conference
failure.(71)   This spurred Marshall to develop a   program   for   the reconstruction of Europe   to   check   the
conditions   which were feared to favor communist expansion.

The U.S.   offer of Marshall aid to Europe as   well
as the Soviet Union was criticized by Stalin as economic   aggression   which served imperialist   interests   in
three ways: first, to exploit Soviet economic weakness
by   seducing   East Europe in an area where the   Soviets
could not compete;   second, to secure American hegemony
in West Europe;   and finally,   to postpone the collapse
of capitalism.(72)   Controversy over the prospects   for
capitalism   had developed within the Soviet Union   following the defeat of Germany.   In 1946,   Eugene Varga,
an eminent Soviet economist,   presented the possibility
that   the   U.S.   economic crisis might be deferred   for
some   time   through increasing governmental   intervention.(73)   He even foresaw the possibility of the   evolution   of   U.S.   capitalism into   socialism.   Varga's
analysis was officially criticized in 1947,   coinciding
with   growing   animosity   between   East   and   West.(74)
Stalin's reparations policy can,   therefore,   be understood   based on the conviction that   capitalism's   collapse   remained inevitable.   Reparations not only aided
the   economic   reconstruction of the Soviet   Union   but
also   served as a catalyst to hasten the   revolutionary
process.   The Marshall Plan countered Soviet hopes that
revolution   would spring from the economic collapse   in
Europe.(75)   More immediately, the Marshall aid program
reflected   the   tremendous imbalance of   strength   with

which the United States and the USSR emerged from World War II.   Only the United States enjoyed economic prosperity and could,   therefore,   expand its political influence through economic aid.

At the end of June 1947,   Foreign Ministers Ernest Bevin,   Georges Bidault,   and Molotov met in Paris   to discuss   the Marshall aid   program.   Molotov   rejected British and French proposals for acquiring and administering   the aid on the grounds that they constituted an interference   in the internal affairs of   the   European states.(76)   At the founding meeting of the   Cominform in   Warsaw,   the   Marshall aid program   was   officially rejected.   Zhdanov   set the tone for a hard-line anti-Western posture with the reintroduction of the two-camp view   of   the world.   The two-camp   formula   not   only explained   the growing hostility between East and   West but   also   gave theoretical expression to the   international power configuration which arose after World   War II.   In   conjunction with this broad change in assessment   of the international situation,   the Kremlin   directed the communist parties in the West to shift   from a   policy of national collaboration to one of   struggle against their respective governments.(77)

Changes   in Allied policy toward Germany also   reflected the growing inability to cooperate.   During the Moscow Conference of Foreign Ministers,   the three Western   participants   signed a separate agreement on   the division of Ruhr coal.   This was the first step toward a common German policy by the three and an open affront to the Soviet Union.(78)   In June the economic division of Germany became clearer with the creation of a standing   German Economic Commission (DWK) in the East   followed   by the creation of an economic council   for   the Anglo-American Zone.   Both exercised coordinative functions   similar to a government agency.(79)   In   August, the   British and Americans revised upward the level   of industry   allowed in Bizonia from the level established by   the Control Council in an effort to make   the   area self-supporting.(80)   This further diminished areas of common Allied policy in Germany.

After   the   failure of the second   London   Foreign Ministers   Conference in   November-December   1947,   the Allies   moved   rapidly apart.(81) In   early   1948,   the Foreign Ministers of only the Western Allies, joined by representatives of the Benelux countries, met in London to   discuss economic and political cooperation of their occupation zones in Germany.   It was decided that   the

Western Zones should participate in the Economic Recovery Program to provide the basis for development of a
democratic Germany.(82)   The Soviets protested the
separate meeting and Western refusal to inform them of
its content. Marshal Vasily Sokolovsky, Commanding
Officer of the Soviet Military Administration since
April 1946, then announced Soviet withdrawal from the
Allied Control Council on 20 March 1948.(83)   This
proved to be the last meeting of the council.

During the second London Six-Power Conference,
agreement was reached on organizing the three Western
Zones into an economic and political entity. The delegates concluded that the Germans were ready and should
be allowed to assume governmental responsibilities.
Therefore, it was agreed to recommend a procedure
whereby a constitutional assembly would be convened to
prepare a constitution which would, in turn, be subject
to approval by the military governors and the participating states.   Creation of an international authority
for control of the Ruhr in which the conference members
and Germany would participate was also recommended.
Despite the obvious divisive nature of the conference
recommendations, the final communique stated that they
"should facilitate eventual four-power agreement on the
German problem" and, in the meantime, "solve the urgent
political and economic problems arising out of the
present situation in Germany."(84)   The Soviet Union
did not share this assessment of the Six-Power Conference.(85)   In response, a meeting of the Soviet Union
and her new East bloc Allies was held in Warsaw 23-24
June. The Warsaw communique denounced the London Conference as a violation of the Potsdam Agreements.   It
cited the recommendations of the meeting as evidence of
the Western powers' decision to eliminate the Council
of Foreign Ministers as well as the four-power machinery in Germany. The Warsaw Declaration stated further
that the decisions taken by the London Conference were
designed to "consummate the division and dismemberment
of Germany." The signatories called for the return to
four-power control of Germany in accordance with Allied
agreements and fulfillment of the main elements of
those agreements: demilitarization of Germany, four-
power control over heavy industry of the Ruhr, formation of a provisional all-German government, conclusion
of a peace treaty, and finally, assurance that Germany
meet her reparations obligations.(86)

In the meantime, relations among the Allies continued to deteriorate ominously. Western military

governors announced a currency reform for the three Western Zones 18 June.(87) The currency reform was considered necessary to stop the drain of goods to the Soviet Zone in order to achieve economic stability and balance within the Western Zones. The Soviets countered with a currency reform in the SBZ which heightened tensions over Berlin.(88) Soviet order no.111 on the implementation of the currency reform included the provision that only the new currency notes of the Soviet Zone would be honored in Greater Berlin, "which is located in the Soviet occupation zone and economically forms a part of it."(89) The commanders of the Western sectors declared the Soviet currency provision for Greater Berlin null and void and ordered, with qualification, the conversion to currency used in the Western Zones in the Western sectors of Berlin.(90)

Mounting tension and hostility climaxed in the Berlin blockade, which began the night of 23 June 1948. Stalin had been testing the vulnerability of Berlin for some time. Traffic to and from the Western sectors had been impeded periodically, and the Soviets had begun claiming all Berlin as part of the SBZ.(91) Interference intensified just prior to the total blockade. Despite the apparent recklessness of their actions, the Soviets proceeded with caution. The interruption of traffic was attributed to technical problems, which provided a path for retreat should the situation become too menacing.(92) The Soviets soon presented their negotiating position. In a meeting of the military governors in early July, Marshal Sokolovsky stated that the "technical difficulties" would continue until plans for a separate West German government had been abandoned.(93) Meanwhile, the Soviets had withdrawn from the Berlin Kommandatura, blaming the West for the breakdown of four power control.(94) The Berlin Kommandatura has been established in response to the special status of Berlin, which was jointly occupied even though the city lay within the SBZ. It provided the instrument for joint administration of the city, much as the Allied Control Council did for the rest of Germany. The Berlin blockade seemed to have two purposes for the Soviets: first, to thwart the establishment of a separate West German state, restoring Soviet access to the Western Zones through renewed four-power control; and second, failing that, to force the Western powers to withdraw from Berlin.

The West responded with the famous airlift and counter-blockade against the SBZ which not only suc-

cessfully thwarted Soviet intentions but also weakened
the Soviet position in Berlin. In Western eyes, the
blockade served to unmask Soviet intentions in Germany
and expose the aggressively hostile nature of Soviet
power generally.(95) Violence in China and the Middle
East, coupled with Soviet pressure on Iran and Turkey,
heightened Western apprehension concerning the reach
and design of Soviet power. The communist coup in
Czechoslovakia, rapid sovietization of East Europe,
threats against Marshal Josip Broz Tito accompanied by
troop movements on the Yugoslav border, strikes in West
Europe supported by the communist parties--all provided
an ominous background against which to assess the
breakdown of the Control Commission and the blockade of
Berlin. Fear of war in Europe was widespread.

Soviet militancy in Europe gave impetus to Western
military cooperation, which only reinforced Soviet
fears. In March 1948, Great Britain, France, and the
Benelux countries signed a mutual defense pact in Brussels. The Brussels Pact was superseded in April 1949
by the North Atlantic Treaty Organization (NATO) which
included the United States. The Soviet offer to join
NATO was rejected. Early in 1949 the CMEA was formed
by Bulgaria, Czechoslovakia, Hungary, Poland, Rumania,
and the USSR, making the institutionalization of opposing camps increasingly visible.(96) The squaring off
of blocs, however, was quickly followed by moves to
dampen tension. The four powers negotiated an end to
the Berlin blockade in May and agreed to convene a
meeting of the Council of Foreign Ministers on 23 May
in Paris.(97) At the conference, Soviet Foreign Minister Andrei Vyshinsky proposed a return to four-power
control of Germany on the earlier basis of the Control
Council and the Allied Kommandantura in Berlin. He
further proposed the creation of an all-German State
Council from the existing economic councils in the
Eastern and Western zones.(98) This arrangement called
for parity representation of "East and West Germany" in
an all-German government, a formula which was unacceptable to the West.(99) According to State Department
communications, the United States had become convinced
that all-German agencies and a central German government would only serve the extension of Soviet influence
throughout Germany. The United States thought the
Soviets would use central administration to hinder
rehabilitation of the Western Zones. This assessment
was the basis for American policy which led to the
establishment of two Germanies.(100)

The dramatic change in Soviet policy toward the West in Germany--from conflict to conciliation and negotiation--underlined the seriousness with which the Soviets sought to prevent the establishment of a West German state. Such a development would not only undermine Soviet interest in influencing all-German conditions but also could threaten an alternative policy option of consolidating a pro-Soviet East Germany.(101) Needless to say, the Soviet diplomatic initiative to restore the status quo ante in Germany failed; the West objected to the proposal as a step backward.(102) In September 1949, the Federal Republic of Germany (FRG) was formally established,(103) followed in October by the German Democratic Republic.(104)

The aggressive anti-Western policy of Zhdanov, lasting from 1946 to 1948 and cued by a hostile Western stance, provided the stimulus toward the formation of a Western military alliance, the establishment of a West German state, and movement toward including Japan and West Germany into the Western alliance. The obvious failure of this policy to promote Soviet interests led to a change, signalled by the mysterious death of Zhdanov in August 1948. A purge of his adherents, known as the Leningrad Affair, followed. The Peace Movement strategy was adopted to expand Soviet support internationally and to bring about a relaxation of tensions between East and West.(105) The emergence of a quasi-right strategy--the use of detente, nationalism, peace sentiment, and anti-imperialism--was not without results.(106) Centrifugal forces within the Western alliance appeared as soon as the perceived Soviet threat diminished. The Europeans feared that the bellicosity of the United States would pull them into another war. Strained relations also developed over colonial policies and West Germany's relationship with NATO. Revived European nationalism began to resent the Americans' domineering leadership.(107)

The Peace Movement and National Front strategies went hand in hand. The communists formed many organizations to further Soviet policy within their respective countries. They were particularly active in the Federal Republic, where they focused on the United States as the enemy of German reunification.

While adverse developments in East-West relations called forth a policy of relaxation of tensions, of peaceful coexistence, the opposite response was elicited from Stalin by unsettling developments in East Eu-

rope.   The United States had been actively encouraging
and covertly supporting anti-communist and anti-Soviet
elements in East Europe.   Growing discord between
Stalin and Tito had culminated in Yugoslavia's expulsion from the Cominform in June 1948.   Tito's independence threatened Stalin's control in East Europe, and
he responded by purging the East European communist
parties of anyone whose allegiance was in   doubt.(108)
The ruthlessness with which the purge was carried out
matched Stalin's determination to prevent Tito from
setting a precedent for other leaders in the bloc.
Another setback for Soviet interests in Europe was the
defeat of communist forces in the Greek civil war in
the autumn of 1949.

     Two   positive developments served to offset these
negative ones and increase Soviet confidence in the
evolving international correlation of forces.   First,
the Soviet Union exploded an atomic bomb, ending the
American monopoly and thereby significantly improving
Soviet prospects for military security.   Second, the
Chinese Communist victory in October 1949, important on
its own merit, served to underline a basic Marxist
tenet that progress and communism are synonomous with
the future.   Furthermore, the Chinese victory drew
attention to the revolutionary potential in Asia.   Nationalist revolts in Indonesia and Indochina, and unrest in the Philippines, Burma, Malaya, Korea, North
Africa, and the Middle East seemed to verify Lenin's
analysis that the collapse of capitalism would be
brought about at its weakest links, i.e., by severing
the colonies from the imperial powers.   The Soviet
Union shifted its focus to areas of unrest in the Third
World which promised to be more receptive to Soviet
influence.

CONFLICT WITHIN THE SOVIET LEADERSHIP;
SOVIET POLICY TOWARD THE SBZ

The Soviet leadership appears to have been divided
over the focus and strategy of foreign policy most
effective in promoting the broad range of Soviet interests.(109) Substantive differences were reflected in
Soviet policy changes toward the SBZ in the early
postwar years. Competing viewpoints have been associated with two groups within the party: one group
identified with Andrei Zhdanov; the other, with
Lavrenti Beria, although clear identification of factions with specific leaders cannot be proven.(110)
Zhdanov's anti-Western policy promoted a decisive confrontation with the West before consolidation of a West
European alliance could be completed and sovietization
of the territories under Soviet control.(111) A competing faction linked to Beria appeared to favor a German
policy which would secure Soviet influence in Europe
without confrontation through a renewal of the Rapallo
Politik, named for the Treaty of Rapallo, which had
allied the USSR and Germany against the West after
World War I.(112) Fluctuations in Soviet policy toward
the Eastern Zone mirror the ebb and flow of influence
of the two approaches in interaction with the changing
policies of the Western powers.

Initial Soviet occupation measures were chaotic
and often contradictory. The occupying army appeared
to disintegrate into virtually independent commands for
a time.(113) Three Soviet agencies were established to
control and direct the economic affairs of the zone:
the Special Committee for Dismantling; the Group of
Soviet Occupation Forces in Germany (GSOVG), engaged in
requisitioning foodstuffs, raw materials, industrial
products, etc., for use of the Soviet army; and the
Soviet Military Administration of Germany (SMAD), responsible for re-establishing a functioning German
economy within given limits and in accordance with
Soviet needs.(114)

The Special Committee for Dismantling had been
established by Georgi Malenkov under the Council of
People's Commissars in 1944 to carry out a policy of
"economic disarmament" in Germany.(115) According to
Vladimir Rudolph, a former Soviet official in occupied
Germany, the purpose of the Special Committee was to
dismantle as much as possible before the armistice was
signed and reparations regulated, indicating that the
Politburo had little confidence in the possibility of

sovietizing even those parts of Germany occupied by Soviet troops.(116) Economic disarmament was to reduce the German economy to a point where it would not be a threat to the Soviet Union for years to come. Both the GSOVG and the SMAD were headed by Marshal Zhukov by virtue of his position as Supreme Commander of Soviet Occupying Forces and Military Governor of the SBZ.(117) The functions of these two organizations brought them into conflict with the Special Committee.(118) The work of the Special Committee for Dismantling was particularly disruptive to the efforts of the other organizations because it was, in itself, so disorganized. Every ministry down to individual Soviet factories had competing requests and even sent their own dismantling brigades to Germany.(119) Wolfgang Leonhard, a young communist who returned to Germany with leaders of the Communist Party of Germany (KPD) and the Soviet military, remarked on the open antagonism between different Soviet authorities. He noted that an officer of the Political Administration of the Red Army referred to reparations gangs as enemies!(120)

In the summer of 1945, Malenkov's policy was called into question when the Potsdam Agreements gave rise to the possibility of prolonged occupation of the SBZ and potential Soviet influence throughout Germany.(121) The desirability of dominating the East German economy for the economic benefit of the Soviet Union gained prominence. The Council of Ministers of the Soviet Union moved to eliminate the conflict by subordinating the Special Committee to the SMAD in the summer of 1946, but the committee continued to interfere with efforts to re-establish normal operations of the economy.(122) At the end of the year the problem was finally resolved when all Soviet employees in Germany were appointed to the Ministry of Foreign Trade, thereby eliminating competing interests and jurisdictions. The Ministry of Foreign Trade then decided on a system of priorities under which dismantled equipment was supplied to the various ministries.(123) Anastas Mikoyan, Minister of Foreign Trade, was not considered a member of either rival Politburo group but was thought to favor a policy of cooperation with the West associated with Beria.(124)

Once Soviet policy settled on an approach which assumed a continued presence in Germany, reflected in the subordiantion of the Special Committee, disagreement as to how Soviet influence might best be brought to bear projected the Zhdanov-Beria rivalry to the forefront. The opposing factions developed proteges among the Soviet occupying personnel in the SBZ. Sergei Tulpanov, Chief of the Information Bureau of the SMAD and leader of the Communist Party of the Soviet Union (CPSU) in the zone from 1945 to 1949, was a leading exponent of the position which favored rapid sovietization.(125)   His nemesis was found in Vladimir S. Semyonov, Political Advisor to the Supreme Commander and Military Governor of the zone.(126)   For Semyonov, a united Germany, even of bourgeois character, seemed more favorable to Soviet security than a divided Germany whose western portion would always present the danger of German revanche and threaten an East German state.(127)   The influence of Tulpanov and Semyonov on German policy varied with the fortunes of their respective "mentors" in Moscow. During 1946 and 1947, Zhdanov and Tulpanov's influence grew in conjunction with the adoption of confrontational strategy vis-a-vis the West.   These policies culminated in the Berlin blockade.   The failure of the blockade and consequent shift to a policy of relaxation of tension coincided with the rising fortunes Beria and Semyonov.(128)

Even as Stalin maintained tension within the Soviet leadership by playing opposing groups against each other, so too were opposing voices maintained in Germany. After Tulpanov's political fortune waned with the sudden death of Zhdanov and purge of his followers, Georgi M. Pushkin, a career diplomat, became chief of the Soviet diplomatic mission to the newly established GDR. He had presided over the transformation of Hungary into a people's republic and represented a renewed presence in support of sovietization in East Germany, a policy then linked with Molotov.(129) However, Semyonov also remained in his position and retained considerable influence in Germany.   U.S. intelligence noted with interest the dual nature of Soviet policy in Germany. A secret memorandum written in March 1950 reported the apparent conflict between Pushkin and Semyonov over appropriate policy toward Germany. This conflict was assumed to reflect parallel divisions within the Politburos in Moscow and Berlin. The strongest evidence for the existence of conflict was found in the confusion of Soviet policy which was visible "all down the line in indecision, demoralization, personal quarrels, etc."(130)

In sum, competing policies toward the SBZ were pursued simultaneously from the early conflict over dismantling versus economic reconstruction to the longer-term tension between sovietization of East Germany and accommodation with the West.   The presence of these competing interpretations of Soviet interest in Germany was maintained by rivalries in Soviet and East German leaderships reflecting the ambivalence of Soviet policy toward Germany as a whole.

THE SED(131)

The Soviets preempted Allied agreement on political activity within the occupation zones by issuing order no. 2, 10 June 1945, allowing the establishment of anti-fascist parties and free trade unions in the SBZ before the Potsdam Conference convened.(132) Four major parties reappeared: the Communist Party (KPD), Social Democratic Party (SPD), Christian Democratic Union (CDU), and Liberal Party (LPD). The Potsdam Conference upheld the Soviet action by emphasizing the prerogative of each occupying power and including only the broad statement "all democratic political parties with rights of assembly and of public discussion shall be allowed and encouraged thoughout Germany" in the political principles set forth in the Protocol of Proceedings.(133)   Thus, there was no common policy on political parties within Germany.   The Soviets favored such a policy, but France, in accordance with its opposition to any moves toward centralization, blocked all efforts to organize parties and trade unions on an all-German scale.(134)   Nonetheless, contact among the parties in the Soviet and Western Zones was common, and interzonal party congresses were held until late 1947. Political parties continued their interzonal contact into the next year.(135)

In the Soviet Zone, the SPD initially pushed for unification with the KPD and for socialization of the economy. There was genuine, widespread support for the unification of the two parties, especially among the rank and file who had shared long years of imprisonment and suffering under the Hitler regime. A consensus had emerged that the rise of Hitler was due to the division of the working class into two competing parties.(136) At first, however, the SMAD and KPD rejected all initiatives of the SPD for unification.   Ironically, the KPD's economic program was more conservative than that of the SPD.   According to the communists, objective conditions were not present for the establishment of socialism, in addition to the fact that the Western

powers would not permit the introduction of socialism
in Germany.(137)   This policy followed the cautious
direction associated with Beria and pursued by Semyonov
in the SMAD and by Anton Ackermann, leading theoreti-
cian of the KPD.(138)   The first executive conference
of the Communist Party in June 1945 called for comple-
tion of the bourgeois-democratic revolution of 1848 and
opposed immediate unity with the SPD.   The communists
perceived the need to build a broad-based party in
order to compete with the socialists.(139)

A series of developments led the Soviets, and
therefore the KPD, to change their position on unification of the two parties in late summer 1945.   First,
the Potsdam Agreements offered the possibility of political influence throughout Germany if a central administration were to be established.   Second, recent
free elections in Hungary and Austria had resulted in a
sound defeat of the communists.   Finally, the growing
strength and popularity of the SPD in the Soviet Zone
made a similar result in the upcoming German elections
seem likely.(140)   Thus, the Soviets sought unification
in order to co-opt the political forces of the SPD.
(141)   In the meantime, the SPD had become increasingly
divided between the Eastern and Western Zones.   Erich
Gniffke, a leading member of the SPD in the SBZ, placed
much of the blame for the split on Kurt Schumacher,
head of the Western SPD.   In early October 1945, Otto
Grotewohl, leader of the Soviet Zone SPD, and
Schumacher met in Hannover.   Each recognized the leadership of the other, but Grotewohl failed to secure
support from the Western SPD.(142)   A January 1946
meeting of the West German SPD adopted the position
that organizational unity of the SPD did not exist;
therefore, decisions taken by the SPD in the Soviet
Zone were not binding on the SPD of the Western Zones.
This position promoted by Schumacher undermined
Grotewohl's position that all-German unity of the SPD
had to precede SPD-KPD unification.(143)   Gniffke
stated that lack of support from the Western sections
of the party and pressure at the local level led the
SPD leadership in the SBZ to agree to unity with the
KPD.   Not surprisingly, the Western SPD rejected unification with the KPD.   SPD leaders in the Soviet Zone
feared that this difference in policy would lead to the
permanent division of Germany.(144)   Nonetheless,
increased pressure from the SMAD and KPD convinced the
SPD leadership that unification was the only way to
save their party from obliteration in the Soviet Zone.
The replacement of Marshal Zhukov by General Sokolovsky

as Supreme Commander and Military Governor in spring 1946 only increased the apprehension.   Zhukov had been seen as something of a protector of the SPD, while Sokolovsky was known to share Tulpanov's enthusiam for rapid sovietization of the zone.)145)   The SPD leadership clung to the hope that as the majority party they would dominate the new unity party.(146)

The KPD and SPD formally united to form the SED in the Soviet Zone on 21 April 1946.   The atmosphere was one of euphoria in the convention hall in Berlin when Wilhelm Pieck, head of the KPD, and Otto Grotewohl, head of the SPD, met at center stage and clasped hands in symbolic recognition of the unification of the German working class.   The first edition of the new party paper, <u>Neues Deutschland</u>, carried the "Manifest to the German People," which stressed the independence of the SED from foreign influence and its identity as a party with its roots in the German working class.(147) Statements by party leaders and the outline of principles and goals of the SED attempted to assuage popular fears of permanent Soviet control exercised through German communists and to disassociate the party as much as possible from the Soviet occupation authorities, with an eye to the upcoming elections.(148)

The last essentially free elections were held in the SBZ in October 1946.   Despite all the advantages the SMAD provided the SED and the Soviet harassment of candidates and supporters of other parties, the SED won less than 50 percent of the votes cast, although leading the competing parties by a substantial margin.(149) The same day, elections were held in Greater Berlin, where the SPD had not joined the KPD.   Those results provided a more accurate measure of SED strength.   The SPD polled 48.8 percent of the vote, while the SED received only 19.7 percent, running a poor third behind the SPD and the CDU.(150)   This was particularly significant because Berlin had long been a communist stronghold.

Growing hostility between East and West throughout 1947, expressed in the Marshall Plan, the Truman Doctrine, and the Cominform, was accompanied by a hardening of opposing positions in Germany.   The failure of the SED to win broad-based support in the October 1946 elections provided the impetus toward the transformation of the party into a party of the "New Type," i.e., a Marxist-Leninist party.   Walter Ulbricht, leader of a hard-line Muscovite faction within the SED, declared

that the process was underway in his report to the SED
Second Party Congress in September 1947, although the
real push came from the Tito-Stalin split in 1948.(151)
In order to preclude further centrifugal trends within
East Europe in the face of hostile East-West relations,
Stalin ordered the transformation of all communist
parties in East Europe to follow the CPSU model. The
Ulbricht faction of the SED was most eager to com-
ply.(152) Tulpanov warned Gniffke and other former SPD
leaders against factionalism and recommended that they
orient their thinking toward Ulbricht's. In July the
Central Secretariat of the SED published a statement
that "the most important lesson of the events in Yugoslavia for us, German Socialists, is to put every
effort into the transformation of the SED into a party
of the New Type."(153) A major purge of the party
which focused primarily on former SPD members was begun
that summer.(154) In January 1949 the First Party
Conference officially abandoned parity between former
KPD and SPD members in the SED, although in reality,
this principle had been overlooked in many cases since
the Second Party Congress in September 1947.(155)   It
was stated that parity was no longer relevant because
distinctions between former SPD and KPD members had
been essentially eliminated and because so many new SED
members had not belonged to either party.(156) The
decline of former SPD members in leading party positions was rapid. In the first party Politburo, which
served from January 1949 to July 1950, there were five
former KPD members and four former SPD members; in the
second Politburo, July 1950 to July 1953, there were
only three former SPD members of a total of fifteen
members and candidates.(157) The Third Party Congress
of the SED in July 1950 adopted new party statutes
modelled after those of the CPSU.(158) Ulbricht's
furtune rose with the sovietization of the party. In
1950 he was elected General Secretary, marking the
dominance of his hard-line faction in the SED.(159)

The balancing of competing factions within the SED
reflected ongoing divisions within the CPSU over appropriate policy toward Germany and the SBZ. U.S. intelligence reports at that time identified two groups
within the SED: the moderates led by Pieck and
Grotewohl, and the radicals led by Ulbricht. In a
breakdown of leading SED personalities and their functions, Grotewohl was seen as the principal authority
for parliamentary and constitutional procedures, while
Pieck was noted to have considerable prestige with the
SMAD and often exercised final authority on internal

party matters. Ulbricht was also perceived to exercise
great power.   He, along with Pieck and Grotewohl, had
regular direct contact with the SMAD.   Ulbricht's importance was attributed to SMAD confidence and a
fiercely loyal faction of supporters within the SED.
Franz Dahlem and Anton Ackermann were also recongized
as wielding considerable influence and authority within
the party.(160) Ackermann represented the most liberal
orientation of those mentioned.   Another intelligence
report on growing tension within the SED supports the
absence of a dominant faction.   It was noted that
tensions within the party were so great that Pieck
decided not to go to Moscow to celebrate Stalin's
birthday, 21 December, but sent Ulbricht alone.   The
radical faction reportedly wanted to get rid of
Grotewohl, and Pieck not only wanted to stay home to
prevent this, but also wanted to ensure Ulbricht's
absence in order to diffuse such an attempt.(161)   It
seems reasonable to conclude, therefore, that although
Ulbricht was certainly a powerful voice from the beginning, competing visions for Germany's future were not
overshadowed by Ulbricht's until a change of circumstances favored the radical faction.

     The transformation of the party went hand in hand
with the increasingly overt alignment of the SED with
the Soviet Union.   Grotewohl had consistently been a
severe critic of Soviet excesses in the zone and a
staunch supporter of Germany's independence.   At the
Second Party Congress in 1947, however, he spoke
against the idea of a neutral Germany serving as a
bridge between East and West--a basic tenet of the
SPD.(162)   In an unexpected move, he also joined his
communist counterparts in paying tribute to Lenin's
achievements: "We will and must learn from the experience of the Russian Workers movement. . . . We must
learn from the achievements of Leninism and adapt those
elements appropriate to Germany."(163)   In the past,
reference had been made only to the Marxist character
of the SED. Grotewohl moved further in recognizing the
Marxist-Leninist nature of the party in his criticism
of Schumacher's efforts to undermine the SED and his
support for the transformation of the SED into a party
of the New Type.   Grotewohl stated,   "In our Party no
one can be a Marxist who is not a Leninist."(164)

     Since its founding, the SED had been cautious in
its admiration of the Soviet Union. The party presented itself first and foremost as a German party serving
the needs and interests of the German people.   The SED

had adopted the "Separate German Road to Socialism" theory formulated by Anton Ackermann and first published in December 1945.(165) First KPD, then SED, official policy held the Soviet model to be inapplicable in Germany due to the advanced stage of industrial development already achieved. The Separate Road thesis was of great significance to virtually everyone in the KPD, including Ackermann and Wolfgang Leonhard, who had become disillusioned with the Soviet system through firsthand experience in the USSR during the war years. It held out the hope that the German communists might eventually be able to disassociate themselves from the harsh policies of the Soviet occupation authorities. Only a small number of officials who completely identified with Moscow, such as Ulbricht, opposed the policy, according to Leonhard.(166)

Separate Roads to Socialism was standard theory throughout East Europe until the summer of 1948. Leonhard notes that many German communists, including himself and Ackermann, did not see this as a tactical device, although it is generally perceived as such in the West. Benefit of hindsight has strengthened the Western assessment, although in this case hindsight seems to distort the realities of the time. The Separate Roads theory represented a period and temper of experimentation which met the dual requirements of the USSR in the immediate postwar period: to expand Soviet influence in East Europe in order to secure a buffer zone with the West, and to avoid conflict with the United States. Given the imbalance of power between the United States and the USSR at war's end, the Soviet Union was in no position to press the sovietization of East Europe against U.S. opposition. It is, therefore, conceivable that the Separate Roads policy would have continued had circumstances not intervened. Yugoslavia's expulsion from the Cominform in June 1948 for crimes of nationalist deviation signalled the policy's end. The Separate Roads theory became treason throughout the bloc. The SED officially denounced Ackermann's thesis. An article on the Yugoslav question in the party press declared that the "mistakes of the Yugoslav Communist Party show [the SED] that a clear and unambiguous pro-Soviet position is the only possibility for every socialist party."(167) Ackermann recanted in September.(168) Repudiation of the Separate Roads theory complemented the transformation of the communist parties throughout East Europe and in East Germany into parties of the New Type, which represented a tightening of Soviet control in the face of Tito's insubordination and consolidation of a united Western position in Germany.

POLITICAL STRUCTURE

The development of the political structure in the SBZ paralleled the evolution of Soviet policy in Germany. In June 1945, new administrations at the local levels were created, followed closely by provincial (Land) administrations. Their tasks were primarily ones of re-establishing order and restoring and rebuilding economic functions.(169) The provincial administrations became the first provisional provincial governments (Landesregierungen).(170)

In July 1945, a central administration for the entire Soviet Zone was ordered to be established. The divisions corresponded to major departments of government. They served as advisory organs to the SMAD.(171)

As events in Germany seemed to be moving toward a divided country, the SED called for an all-German People's Congress for Unity and a Just Peace to convene. All anti-fascist, democratic parties, unions, and other mass organizations from all over Germany were invited to the first People's Congress (Volkskongress) in December 1947 in Berlin. Over twenty-two hundred delegates attended, of whom more than six hundred came from the Western Zones.(172) The congress called for the creation of a central German government, the election of a National Assembly, and a national referendum on the reunification issue.(173) The Second People's Congress met in March 1948 and elected an executive body, the German People's Council (Deutscher Volksrat) to function between Congresses. The council was authorized to appoint a committee to work out guidelines for the establishment of a German democratic republic.(174) The committee produced a constitution based on an original draft by the SED in November 1946, which was accepted by the Third People's Congress in May 1949.(175)

In a move toward centralization of the government, the German Economic Commission (DWK) was established by the SMAD in June 1947. Although the economic functions of the DWK were generally stressed, it was actually similar to a government central executive. The majori-

ty of all-German administrations were directly subordinate to it.(176)   The administrations covered all basic
societal functions: transportation, post and telegaph,
fuel and power, agriculture, education, justice,
etc.(177)   Thus, it is clear that DWK authority ex-
ceeded economic matters.   The effect was to reduce the
authority of the Länder governments.

Following the formal announcement of the creation
of a West German government, a provisional government
of the GDR was established.   The administrative divisions of the DWK were transformed into ministries of
the GDR.   Otto Grotewohl headed the new government,
although Ulbricht was soon recognized as the dominant
German in the SBZ.   Wilhelm Pieck was elected
President.

General Chuikov, who had replaced Sokolovsky as
head of the SMAD in March, turned over to the provisional government the administrative functions of the
Soviet Military Administration on 10 October 1949.(178)
The Soviet Union and the GDR exchanged diplomatic missions on 15 October--a move quickly followed by the
other East bloc countries.(179) In November, the SMAD
was reorganized as the Soviet Control Commission, with
reduced formal authority in official recognition of
East Germany's new status.

The government functioned as an instrument of the
party, and the leading positions in each were held by
the same persons. It must be recognized, however, that
real power flowed from the Soviet Union until Stalin's
death.   Evidence for this includes instructions from
Moscow to top SED leaders on most issues and difficult
shifts in policy, such as abandonment of a nationalist
orientation expressed in the German Road to Socialism
in favor of adherence to the Soviet model, and the
shift from rejection to acceptance of the Oder-Neisse
border.   The uniformly unpopular Soviet policy of dismantling (discussed in Chapter 3) as well as the Soviet
failure to repatriate thousands of German POWs until
the mid 1950s shows the lack of German communist influence with the Soviet occupiers.(180) Stalin was known
to have been particularly wary of the German communists
because they had failed to prevent Hitler's rise to
power, even though Stalin's own policy instructions to
the KPD through the Comintern had been critical to that
development. At the same time, he was mistrustful of
those German communists who had remained in Germany and
attempted to organize resistance against Hitler.   In

addition, the uncertainty of Germany's future and conflicting Soviet interests reduced the SED to an instrument of Soviet policy to a greater degree than in the
rest of East Europe.   At the same time, however, the
SED enjoyed much greater administrative authority in
the SBZ than any German political party in the Western
Zones in the early postwar period.   Nonetheless, it
must be concluded that the Soviets developed their
policy toward Germany largely irrespective of the
interests or fortunes of the SED, although major shifts
in policy orientation struck a responsive chord with
some factions of the party.

CONCLUSIONS

The establishment of two German states in 1949
dramatically symbolized the perceived irreconcilability
of interests of East and West.   The division cannot be
said to have occurred as a result of a plan on either
side, but rather, to have developed in conjunction with
the dynamic spiral of international tension between the
two systems.

The proceedings of the Yalta and Potsdam conferences illustrate the lack of understanding of competing
postwar goals while bringing to light the issues of
fundamental disagreement which would ultimately undermine the alliance. Stalin himself prophetically stated
toward the close of the Yalta Conference: " It is not
so difficult to keep unity in time of war since there
is a common aim to defeat a common enemy. . . . The
difficult task will come after the war when diverse
interests tend to divide the Allies. . . ."(181)

Charges that the United States "gave away" too
much at Yalta were common in the 1950s as well as
today.   They seem to reflect a perspective which accords no legitimacy to Soviet interests or security
requirements.   It must be noted that at the time, U.S.
concessions on reparations and Poland seemed to Roosevelt and Churchill to be matched in importance by
Soviet concessions on the United Nations and French
participation in the occupation of Germany.   Stalin's
preoccupation with the reparations and Polish issues
was due to their direct importance to Soviet national
security.   By contrast, U.S. national security was not
directly threatened by any of the matters at issue, as

evidenced by the American absorption with formation of
the United Nations, the intended forum for postwar
cooperation. In addition, Roosevelt expressed particular sympathy toward Soviet interests because of the
USSR's terrible sacrifices during the war, Stalin's
formal commitment to enter the war against Japan three
months after Germany's surrender, and Stalin's support
for U.S. proposals concerning the United Nations. The
tentative nature of the Yalta Agreements made them
subject to differing interpretations which, when altered because of new conditions and a more hostile U.S.
disposition toward the USSR at Potsdam, fostered resentment and distrust.

     But the issues run much deeper than trading con-
cessions. The burgeoning difficulties which finally
broke the alliance had no specific starting point; they
were inherent in fundamental differences between the
two systems which had only been partially submerged in
the interest of fighting a common enemy. That the West
and the USSR had conflicting visions of an acceptable
postwar order is clearly represented in their opposing
conceptions of democracy. The West apparently expected
the USSR to acquiesce to the reimposition of an order
akin to the status quo ante bellum in Europe, which had
been decidedly anti-Soviet. Because the Soviet search
for security could be equated with the spread of communism, Western leaders interpreted Soviet expansion as
ultimately threatening their own security. In turn,
the United States shifted from a traditional policy of
isolation to one of international involvement to check
the communist advance. There can be no illusion of a
grand design on either side. The Soviet Union, in
dramatic contrast to the United States, was acting from
a position of economic devastation and absolute military vulnerability. The Kremlin's reparations policy,
rejection of Marshall aid, and the Berlin blockade were
all expressions of weakness. They were interpreted in
the West, however, as hostile and aggressive actions
which spurred the consolidation of the Western Zones of
Germany and their incorporation into the Western alliance. The United States initiated each step in the
series of consequent actions discussed in this chapter
which resulted in the formation of two German states.

     Stalin's priorities in Germany were to rebuild the
Soviet economy through use of German resources, eliminate German military capability, ensure that Germany
would never become a member of an anti-Soviet alliance,
and, if possible, win Germany to the Soviet vision of a

new postwar order.   These competing and often conflicting goals reflect the fundamental dilemma facing the
USSR in the postwar period as an emergent powerful
nation state and as the leader of an international
revolutionary movement.   Soviet uncertainty as to how
to achieve the strongest possible position in Germany
in order to attain these goals was reflected in the
conflicting voices within the Soviet leadership which
promoted competing occupation policies and the major
policy shift vis-à-vis the Western powers from confrontation to negotiation in the late 1940s.   The policy
shift to peaceful coexistence resulted from a broad-
range assessment of the failure of militancy to improve
the Soviet position or enhance socialist prospects.
The German communists mirrored these fluctuations in
their role as an instrument of Soviet policy.

In sum, the deterioration of the alliance and the
escalation of tensions internationally were due to a
fundamental clash of interests of the dynamic, new
world powers.   The dishonesty, hostility, and aggres-
siveness perceived on both sides intensified and accelerated these trends.

NOTES

1.   The literature on the breakdown of the alliance is voluminous. The ongoing controversy over the interpretation of events can only be touched upon here. Some of the more interesting works on the subject include: Daniel Yergin A Shattered Peace: The Origins of the Cold War and the National Security State (Boston: Houghton Mifflin, 1977); Joyce Kolko and Gabriel Kolko, The Limits of Power: The World and United States Foreign Policy, 1945-1954 (New York: Harper & Row, 1972); Boris Meissner, Russland, die Westmächte und Deutschland: Die sowjetische Deutschlandpolitik, 1943-1953 (Hamburg: H.H. Nölke Verlag, 1953); Herbert Feis, Churchill Roosevelt Stalin (Princeton, N.J.: Princeton University Press, 1957); W. Averell Harriman, Special Envoy to Churchill and Stalin, 1941-1946 (New York: Random House, 1975); John Lewis Gaddis, The United States and the Origins of the Cold War (New York: Columbia University Press, 1972); Ivanovich Orlik, Imperialisticheskiye Derzhavy i Vostochnaya Evropa, 1945-1965 (Moscow: Academy of Sciences, 1968). Orlik provides a valuable source for a Soviet perspective.

2.   A Decade of American Foreign Policy: Basic Documents, 1941-49 (New York: Greenwood Press, 1968), p. 10 (hereafter cited as Basic Documents).

3.   Diane Shaver Clemens, Yalta (New York: Oxford University Press, 1970), pp. 40-42. Philip Mosely, a representative to the European Advisory Commission (EAC), attributes this to the deep differences between the President's political and military advisors. Mosely, The Kremlin and World Politics (New York: Vintage Books, 1960), pp. 158-59, 202. Secretary of State Cordell Hull recounts in his memoirs that EAC functions were limited to the terms of surrender and plans for their execution, reflecting the U.S. preference for delaying peace arrangements until the end of the war.   Hull, The Memoirs of Cordell Hull, 2 vols. (New York: The Macmillan Co., 1948), 2:1642.

4.   The Italian armistice was negotiated between the United States, Great Britain, and the Supreme Allied Commander of the Mediterranean without Soviet participation.   The State Department prophetically protested this, saying it would allow the Soviets to

exclude American and British participation in armi-
stices in East Europe, where their troops were not
present. Mosely, The Kremlin and World Politics,
p. 203. Only token Soviet participation on the Allied
Control Commission in Italy was allowed. Basic Documents, p. 458. At Potsdam, when the United States and
Great Britain complained about lack of access and information in East Europe, specifically Rumania, Bulgaria, and Hungary, Stalin countered that the Soviets
had no rights in Italy. U.S. Department of State,
Foreign Relations of the United States: Diplomatic
Papers: The Conference of Berlin (Potsdam) (Washington,
D.C.: Government Printing Office, 1960), pp. 358-63
(hereafter cited as Potsdam Documents).

5.   The Soviet army sat on the other side of the
Vistula while the retreating Nazi army slaughtered the
Polish resistance in the Warsaw uprising. George
Kennan reports that, in addition, Stalin denied U.S.
Ambassador Harriman permission to use the American
shuttle base in the Ukraine to drop supplies to the
Poles. Kennan was a member of the U.S. Embassy staff
in Moscow at the time. George F. Kennan, Memoirs,
1925-1950 (Boston: Little, Brown and Co., 1967),
pp. 210-11. Secretary Hull remembers that Stalin gave
permission for one flight on 18 September and for one
other which never took place. Hull, Memoirs, 2:1447.

6.   Sir Winston S. Churchill, Triumph and Tragedy
(Boston: Houghton Mifflin, 1953), pp. 227-33.
Churchill contends that the division was in no way
intended to prescribe the representation on control
commissions in any of the countries nor to establish
rigid spheres of influence. Hull notes that Stalin
assumed the United States had agreed to this division
of Europe since Roosevelt agreed to the division of
military responsibilities. Hull, Memoirs, 2:1458. At
a meeting with Yugoslav communist leaders in April
1945, Stalin said that each side would impose its own
social system on the territory its forces occupy.
Milovan Djilas, Conversations with Stalin (New York:
Harcourt, Brace & World, 1962), p. 114.

7.   W. Averell Harriman, Peace with Russia (New
York: Simon & Schuster, 1959), pp. 3-4; Kennan, Memoirs, pp. 256-58.

8.   Secretary Hull recounts his impression, after
meeting Stalin in October 1943, that an American with
Stalin's personality and approach might well reach high

public office in the United States.   He added that
Roosevelt looked forward to meeting Stalin with the
enthusiasm of a boy.   Hull, Memoirs, 2:1311-13.

    9.   Wolfgang Leonhard,   Child of the Revolution
(Clinton, Mass: Colonial Press, 1958), p. 271

    10.   Clemens's Yalta presents a revisionist anal-
ysis of the Yalta Conference and Allied difficulties.
The author examines the major issues dividing the powers prior to and during the conference topically, based
on extensive use of primary sources, including Soviet
documents first published in International Affairs
(Moscow, 1965).

    11.   Churchill pushed to include France as a full
partner in the occupation of Germany.   Roosevelt's
statement at the first plenary meeting at Yalta that
the U.S. occupation would be limited to two years
aroused fears of creating a power vacuum in Europe
which the Soviets would rush to fill.   Churchill,
Triumph and Tragedy, p. 353. Roosevelt's public statement of intention also led Churchill to oppose Stalin
and the President on the dismemberment and reparations
issues.
    Charles Bohlen, a career foreign service officer
who served in Moscow and was Roosevelt's interpreter at
the Yalta Conference, recounted that Stalin's acceptance of France as a full occupying power reinforced
Roosevelt's notion that he exercised great personal
influence over Stalin.   Bohlen further speculated that
Stalin's acquiescence on France may have influenced
Roosevelt's position on reparations.   Charles E.
Bohlen, Witness to History, 1929-1969 (New York: W.W.
Norton & Co., 1973), p. 185.

    12.   The Control Council would be composed of the
three Commanders-in-Chief.   Its functions were

    to ensure appropriate uniformity of action by
    the Commanders-in-Chief in their respective
    zones; to work out military, political, eco-
    nomic and other problems affecting Germany as
    a whole based on instructions received from
    their respective home governments; to control
    the German central administration; and to di-
    rect the administration of Greater Berlin.

The Control Council was to meet at least once in ten
days and meet upon the request of any one member.   All

decisions were to be unanimous. U.S. Department of
State, Foreign Relations of the United States: Diplomatic Papers: The Conferences at Malta and Yalta, 1945
(Washington, D.C.: Government Printing Office, 1955),
pp. 124-25,970 (hereafter cited as Yalta Documents).

In discussions of possible French participation in
the Control Commission, Churchill argued there was no
danger that the commission would make basic policy for
Germany. Stalin countered that the commission would be
involved in the daily work of administering Germany and
that the effect would be that of policymaking. Yalta
Documents, pp. 618-19.

13. "The Yalta Conference Protocol of Proceedings," Article III, "Dismemberment of Germany," Basic
Documents, pp. 29-30.

14. Roosevelt and Churchill had approved the
Morgenthau Plan for pastoralization and dismemberment
of Germany at the second Quebec Conference in late
summer 1944, although the plan was dropped by the time
of Yalta. Feis, Churchill Roosevelt Stalin, p. 534;
Mosely, "Dismemberment of Germany," Foreign Affairs
(April 1950), p. 491. Discussions of possible dismemberment of Germany may have begun as early as December
1941 between Churchill and Roosevelt. Formal discussions began in the spring of 1943. The issue was
allowed to fade between Yalta and Potsdam. Mosely,
"Dismemberment of Germany,", p. 488. Stalin publicly
repudiated dismemberment and destruction of Germany on
the day following the German surrender. Josif Stalin,
Über den grossen vaterländischen Krieg der Sowjetunion
(Berlin: Dietz Verlag, 1950), pp. 221-23.

15. Yalta Documents, pp. 620-21, 707. The Soviets
deferred to Western objections to reparations in cash
based on the post-World War I experience, and since
1943, spoke only of reparations in kind. Clemens,
Yalta, p. 37.

16. Yalta Documents, p. 622. As early as the
Moscow Foreign Ministers Conference in October 1943,
the United States expressed its intention to honor
Soviet reparations claims. Hull, Memoirs, 2:1286.

17. John Backer, The Decision to Divide Germany
(Durham, N.C.: Duke University Press, 1978), p. 67.

18. Yalta Documents, pp. 901-02.

19.   Ibid., pp. 978-79. (See Appendix A for complete text.) There is no firm evidence in the minutes of the meetings to support the claim that the United States agreed to the Soviet reparations figure in exchange for Stalin's concurrence on the voting procedure in the United Nations' Security Council made by Adam Ulam in The Rivals: American & Russia Since World War II (New York: Viking Press, 1971), pp. 53-54. Stalin's concession was linked in discussion with winning admission of two or three Soviet Republics to the United Nations. Yalta Documents, pp. 711-15. Bohlen felt Roosevelt's support for Stalin on the reparations issue might have been linked to the admission of France as an occupying power. Bohlen, Witness to History, p. 185. Roosevelt and Churchill viewed Stalin's agreement on the voting procedure a significant concession when, in fact, Stalin seemed little interested and uninformed about the issue, reflecting his gauge of its importance. Yalta Documents, pp. 660-67; James F. Byrnes, Speaking Frankly (Westport, Conn.: Greenwood Press, 1974), p. 37; Gaddis, Origins of the Cold War, p. 354. Because of Roosevelt's valuation of Stalin's concession, it is, however, not unreasonable to link his support for Stalin on the reparations issue with the voting issue, among others, out of a feeling of gratitude.

20.   Churchill, Triumph and Tragedy, p. 366.

21.   Bernt Conrad, "How Definitive Is the Oder-Neisse Line?" from Die Welt (24 December 1984), in The German Tribune 51 (21 April 1985), p. 14.

22.   Yalta Documents, pp. 728, 805-6.

23.   Article VI of the final communique called for a reorganization of the government "which is now functioning in Poland." Yalta Documents, p. 974. Furthermore, the United States had withdrawn its insistence on Allied supervision of elections. Bohlen, Witness to History, p. 192.

24.   Feis, Churchill Roosevelt Stalin, pp. 285-87; Conrad, "How Definitive Is the Oder-Neisse," p. 14.

25.   Yalta Documents, p. 709.

26.   Ibid., p. 974.

27.   Thomas G. Paterson, "The Sources of the Cold War," in Major Problems in American Foreign Policy, Documents and Essays, Vol. II, 2nd edition, ed. by Thomas G. Paterson, (Lexington, Mass: D.C. Heath & Co., 1984), pp. 356-57; "Harry Hopkins and Josef Stalin Discuss Lend-Lease and Poland, 1945," in Paterson, ed., Major Problems in American Foreign Policy, pp. 289-92.

28.   Byrnes, Speaking Frankly, p. 82.

29.   Backer, Decision to Divide Germany, pp. 35-45.

30.   Potsdam Documents, pp. 903-4, 950.

31.   Ibid., pp. 295-97, 428-32, 473. The transfer of Silesia to Poland will be discussed in conjunction with the issue of Poland's western frontier.

32.   Ibid., p. 297.

33.   Ibid., p. 474.

34.   Ibid., pp. 1485-86; Backer, Decision to Divide Germany, pp. 162-63.

35.   Potsdam Documents, pp. 472-76, 514.

36.   Ibid., p. 1485.

37.   Mosely, Kremlin and World Politics, p. 212; Feis, Between War and Peace: The Potsdam Conference (Princeton, N.J.: Princeton University Press, 1960), p. 36. Stalin justified the recognition to Hopkins on the grounds that the Red Army needed the Warsaw government's cooperation. Feis, Between War and Peace, pp. 102-3.

38.   Mosely, Kremlin and World Politics, p. 212; Feis, Between War and Peace, p. 105. Not all important Polish political leaders agreed to participate in the conference. Wincenty Witos, head of the popular Peasant Party, declined an invitation but was, nonetheless, given a position in the new government. Feis, Between War and Peace, pp. 205-8.

39.   Feis, Between War and Peace, p. 208.

40.   Ibid., p. 214.

41.   Potsdam Documents, p. 1110.

42.   Ibid., p. 1490.

43.   Byrnes, Speaking Frankly, pp. 79-80; Mosely, Kremlin and World Politics, p. 212; Feis, Potsdam Conference, p. 36.

44.   Potsdam Documents, pp. 210-14. Churchill replied that at least two and a half million Germans were still there.

45.   Ibid., pp. 1491-92. See Appendix B for complete text.

46.   Ibid., pp. 1495-96; Beate Ruhm von Oppen, ed., Documents on Germany under Occupation, 1945-54 (London: Oxford University Press, 1955), pp. 159, 161-63 (hereafter cited as Documents on Germany); Manuel Gottlieb, The German Peace Settlement and the Berlin Crisis (New York: Paine-Whitman, 1960), p. 137. The East German leadership acquiesced to this loss of territory in a 1950 agreement with Poland. The border remained officially unrecognized by the Western powers until the 1970s.

47.   Potsdam Documents, p. 1481.

48.   Ibid., p. 1483.

49.   Ibid., p. 1485.

50.   Ibid., p. 1484. The distribution of commodities was also tied into the reparations formula, which was to cause significant trouble among the Allies later.

51.   The Council of Foreign Ministers was established at the Potsdam Conference to meet not later than 1 September 1945 to prepare treaties of peace with the European enemy states for submission to the United Nations. The council included the Foreign Ministers of the Five Great Powers: the United States, the United Kingdom, USSR, France, and China. Potsdam Documents, pp. 1478-80.

52.   Byrnes, Speaking Frankly, pp. 93-107; Basic Documents, pp. 51-58.

53.   Erich Gniffke was a high-ranking member of
the former SPD, close to Grotewohl, the Party Chairman,
and thereby was included in the leadership circle of
the SBZ.   In March 1948, he was elected General Secretary of the Deutsches Volksrat.   He details the early
postwar years in the Soviet Zone with the benefit of
access to the highest echelons of government and party
until his defection in 1948.   Gniffke, _Jahre_ _mit_
Ulbricht (Cologne: Verlag Wissenschaft und Politik,
1966), p. 123.

54.   At the same time, there was no food surplus
in the SBZ to help feed the West Germans, but the SBZ
was expected to exchange food for a percentage of
reparations received from the Western Zones.   The trade
between a fixed amount and a percentage would work to
the Soviet disadvantage.   Gottlieb, _German_ _Peace_ _Set-_
tlement, pp. 123-38.
A Department of State paper for the President on
recommendations for the economic treatment of Germany
included the evaluation that the Soviet Zone was a food
surplus area with little bomb damage. _Yalta_ _Documents_,
p. 169.

55.   Lucius D. Clay, _Decision_ _in_ _Germany_ (Garden
City, N.Y.: Doubleday & Co., 1950), pp. 120-21; Backer,
Decision _to_ _Divide_ _Germany_, pp. 141-42.

56.   Hugh de Santis, _The_ _Diplomacy_ _of_ _Silence:_
The _American_ _Foreign_ _Service,_ _the_ _Soviet_ _Union_ _and_ _the_
Cold _War,_ _1933-1947_ (Chicago: The University of Chicago
Press, 1980), p. 179.

57.   General Clay viewed this as the first important break with Soviet policy in Germany.   Clay, _Deci-_
sion _in_ _Germany_, p. 120.   Adam Ulam concurs with this
assessment and sees it as the beginning of a progressive erosion of Allied unity.   Ulam, _Expansion_ _and_
Coexistence: _The_ _History_ _of_ _Soviet_ _Foreign_ _Policy,_
_1917-1967_ (New York: Praeger, 1968), p. 443.

58.   J.P. Nettl, _The_ _Eastern_ _Zone_ _and_ _Soviet_
Policy _in_ _East_ _Germany,_ _1945-1950_ (London: Oxford University Press, 1951), p. 157.

59.   _Documents_ _on_ _Germany_, pp. 146-47.   The Soviets had proposed four-power control of the Ruhr at
Potsdam. _Potsdam_ _Documents_, pp. 451-52, 521-22.

60.   _Basic_ _Documents_, pp. 84-85.

61.   <u>Documents on Germany</u>, p. 158.

62.   Ibid., pp. 195-99. A practical incentive for the fusion of the two zones was to allow the United States to pay much of British occupation costs. Britain was destitute, but the U.S. Congress was in no mood to finance the British Zone. The fusion obviated the political problem.

63.   Ibid., pp. 211-17. Complete text of Marshal Sokolovsky's remarks on cited pages.

64.   Zhdanov was a member of the Secretariat and the Politburo. As head of the Leningrad party organization, he also had a strong power base from which to pursue his political interests. He was considered third in line in the party hierarchy behind Stalin and Malenkov.

65.   Soviet and Western interests, often historically based, clashed in Iran, Turkey, and Greece. Oil and an autonomous Azerbaidzhan provided the focal points for conflict in Iran. In Turkey, the United States thwarted the age old Russian interest in controlling the Dardenelles. Walter LaFeber, <u>America, Russia and the Cold War</u> (New York: John Wiley and Sons, 1967), pp. 27-8. At Yalta and Potsdam, the British were supportive of the Soviet request for revision of the Montreaux Convention which allowed Turkey control over the Straits. <u>Yalta Documents</u>, pp. 328, 903-5; <u>Potsdam Documents</u>, pp. 301-5. The United States had been less supportive but not adverse.
The U.S. failure to send clear signals to Stalin regarding its national security interests in Iran and Turkey, and the British withdrawal from Greece gave the impression of opportunities for Soviet expansion of influence. In Asia, the Soviets and Americans supported opposing sides in China's civil war and faced off at the 38th parallel in Korea.

66.   DeSantis, <u>The Diplomacy of Silence</u>, p. 172. The Cominform was organized in September 1947. The SED was not included as a member, but the Party was, nonetheless, bound by Cominform decisions.

67.   N.S. Khrushchev, <u>Khrushchev Remembers</u> (Boston: Little, Brown & Co., 1970), p. 393.

68.   Vyacheslav Mikhailovich Molotov, <u>Problems of Foreign Policy: Speeches and Statements</u> (Moscow: For-

eign Languages Publishing House, 1949), pp. 381-85.

69.   Basic Documents, p. 101.

70.   Ibid., pp. 99-100.

71.   Bohlen, Witness to History, pp. 262-63.

72.   Marshall D. Shulman, Stalin's Foreign Policy Reappraised (Cambridge: Harvard University Press, 1963), pp. 14-15, 35.

73.   Eugene Varga, Changes in the Economy of Capitalism Resulting from the Second World War (Moscow, 1946).

74.   Soviet Views on the Post-War World Economy: An Official Critique of Eugene Varga's Changes in the Economy of Capitalism Resulting from the Second World War. Translated by Leo Gruliow. (Washington: Public Affairs Press, 1948).

75.   Studiengesellschaft für Zeitprobleme, Die sowjetische Deutschlandpolitik, 4 parts (Duisdorf bei Bonn: Studiengesellschaft für Zeitprobleme, 1962-1963) 2:111-12.

76.   Molotov, Speeches and Statements, pp. 459-62, 468-69.

77.   Shulman, Stalin Reappraised, p. 15; LaFeber, Cold War, p. 62; Carola Stern, Porträt einer bolsche-wistischen Partei (Cologne: Verlag für Politik und Wirtschaft, 1957), p. 77.

78.   Gniffke, Jahre mit Ulbricht, p. 224.

79.   Franz L. Neumann, "Soviet Policy in Germany," American Academy of Political and Social Science Annals (May 1949), p. 170; DDR: Werden und Wachsen (Berlin: Dietz Verlag, 1975), p. 115.

80.   Backer, Decision to Divide Germany, p. 100; Documents on Germany, pp. 239-45.

81.   Documents on Germany, pp. 261-63; Studienge-sellschaft, Deutschlandpolitik, 2:119-24; Werden und Wachsen, p. 115.

82.   Werner Weber and Werner Jahn, _Synopse zur Deutschlandpolitik, 1941 bis 1973_ (Göttingen: Verlag Otto Schwartz & Co., 1973), p. 44.

83.   See _Dokumente zur Deutschlandpolitik der Sowjetunion_, 3 vols. (Berlin: Rütten & Loening, 1957), 1:181-83, for complete text of Marshal Sokolovsky's statement before the Control Council.
It is possible that the Soviets thought the West would make concessions on uniting the Western Zones rather than risk breakup of the Control Council. Studiengesellschaft, _Deutschlandpolitik_, p. 149. Otto Grotewohl, joint chairman of the SED, criticized the actions of the Western powers at the Second German People's Congress, 17 March, holding Western attempts to link the Western Zones with the Western bloc and to integrate them into the Marshall Plan responsible for the final division of Germany. _Documents on Germany_, pp. 280-81. General Clay contends that the failure of the Allies to agree on economic issues led to the breakup of the quadripartite government in Germany. Clay, _Decision in Germany_, p. 41.

84.   A communique was issued by the conference on 7 June 1948 which reaffirmed the recommendations of the first meeting at the end of 1947. For complete text of communique, see _Documents on Germany_, pp. 286-90.

85.   The intentions of the Western powers appeared more ominous by the signing of the Brussels Pact in March 1948. The pact was signed by Great Britain, France, and the Benelux countries. It was seen by the West as a defensive alliance against communist aggression, the fear of which was heightened by the communist takeover in Czechoslovakia. Weber and Jahn, _Synopse_, pp. 44-45.

86.   _Dokumente zur Deutschlandpolitik der Sowjetunion_, 1:183-94. In fact Potsdam and Yalta did not include provisions for four-power control of the Ruhr or establishment of an all-German government.

87.   It will be recalled that the Soviets began printing extra currency to circumvent the cutoff in reparations deliveries from the Western Zones in spring 1946. For the text of the first monetary reform law, see Johannes Hohlfeld, ed._Dokumente der deutschen Politik und Geschichte von 1948 bis zur Gegenwart_, 8 vols. (Berlin: Dokumenten Verlag, 1951-56), 6:283-90 (hereafter cited as _Dokumente der deutschen Politik und_

Geschichte).

88.   Ibid., pp. 291-93.

89.   Ibid., p. 291, n. 3.

90.   Ibid., pp. 295-97.

91.   Documents on Germany, pp. 312-13; Gniffke, Jahre mit Ulbricht, pp. 313-14; Studiengesellschaft, Deutschlandpolitik, 2:142-45.

92.   Dokumente der deutschen Politik und Geschichte, 6:298-99.

93.   Clay, Decision in Germany, p. 367.

94.   Documents on Germany, pp. 314-15.

95.   Clay, Decision in Germany, pp. 360-61.

96.   Albania joined in April 1949, and the GDR became a member in September 1950.

97.   This was the same day the Grundgesetz (Basic Law) went into effect for West Germany. Weber and Jahn, Synopse, p. 76.

98.   Dokumente zur Deutschlandpolitik der Sowjetunion, 1:217-18, 222-23.

99.   Studiengesellschaft, Deutschlandpolitik, 2:167.

100.   Telegram from Smith in Moscow to the Secretary of State, 7 January 1947. National Archives documents.

101.   Studiengesellschaft, Deutschlandpolitik, 3:13.

102.   The Americans did not go into the meeting with an open mind. General Clay, in a press conference on 5 May, said that despite the upcoming Foreign Ministers' Conference, the Western Allies would support the establishment of a West German state with the same decisiveness as before. Weber and Jahn, Synopse, p. 74.

103.   In August the first West German Bundestag was elected. In September, Theodor Heuss was elected

the first Presdient by the Bundesversammlung and Konrad
Adenauer was elected the first Chancellor.

104.   The GDR was established after the Federal
Republic to make sure the West was blamed for the
division of Germany.   Nettl, Eastern Zone, p. 111;
Studiengesellschaft,   Deutschlandpolitik,   3:18;
Meissner, Russland, die Westmächte und Deutschland,
p. 212.   Schulz attributes Stalin's hesitation to the
fact that he still wanted influence in West Germany and
especially in the Ruhr.   Eberhard Schulz, "Die DDR als
Element   der   sowjetischen Westeuropa-Politik,"   Europa
Archiv (25 December 1972), p. 836.

105.   The new strategy should also serve to hasten
the   collapse of capitalism by   exacerbating tensions
within the system caused not only by internal contradictions by also by recession.

106.   Shulman judges this move toward moderation a
qualitative change in the direction of Soviet policy
most   often   attributed to the post-Stalin leadership.
Stalin Reappraised, p. 264.   A differing interpretation
finds the cooptation of the Peace Movement merely a
tactical shift in the hard line embarked upon in 1946.
Studiengesellschaft, Deutschlandpolitik, 2:170-71.

107.   Shulman, Stalin Reappraised, pp. 109-10.

108.   Wladyslaw Gomulka in Poland, Laszlo Rajk of
Hungary,   and   Traicho Kostov of Bulgaria were all victims of the purge.

109.   For a detailed description of party conflict
over German policy, see Walter Osten, "Die Deutschlandpolitik der Sowjetunion in den Jahren 1952/53," Osteuropa (January 1964), pp. 1-13; "Männer und Kräfte des
Politbüros," PZ Archiv, nos. 4, 5, 7, 1951.   One of the
most riveting accounts of the SBZ period is Leonhard's
Child of the Revolution.

110.   Beria, a candidate member of the Politburo,
had been appointed Commissar for Internal Affairs in
1938 and remained head of the security forces until he
was purged in 1953.   He had become a full member of the
Politburo in 1946.

111.   "Männer und Kräfte des Politbüros," no. 5,
p. 4.

112.   Ibid., pp. 4, 6. Klaus Erdmenger, _Das folgenschwere Missverständnis_ (Freiburg i. Br.: Verlag Rombach, 1967), p. 142.

113.   Gregory Klimov, Major in the Soviet Army, worked in the Administration for Economy within the SMAD as an aide to General Shabalin. Klimov, _Berliner Kreml_ (Cologne: Kiepenheuer und Witsch, 1951), pp. 120-21; Nettl, _Eastern Zone_, p. 59.

114.   Vladimir Rudolph, "The Administrative Organization of Soviet Control," in _Soviet Economic Policy in Postwar Germany_, ed. by Robert M. Slusser (New York: Research Program on the USSR, 1953), pp. 18, 31.

115.   Malenkov was a full member of the Politburo and Deputy Chairman of the Council of People's Commissars.

116.   Rudolph, "Administrative Organization of Soviet Control," p. 19.

117.   Zhukov was replaced as Commander in Germany in April 1946 by General Sokolovsky, who soon after became Marshal.   Sokolovsky was, in turn, succeeded by General Chuikov in March 1949.

118.   Klimov was commissioned to gather evidence against the Special Committee for the Administration for Reparations of the SMAD in an investigation headed by Mikoyan.   Klimov, _Berliner Kreml_, pp. 364-65; Rudolph, "Administrative Organization of Soviet Control," pp. 27-29, 31.

119.   Klimov, _Berliner Kreml_, p. 367; Rudolph, "Administrative Organization of Soviet Control,", pp. 20-21.   According to one report, at the height of dismantling, between 60,000 and 70,000 workers from enterprises, factories, etc., were added to army personnel roles and sent to Germany to carry out dismantling operations.   Valentin L. Sokolov, _Soviet Use of German Science and Technology_ (New York: Research Program on the USSR, 1955), pp. 1-2.   Sokolov was sent as one such worker to Germany in May 1945 by the Soviet Commissariat for the Aviation Industry to take part in dismantling.

120.   Leonhard, _Child of the Revolution_, p. 345.

121.   According to Rudolph, rumors were rampant among Deputy Ministers in Berlin that Malenkov's career was waning, e.g., Special Committee telegrams were no longer addressed to Malenkov. "Administrative Organization of Soviet Control," p. 42.

122.   Ibid., pp. 32-33. Commissars were renamed Ministers in March 1946.

123.   Ibid., pp. 34, 54.

124.   "Männer und Kräfte des Politbüros," no. 7, p. 4.

125.   Osten, "Deutschlandpolitik der Sowjetunion," p. 5; Die sowjetische Besatzungszone Deutschlands in den Jahren 1945 bis 1954 (Bonn: Bundesministerium für Gesamtdeutsche Fragen, 1956), p. 9 (hereafter cited as SBZ 1945-54).

126.   Semyonov had a long political career in Germany and was considered a specialist on German affairs. Before World War II, he was a member of the Soviet diplomatic corps at the embassy in Berlin. As Political Advisor, he was responsible for implementing the political policy of the Kremlin in Germany and supervised all the measures taken by the Supreme Commander. The importance of the position is indicated by Klimov's account that Molotov always met with the Political Advisor before the Commander when he was in Berlin. Klimov, Berliner Kreml, pp. 205-6; Osten, "Deutschlandpolitik der Sowjetunion"; Paul R. Willging, Soviet Foreign Policy in the German Question: 1950-1955 (Ph.D. diss., Columbia University, 1973), pp. 28-33.

127.   Osten, "Deutschlandpolitik der Sowjetunion," p. 4; "Männer und Kräfte des Politbüros," no. 7, p. 5.

128.   "Männer und Kräfte des Politbüros," no. 7, p. 6; Elizabeth Allen, "Soviet Control of Eastern Zone Government through the SCC of the SED," 6 January 1950, Intelligence Division, European Command, National Archives documents.

129.   "Männer und Kräfte des Politbüros," pp. 6-7; Werden und Wachsen, p. 168.

130.   Memorandum "Dual Soviet Policy in Germany," 16 March 1950. National Archives documents.

131.   An important work on the creation of the SED and the interplay between Soviet and German leaders is Henry Krisch's German Politics under Soviet Occupation (New York: Columbia University Press, 1974).   Ruth Fischer's Stalin and German Communism: A Study in the Origins of the State Party (Cambridge: Harvard University Press, 1948), provides a detailed personal account of German and Russian communist relations before the war.

132.   Documents on Germany, pp. 37-38.

133.   Potsdam Documents, p. 1482; Krisch, German Politics, p. 24.

134.   Molotov, Speeches and Statements, p. 356; Krisch, German Politics, p. 25.

135.   Nettl, Eastern Zone, pp. 260-61.

136.   Heinz Brandt, The Search for a Third Way (Garden City, N.Y.: Doubleday & Co., 1970), p. 163. Brandt was propaganda secretary for the Berlin district administration of the SED until he left for West Germany in the autumn of 1958.   Dietrich Staritz, Sozialismus in einem halben Land (Berlin: Verlag Klaus Wagenbach, 1976), pp. 35-36.

137.   Anton Ackermann, "Wohin Soll der Weg Gehen?" Deutsche Volkszeitung (14 June 1945); "Aufruf der kommunistischen Partei Deutschlands," Tägliche Rundschau, (14 June 1945); Stern, Porträt, pp. 21-22.

138.   SBZ 1945-54, p. 9.

139.   Jean Edward Smith, Germany Beyond the Wall (Boston: Little, Brown and Co., 1969), pp. 186-87.

140.   Krisch, German Politics, pp. 101-3.

141.   Stalin pursued a policy of unification of communist and social democratic parties in all East European countries.

142.   David Childs, Moscow's German Ally (London: George Allen & Unwin, 1983) p. 16.   Schumacher was a nationalist who opposed association with any of the occupying powers.   He opposed cooperation with German communists as collaborators with the USSR.   Lewis J. Edinger, Kurt Schumacher: A Study in Personality and

Political Behavior (Stanford,   Calif.: Stanford University Press, 1965), pp. 156-58.

143.   Staritz, *Sozialismus in einem halben Land*, p. 76.

144.   Gniffke, *Jahre mit Ulbricht*, pp. 138-45. Ernst Lemmer, a Christian Democrat leader, writes that Schumacher distrusted Otto Grotewohl because he was under Soviet occupation.   West German members of the SPD supported Schumacher's decision to reject unification with the KPD. As a result of Schumacher's action, Grotewohl reportedly felt isolated and hurt.   Grotewohl then convinced himself, according to Lemmer, that only in an independent party leadership in the zone could he play a significant role.   Lemmer, *Manches War Doch Anders: Erinnerungen eines deutschen Demokraten* (Frankfurt am Main: H. Scheffler Verlag, 1968), p. 270.

145.   Gniffke, *Jahre mit Ulbricht*, p. 184.   Zhukov was recalled primarily because of the fears his popularity and ability to build a power base aroused in the Kremlin.   Sokolovsky, said to be a gifted administrator, did not generate the same fears.   Klimov, *Berliner Kreml*, p. 205.

146.   Gniffke, *Jahre mit Ulbricht*, p. 148.

147.   "Manifest an das deutsche Volk," *Neues Deutschland*, (23 April 1946).

148.   "Grundsätze und Ziele der neuen Partei," *Tägliche Rundschau* (23 April 1946); Wilhelm Pieck, "Der demokratische Weg zur Macht," *Tägliche Rundschau* (23 April 1946).

149.   Percy Stulz and Siegfried Thomas, eds., *Die Deutsche Demokratische Republik auf dem Wege zum Sozialismus: Dokumente und Materialen*, 2 parts, (Berlin: Volk und Wissen Volkseigener Verlag, 1959), 1:140.

150.   *Tägliche Rundschau* (21 October 1946).

151.   *Protokoll der Verhandlungen des II Parteitages der Sozialistischen Einheitspartei Deutschlands* (Berlin: Dietz Verlag, 1947), p. 479.

152.   Stern, *Porträt*, p. 81.   Ulbricht was an early proponent of the recognition of two separate

German states and was generally allied with the Zhdanov-Tulpanov position on Soviet policy toward Germany.
    The Berlin blockade was in its early, uncertain stages at this time. The three Western Zones had united and adopted a common currency separate from the SBZ.

153.   "Erklärung des Zentralsekretariats der SED zur jugoslawischen Frage," Neues Deutschland (1 July 1948).

154.   Martin McCauley, Marxism-Leninism in the German Democratic Republic (New York: Barnes & Noble, 1979), pp. 54-57; Childs, Moscow's German Ally, p. 22.

155.   Stern, Porträt, p. 90.

156.   Otto Grotewohl, Die Politik der Partei und die Entwicklung der SED zu einer Partei neuen Typus (Berlin: Dietz Verlag, 1949), p. 52.

157.   Stern, Porträt, p. 92.

158.   Protokoll der Verhandlungen des III Parteitages der Sozialistischen Einheitspartei Deutschlands (Berlin: Dietz Verlag, 1951), 2:307-21.

159.   Childs, Moscow's German Ally, p. 22.

160.   "On Personnel and Functions of SED Leadership," 28 December 1949; "Groups within the SED," 10 June 1950, Intelligence Division, European Command, State Department documents, National Archives.

161.   "Growing Tension in the SED," 15 March 1950, Intelligence Division, European Command, State Department documents, National Archives.

162.   Protokoll der Verhandlungen des II Parteitages, pp. 252-54; Gniffke, Jahre mit Ulbricht, p. 255.

163.   Protokoll der Verhandlungen des II Parteitages, p. 292.

164.   Grotewohl, Die Politik der Partei, pp. 48-50.

165.   Leonhard, Child of the Revolution, p. 441. Anton Ackermann was the chief party ideologist and was

later State Secretary of the Foreign Ministry.

166. Ibid., pp. 347-49.

167. "Erklärung des Zentralsekretariats der SED zur jugoslawischen Frage," Neues Deutschland (4 July 1948).

168. Anton Ackermann, "Über den einzig möglichen Weg zum Sozialismus," Neues Deutschland (24 September 1948).

169. Werden und Wachsen, p. 41.

170. Ibid., p. 42.

171. Ibid., p. 122.

172. Ibid., p. 123.

173. Ibid.

174. Kurt Sontheimer and Wilhelm Bleek, The Government and Politics of East Germany (New York: St. Martin's Press, 1975), p. 32.

175. Ibid.

176. Stern, Porträt, p. 139.

177. Nettl, Eastern Zone, pp. 58-59.

178. Dokumente zur Deutschlandpolitik der Sowjetunion, 1:236-38.

179. Werden und Wachsen, p. 168.

180. Fritz Schenk, Im Vorzimmer der Diktatur (Cologne: Kiepenheuer & Witsch, 1962), p. 221; Childs, Moscow's German Ally, p. 25; Leonhard, Child of the Revolution, p. 364.

181. Yalta Documents, p. 798.

3
The Question of Exploitation

In this chapter, Soviet economic policy toward the SBZ will be examined as a key to the complexity of Soviet policy toward Germany as a whole. The question of exploitation will be discussed in reference to the Yalta and Potsdam agreements which defined the relations between Germany and the Allies. Direct policies of dismantling, extracting reparations and forming joint stock companies as well as direct effects such as restructuring the economy and reorientation of trade must be considered. The generally unrecognized ambivalence of Soviet policy toward East Germany becomes clear when these harsh measures are juxtaposed with Soviet economic aid to the zone, toleration of private enterprise, early rapid economic recovery, and emphasis on improving the standard of living as reflected in consumption/investment data, household income, and consumption statistics. The apparent contradiction in policies illustrates a parallel conflict in Soviet national policy interests perceived in terms of economic recovery and eliminating Germany as a future threat while, at the same time, keeping all policy options open vis-à-vis West Germany. These elements underscore the tentative nature of Soviet policy toward Germany at the time.

THE GDR'S ECONOMIC POTENTIAL

An overview of East Germany's prewar economic situation and damage suffered during World War II is necessary in order to assess the impact of Soviet economic policy. Contrary to popular conception, the area that is now the GDR was highly industrialized before World War II. The area's lack of raw materials, however, made it dependent upon the western regions of Germany, particularly for hard coal and steel.(1) The economy was based on processing raw materials into high-quality finished products for export. Industrial structure naturally followed factor endowments. Most of basic industry and heavy machine building was con- centrated in western Germany by virtue of supplies of hard coal and iron ore.(2) Eastern Germany did, how- ever, produce her share of industrial output relative to the population: figures vary slightly, but roughly one-quarter of the population produced better than one- quarter of the national industrial output.(3) In basic industry, the area was an important supplier of heavy chemicals, synthetic rubber, gasoline, and building materials, contributing 23 percent to the nation's total production.(4) The chemical industry was based on abundant lignite, as was the extraction of aluminum and magnesium which was concentrated here. Eastern Germany produced 28 percent of metalworking production and 33 percent of light industry production.(5) The area also excelled in the production of precision ma- chinery and in manufacturing. Textile and office ma- chinery, airplanes, and optics were especially well known.(6)

In agricultural production, eastern Germany was better off than the western regions of the country.(7) Before the war, Germany was unable to feed herself. A high of 83 percent self-sufficiency was reached in 1939.(8) The loss of territory east of the Oder-Neisse significantly worsened Germany's situation because this meant a loss of approximately 25 percent of Germany's arable land. This was the only region which produced a food surplus.(9) Eastern Germany, however, was self- sufficient in food production. In 1936, the area pro- duced 27 percent of total food, drink, and tobacco industry output.(10) Eastern Germany, including East Berlin, accounted for 30.6 percent of postwar German territory. It concentrated more on the production of grains and raising pigs, sheep, and goats, while west- ern Germany produced more cattle, milk, chickens, and eggs.(11)

     During the war the volume of industrial output in
eastern Germany increased substantially due to increased investment and also to the transfer of industry
within Germany to the east.(12) Dramatic changes in
structure resulted from wartime demands.   The chemical
industry increased in relative importance due to military demand for rubber products, gasoline, pharmaceuti-
cals, and ammunitions.   Also, the metalworking industries' share of industrial production soared from 27
percent in 1936 to 46.5 percent in 1944.   By contrast,
the light industries' share declined precipitously from
35.8 percent in 1936 to 19.8 percent in 1944, although
eastern Germany's share of national production in light
industry increased.(13)

     War damage and its effect on the economy varied
from region to region.   According to the United States
Strategic Bombing Survey, eastern Germany was not
bombed as extensively as the western and southern
areas.(14) The Ruhr drew particularly heavy bombing by
virtue of its position as the industrial heartland of
Germany.   This was to become part of the British occupation zone. Targets in eastern Germany included chemical and synthetic rubber plants as well as aircraft
factories.   The transportation system was the main
target of Allied bombing throughout Germany.   It suffered the greatest damage and brought about serious
distribution problems, creating severe shortages of
critical food and other supplies.(15) Coal supplies
necessary for most production became scarce by the end
of 1944.   From December 1944, all sectors of the national economy were in rapid decline. The breakdown in
the transportation system was probably the greatest
single contributor to the final collapse of the German
economy.(16)

     Contrary to initial visual impressions and popular
conception, military actions did not do intensive damage with long-term impact to Germany's productive
capacity.   German industry proved itself amazingly
resilient and well protected against bombing raids.(17)
It is estimated that war damage reduced industrial
capacity in eastern Germany to approximately 1936
levels.(18) Of this destruction, basic industries were
to have suffered proportionately less: 3 percent in
coal, 8 percent in metallurgy, and 15 percent in the
chemical industry.(19) Exact calculations of war damage were virtually impossible, however, because of the

dismantling activity of both Soviet and Western troops upon their entry onto German soil.

Factors of Production

The Soviet occupation zone was considered the most economically balanced of the four zones in terms of population, arable land, and manufacturing capacity. At Potsdam, the United States calculated 50 percent of German wealth was in the Soviet Zone. The Soviets estimated somewhat lower, at 42 percent. Either figure signifies a perception of considerable wealth.(20) As previously noted, the SBZ comprised 30.6 percent of postwar German territory. In 1946, it had the highest ratio of land under cultivation per one hundred inhabitants. The SBZ had 34.3 hectares of cultivated land per one hundred inhabitants, compared with 26.8 in the British Zone, 32.8 in the American Zone, and 34.2 in the French Zone. At the same time, the Soviet Zone had only nineteen head of livestock per one hundred inhabitants, compared with twenty-four in the British Zone, thirty-two in the American Zone, and twenty-nine in the French Zone. The reduction in livestock in the SBZ, due in large part to Soviet requisitions, meant more grains for direct nourishment of the population.(21) This would not be satisfactory for the long term, but in the short term it inadvertently favored the well-being of the East Germans. The population/food production ratio improved in the Soviet Zone when the occupying powers assumed responsibility for feeding their respective sectors in Berlin, relieving the SBZ of that burden. The Western Zones were not well divided in terms of ability to feed their populations. They occupied a large portion of land which could not be put under cultivation.(22) The loss of territory east of the Oder-Neisse, which had been the breadbasket of Germany, and generally unfavorable economic conditions led to a drop in agricultural production in 1947 throughout Germany to approximately 50-55 percent of the prewar years 1935-1939. Added to that, the large influx of German refugees from the east in the immediate postwar period meant there were no food surpluses in any zone, even the more prosperous SBZ.(23)

All occupation zones, except the French Zone, experienced an increase in population between 1939 and 1946 due to the expulsion of Germans from the territory turned over to Poland as well as from other East European countries.(24) The East German population in

creased from a level of 16.160 million in 1936 to
18.057 million in 1946, an increase of roughly 12
percent.(25)   This increased the burden on the reduced
amount of land but added about one-half million men,
bringing the number of men back to 1939 levels.   The
percentage of males in the population declined, nonetheless.   In May 1939, 51.4 percent of the East German
population was female, compared to 57.5 percent in
October 1946.(26)

       From 1946, the SBZ lost population due to migra-
tion to the Western Zones.   An estimated 130,000 left
the Soviet Zone in 1947; 150,000 in 1948.   Large numbers continued to leave East Germany until the Berlin
Wall was built in August 1961.(27)   The result was a
net decrease in population from 1946 to 1958, due not
only to the refugees from East Germany but also to the
low birth rate.   The total population has been declining since 1949.   The impact on the labor force has been
detrimental.   Generally, men in the most productive age
group comprised the majority of East German refugees.
Table 1 shows the change in the East German labor
force.

Table 1
Persons of Working Age, East Germany

		Total	Percent of population	Percent of men of working age
May	1939	11,309,700	67.5	50.6
Oct.	1946	11,552,400	62.5	41.0
Aug.	1950	11,656,100	63.3	44.5
Dec.	1955	11,269,400	63.2	45.7
Dec.	1957	10,899,300	62.6	46.2
Dec.	1958	10,781,500	62.3	46.6

Source: Wolfgang S. Stolper, The Structure of the East
German Economy (Cambridge: Harvard University Press,
1960), p. 27.

       In East Germany men from the ages of fifteen to
sixty-four and women from the ages of fifteen to fifty-
nine, inclusive, were considered of working age.   The
figures show that the number of persons of working age
declined between 1946 and 1958 in absolute terms and as
a percentage of the total population.   Also, the balance between men and women in the working-age population in 1939 was never restored.   The working-age popu-

lation as a percentage of total population is smaller
in East Germany than in West Germany. The imbalance of
men and women of working age is also greater in East
Germany.(28)

The distribution of the labor force by economic
sector is represented in Table 2. The sharp increase
in percentage of the labor force in agriculture between
1939 and 1950 was due to the influx of refugees from
the east, most of whom were farmers. This in turn
caused the decline in percentage of labor force engaged
in industry and crafts, despite the emphasis on rebuilding and expanding the Soviet Zone's industrial
base. In absolute numbers, the SBZ labor force approached the 1939 level in 1954 but receded in later
years because of emigration.(29) Labor shortage remains an important economic problem in the GDR.

Table 2
Employment in the GDR by Economic Sector

| | Percent of total | | | |
	1939	1950	1953	1955
Industry & artisans	42.17	38.21	41.46	40.57
Construction	5.71	5.25	6.39	5.93
Agriculture	20.24	26.64	21.03	21.56
Transportation & communications	6.93	6.10	6.75	6.80
Trade	11.17	8.54	10.87	10.98
Private & public service	13.77	15.26	13.61	14.15

Source: Stolper, Structure of the East German Economy,
p. 37.

Loss of capital was also a critical problem in the
SBZ in the early postwar years. As previously noted,
war destruction is estimated to have reduced industrial
capacity in East Germany to 1936 levels. The most
significant loss of capital, however, was the result of
"trophy campaigns" and dismantling and reparations
policies of the Soviet Union in the Eastern Zone.(30)
Total loss of industrial capacity through all those
causes is estimated to be 40 percent of the 1936
level.(31) In addition, reparations obligations to the
USSR kept investment very low, delaying the replenish-
ment of depleted capital stock.

An overview of the Eastern Zone's economic capabilities shows it to have been the most viable of the occupation zones. Table 3 illustrates the favorable balance of land, population, and manufacturing capacity.

Table 3
Economic Data on Potsdam Germany in 1936

Area	Mil. ha.	%	Arable land	%	Popula- tion	%	Manuf. Mil. RM	%
SBZ + Berlin	10.9	30.5	5.1	36.7	18.9	32.7	11.2	32.9
Germany	35.8	100	13.9	100	58.8	100	32.0	100

Source: J.P.Nettl, The Eastern Zone and Soviet Policy in Germany, 1945-1950 (London: Oxford University Press, 1951), p. 147.

Statistical evidence such as this does not provide an entirely accurate basis for projecting the economic viability of the SBZ, however, because the prewar performance relied on the free exchange of goods within Germany. Eastern Germany's lack of raw materials, particularly iron ore and hard coal, makes development of a modern industrial economy very difficult.(32)

SOVIET ECONOMIC POLICY TOWARD THE SBZ

Reparations

Soviet economic policy toward the SBZ is generally equated with the extraction of reparations. Despite a general recognition of the Soviet right to reparations from Germany, the amount and kinds exacted are widely perceived as exploitive. Exploitation is a common characterization of Soviet treatment of East Germany in general. Although Soviet policy was harsh compared with Western treatment of their zones, the validity of characterizing it as exploitive must be examined in light of the Allied agreeement on reparations. It will be recalled that at Yalta, The British, Americans, and

Soviets agreed to reparations in kind from dismantling, current production, and German labor. Amounts were left undecided, although the Americans recognized the proposed Soviet figure of $20 billion as a basis for discussion. The Potsdam Agreements, on the other hand, only established a formula for dismantling and exchange of goods between zones. No mention was made of the use of German labor or reparations from current production. The First Charge principle, insisted upon by the Americans during interim negotiations, was included in the Potsdam Protocol, which, in effect, denied reparations from current production.

In administering their reparations policy, the USSR interpreted the Potsdam Agreements as supplemental to Yalta. The Western powers, on the other hand, viewed Potsdam as superseding Yalta, a polition which led to the quick characterization of Soviet policy as exploitive. Soviet policy toward East Germany will be evaluated in this study from the Soviet perspective, bearing in mind that the Soviets asked for one-half of total reparations, or $10 billion. The Potsdam Agreements stipulated that Poland was to receive 15 percent of total reparations deliveries to the USSR. In attempting to judge Soviet policy, it is also useful to recall that Stalin's Yalta plan was much more modest than demands for reparations following World War I. At that time, reparations in the amount of $35 billion in gold marks were imposed on Germany. This equalled about $55 billion in 1947.(33) In this light, Soviet demands appear less harsh.

How did the actual administration of Soviet policy conform to their reparations proposal? During the early years after World War II, chaos reigned in Soviet implementation of their reparations proposal.(34) Special "trophy" units were organized within the Soviet army to confiscate a large variety of industrial and consumer goods to send back to the Soviet Union.(35) This occurred before the Potsdam Conference and, therefore, before any Allied agreement on reparations. The first removals from Germany of war booty were not counted by the Soviets as reparations.(36) Soviet soldiers loaded trains returning to the USSR with everything imaginable for their families.(37) The loss to Germany from these unofficial collections was considerable, estimated at two to eight million reichsmark at current prices.(38)

Dismantling troops followed directly on the heels of the occupying Red Army and began a series of campaigns which lasted until the spring of 1948. The first wave of dismantling occurred in the spring of 1945 before the Western Allies had entered Berlin. The second wave, in the fall of 1945, did not follow the Potsdam Agreements, which had specified only those industries of military potential to be subject to dismantling. A conservative estimate of official dismantling of industrial installations is $4 billion in 1955 prices, which represented about one-fourth of East Germany's postwar industrial capacity.(39) Dismantling concentrated on removal of heavy industry capacity, leaving the area with a manufacturing capacity, primarily in light and food industry, similar to its prewar structure. The impact of dismantling on specific industries is presented in Table 4. Additional industries of importance not listed which were affected by dismantling were the chemical and brown coal industries. Losses in the chemical industry were estimated at roughly two-thirds of 1936 capacity.(40) A considerable portion of brown coal production was also lost, but an amount was not specified.(41)

Table 4
Capacity Reductions through Dismantling

	% (1936)=(100%)
Metallurgy	64
Iron works and rolling mills	80
Mechanical engineering	53
Vehicles	54
Electrical industry	60
Precision instruments and optics	63
Cement	40
Gypsum and construction material	35
Glass and ceramic	35
Flint	100
Plywood	100
Cellulose and paper	45
Rubber	95-100
Textiles	15
Sulfuric acid	100
Sodium hydroxide	60
Leather goods	25

Source: Franz Rupp, Die Reparationen der sowjetischen Besatzungszone in den Jahren 1945 bis Ende 1953 (Bonn: Bonner Berichte, 1954), p. 15.

Dismantling in the SBZ was much more thorough than in any of the Western Zones. One source estimates removal of industrial capacity in the Western Zones at 8 percent, compared to 45 percent in the SBZ.(42) Dismantling in the Eastern Zone resulted not only in a direct reduction of industrial capacity but also in a shift in the proportions or balance of industry. These effects were more strongly felt after the separate currency reforms in 1948 and the blockades which reduced the flow of goods between East and West Germany to a trickle. The result was to weaken the economic potential of the SBZ and to increase the zone's dependence on the Soviet Union, especially for raw materials.

The Soviet Union, however, did not benefit in equal amount to capacity lost in East Germany through dismantling. As is well known, a significant share of the plants and equipment sent to the USSR did not arrive, or at least did not arrive intact. Much of the materiel rusted by railroad sidings, the transportation system having been so severly impaired by Allied bombing that it could not handle the traffic. Items that did arrive were often incomplete, without operating instructions, or rendered useless by the lack of appropriately skilled workers. Losses which occurred between dismantling in Germany and operation in the Soviet Union are numbered in the millions of dollars.

In order to make better use of German skills and industrial capacity, the Soviets decided to leave important industries in the SBZ but appropriate their production.(43) Some 213 enterprises earmarked for dismantling were transformed into Sowjetische Aktiengesellschaften (SAGs), enterprises operated under joint Soviet-German ownership, to ensure deliveries from current production.(44) The SAGs accounted for roughly one-quarter of zone production, although some estimates run as high as 35 percent.(45) SAGs were particularly dominant in the production of liquid fuels, vehicles, rubber, and asbestos and provided roughly half of the zone's production in the chemical and electrical industries. Many of these enterprises were placed directly under the Ministry of Foreign Trade in Moscow.(46) Table 5 details the breakdown of SAGs in terms of capacity and production.

Table 5
SAGs in the East German Economy, 1947

Industry	% of total production	% of total capacity
Coalmining	15-20	15-20
Potash mining	40	40
Liquid fuels	80	70
Chemicals	55	40
Vehicles	70	60
Machines	40	30
Rubber and asbestos	70	55
Electrical	50	35
Metal goods	40	20
Metal ore and refining	40	30
Synthetic fibers and paper	30	15
Building materials	18	8
Textiles	5	2
Ceramics	8	5
Total industry	25	15-17

Source: Nettl, Eastern Zone, p. 222.

The productivity of the SAGs was much higher than other enterprises because they enjoyed priority in supply and quality of materials and workers.(47) Neues Deutsch-land, the official East German newspaper, called them "the very heart of the economy and the most productive of all plants.(48) The paper did, however, credit the Soviets with rebuilding the plants from nothing.

The only totally Soviet-owned company was Wismut, A.G., the uranium company started by the Soviets.(49) Although the SAGs were formally under joint Soviet-German ownership, the Russians managed the companies and disposed of their production. SAG production was figured into the reparations account, some of which was sold in the SBZ. Nearly one-half of the joint com-panies, the least important ones, were returned to the East Germans in 1947.(50) The rest were returned in stages: twenty-three in 1950, sixty-six in 1952, and the remaining thirty-three on 1 January 1954. Wismut became a jointly owned company in 1954. With the exception of the final thirty-three, the Soviets sold their shares of those enterprises to the East German government at inflated prices.(51) In addition, before turning the SAGs over, stocks and equipment were removed.(52)

Soviet claims on current production for the reparations account also lasted until 1 January 1954. In
addition to the SAGs , every firm in the zone could be
ordered to produce to fill reparations orders on short
notice. During the late 1940s and early 1950s, deliveries to the Soviets from current production averaged
20 percent of gross industrial production, imposing a
heavy burden on East German efforts for reconstruction.(53) A convoluted payments process was created
whereby the East Germans paid for the reparations deliveries in full while giving the appearance that the
Soviets paid for goods received.(54) The goods delivered to the Soviets were valued much below official
German prices as well as below the cost of production
to further obfuscate the actual transfer of wealth.
The effect was to extend Soviet claims to East German
production.(55)

The strain of reparations from current production
on the SBZ economy was great enough that the Central
Committee of the SED, along with Minister President
Grotewohl, requested a reduction in payments to the
Soviet Union in May 1950.(56) Stalin responded that
the Soviet Union and Poland agreed to reduce their
remaining claims by half.(57) According to Soviet
calculations, the SBZ had delivered goods worth $3.658
billion of the total $10 billion.(58) Thus, the Ger-
mans were to deliver an additional $3.171 billion worth
from current production, the payment period to be extended for fifteen years, i.e., until 1965. This allegedly generous settlement was far from advantageous
to the GDR. As noted before, deliveries had been
undervalued such that reparations already paid were
worth more than the $3.568 billion for which they were
credited.(59) According to one estimate, by 1950 the
SBZ had paid $10.7 billion in all forms of reparations,
excluding occupation costs.(60) This was more than the
Soviets had demanded at Yalta from all of Germany over
a twenty-year period. As a result of Stalin's action,
SBZ reparations payments were actually increased over
1946-1948 levels.(61) At that time, however, the East
Germans published official statistics showing that the
percentage of output allotted to reparations deliveries
was declining due to the rapid growth of industrial
production. Reparations which reportedly accounted for
only 10 percent of gross industrial production in 1948
were projected to decline to only 4.4 percent of
planned production for 1950. By the same token, occu-

pation costs were to decline from 14.6 percent in 1948 to a projected 6.3 percent of gross industrial production in 1950.(62) Direct deliveries to the SMAD included not only goods for the maintenance of troops in the SBZ but also goods sent directly to the USSR or exported abroad on the Soviet account. These goods were not officially labeled reparations but should be considered as such.(63)

Western experts estimate total reparations paid to the Soviet Union by the GDR, including occupation costs, reached approximately $19 billion, roughly twice the amount demanded at Yalta.(64) Of that figure, dismantling accounted for $4 billion; deliveries from current production accounted for more than $6 billion; deliveries to the Red Army, which continued until the end of 1958, accounted for approximately $4 billion; other deliveries, such as uranium and inventory depletions from SAGs, accounted for another $4 billion. The bulk of payments ended as of 1 January 1954. From 1945 until 1954, reparations deliveries are estimated to have equalled from one-fifth to one-third of the East German GNP(65) Per capita reparations burden in the SBZ is estimated at two hundred times that in the Western Zones.(66)

In addition to quantifiable costs of reparations and troop maintenance, the East German economy suffered loss of manpower due to Soviet policies. Approximately 40,000 German scientists, engineers, and technicians were deported to work in the Soviet Union after the poor showing of the SED in the October 1946 elections.(67) Individuals with needed skills were given contracts for five years of work to give the transfer a voluntary appearance, but all preparations were made in secret.(68) It should be noted that U.S. forces also ordered many people from the universities and industries to go with them as they withdrew from the SBZ.(69) Many German prisoners of war were detained in the USSR and contributed to the Soviet labor force long after the war was over.

Economic Aid

Soviet economic policy toward the SBZ was not merely one of reparations, although that aspect of policy has received the greatest attention. Economic aid to the SBZ was part of the total economic policy. The apparent inconsistency of reparations and economic aid reflects concretely the fundamental ambivalence of Soviet intentions in Germany. Economic aid served both economic and political interests of the USSR. On the one hand, foodstuffs and raw materials delivered to the SBZ on the one hand, ensured that the East Germans had the means to meet their reparations obligations. On the other, and equally important, economic aid complemented the cooperation in reconstruction between Germans and Soviets, which was much more advanced than in the Western Zones in the early years. This positive cooperation was designed to show that the Soviet and German peoples could work together as allies in postwar development.

Immediately following the cessation of hostilities, the USSR delivered foodstuffs to the SBZ and Berlin, despite its own tremendous shortages. The following goods were delivered to Berlin in September 1945:(70)

flour	27,638	tons
sugar	2,496	"
potatos	45,067	"
meat	2,076	"
groats	3,131	"
salt	645	"

The Soviets were supplying the Western sectors of Berlin as well as their own with foodstuffs at the time.

In 1946 a severe drought throughout the European area of the Soviet Union led to famine and starvation, even in the Ukraine, the country's breadbasket.(71) All the while, according to Nikita Khrushchev, Stalin sent food to Germany and Poland.(72) In addition, cotton and iron necessary for East German economic recovery were delivered.(73) Nonetheless, living conditions were so difficult that in July, the SED felt impelled to request an increase in rations from the SMAD. Sokolovsky agreed.(74) The cessation of reparations deliveries from the American Zone by General Clay in the spring of 1946 contributed to the difficult economic situation in the SBZ.

In the month preceding the currency reform in the Western Zones and the imposition of the Berlin block- ade, the Soviets stepped up grain deliveries to the SBZ.   Some 40,000 tons of bread and feed grains were scheduled for delivery in the month of June in addition to the more than 22,000 tons delivered between 16 May and 9 June.   Wheat, rye, and barley were the primary grains supplied.(75)   After the blockade went into effect, the Soviets tried to meet essential SBZ needs for raw material and other foods formerly procured in the West. Deliveries from other people's republics were increased as well. (76) The Berlin blockade and Western counterblockade, which became increasingly effective in the early part of 1949, had severe economic effects on the SBZ, East Europe, and the Soviet Union. The USSR suffered shortages of grain and livestock, steel, rail transport, and housing.(77) Nonetheless, the Soviets granted the East Germans a credit of 100 million rubles for imports of fat, grain, agricultural machinery and trucks, at 2 percent interest.(78) Substantial deliv- eries of foodstuffs and cotton were promised in the summer of 1950 in addition to those goods already guaranteed in the Soviet-East German trade agree- ment.(79)

That Soviet economic aid was more than an economic policy is evident in the cost it imposed on her own struggling reconstruction.   The policy makes sense primarily as a means for courting the German population as a whole, to demonstrate Soviet friendship in deed as well as word.   As East-West relations deteriorated, Soviet economic aid could build solidarity with the East German population based on commonly experienced Western hostility and could serve as a positive example of cooperation for the rest of the German population.

RAMIFICATIONS OF SOVIET POLICY

Restructuring the Economy

The overall structure of the East German economy did not change dramatically from prewar to postwar years. Only construction declined significantly in its share of GNP between 1936 and 1950. Agriculture declined slightly, while industry, trade, transporation, and communication all increased slightly during the same period.(80)

The significant changes were made within the industrial sector. As previously noted, substantial increases in the metalworking industries as well as the chemical industry made between 1936 and 1944 in response to war needs substantially altered the production structure within industry. As a result of Soviet dismantling, these changes were more than reversed. Dismantling focused on chemicals and metallurgy as well as the capital stock of metalworking industries. The metalworking industries' share of total industrial production in 1946 was reduced to 8.5 percent from a high of 46.5 percent in 1944.(81) Basic, light, and food industries as a whole produced at roughly 1936 levels or better in 1946. Ensuing developments produced an industrial structure similar to the war years but very different from the prewar economy.(82) Particular attention was given to restoring and expanding metalworking industry at the expense of light industry. Basic industry, although declining during the 1950s, was still substantially above the 1936 level. The changes in industry structure are presented in Table 6.

Table 6
Percentage Share of Major Industry Groups
in Industrial Production, 1936 Prices

Industry	1936	1950	1951	1952	1953	1954	1955	1956
Basic	37.2	47.7	46.1	45.7	43.4	42.6	43.9	43.8
Metal-working	26.8	23.8	23.8	24.3	28.2	29.0	28.7	30.4
Light	28.1	17.8	18.3	18.2	17.0	17.2	16.3	15.5
Food	12.3	10.8	11.8	11.8	11.4	11.3	11.1	10.2

Source: Stolper, Structure of the East German Economy, p. 262.
Note: Basic industry is defined as the energy, mining, gas, matallurgy, chemical (including fuel and fiber), and building materials industries. Metalworking industry includes machine, electrical engineering, fine mechanics and optics industries (corresponds to investment goods in Western terminology. Light industry includes woodworking, textiles, leather and shoe, clothing, cellulose and paper, and printing industries.

These changes occurred in response to Soviet reparations claims and in order to fill the important gaps created by the effective division of the East and West German economies. The attempt was made to build as full a complement of industries as possible, a policy followed throughout East Europe. Steady growth of the metalworking industry responded to the desperate need for investment goods in the USSR and in the bloc, of which the GDR became the main supplier.(83) Expansion of the small steel industry and production of heavy machinery, electrical machinery, and railroad equipment were initial priorities. An entirely new shipbuilding industry was created to meet Soviet needs. Traditional industries were allowed to stagnate.(84)

Hand in hand with restructuring of productive capacity went restructuring of economic organization. Economic planning and nationalization of important industries changed the character of economic life. In the early postwar period, banks, insurance companies, railroads, and postal and news services were nationalized. The coal industry, its branch industries, and all utilities were also nationalized.(85) Central German administrative organs were formed to organize social and economic life.(86) For a while dismantling ran parallel with efforts at reconstruction, although the worst ended in 1946. Soviet interest in rapid reconstruction increased after General Clay stopped reparations deliveries in May 1946. The Soviet order creating the SAGs, issued on 5 June, marked an important reduction in dismantling. Clay's action was cited by the Soviets as justification for transforming the major industrial enterprises of the SBZ into joint companies in order to guarantee German fulfillment of reparations obligations. A referendum held on 30 June 1946 in Saxony overwhelmingly approved the nationalization of businesses and property of Nazis and war criminals.(87) This referendum provided the legitimization for a policy of nationalization thoughout the SBZ which led to the conversion of approximately 3,000 properties into state owned businesses (Volkseigene Betriebe or VEBs) by 1948. These nationalized enterprises accounted for 20-30 percent of total industrial output in the zone.(88) Until the spring of 1948 these enterprises were under the authority of the provincial or Länder governments. During the early period most economic and administrative authority was dispersed to the Länder governments.(89) The difficulties this structure presented to efforts to coordinate economic planning throughout the zone led the SMAD to move toward centralization. In April 1948 all the larger and most important VEBs were reorganized into unions of state-owned enterprises (Vereinigungen Volkseigener Betriebe or VVBs) under the authority of the DWK by order of the SMAD.(90) The result was a centralization of control at the expense of the Länder, which complemented governmental centralization.

Until 1948, a Soviet plan, a central German plan, and provincial economic plans were drawn up independently. The Soviet plan was predominant in the amalgamating process of creating a final economic program.(91) Economic authority was gradually transferred to the DWK. In 1948 the commission assumed several functions which had been performed by the SMAD, including the right to conclude commercial treaties.(92) There was no real economic planning in the SBZ until the half-year plan for the second half of 1948.(93) Two one-year plans and the First Five Year Plan (1949, 1950, and 1951-1955) focused on the reconstruction and development of those industries desired by the Soviet Union.

A program for the Construction of Socialism in the GDR was adopted by the Second Party Conference of the SED in July 1952. The program called for rapid indus-

trial construction and collectivization of agriculture,
modelled after Stalin's First Five Year Plan of 1928.
These measures were to be accompanied by extensive
administrative reform. Liquidation of private ownership in industry, trade, and crafts was a hallmark of
the transformation. The impact of the policy is visible in Table 7.

Table 7
Contribution to Total GDR Production
According to Ownership

| Forms of ownership | Total Production* | | | | | |
	1950	1951	1952	1953	1954	1955
gross production						
All forms	52,316	63,775	70,391	75,982	83,536	89,085
State	27,616	35,561	40,876	47,671	51,826	55,713
Coop.	1,895	2,280	2,917	3,929	4,465	5,146
Private	22,805	25,934	26,598	24,382	27,245	28,226
net production						
All forms	30,662	36,513	39,745	41,521	46,365	49,819
State	14,738	19,448	21,981	24,377	26,758	29,479
Coop.	1,480	1,719	2,080	2,553	2,942	3,213
Private	14,444	15,346	15,684	14,591	16,665	17,127

Source: Statistisches Jahrbuch der Deutschen Demokratischen Republik (Berlin: VEB Deutscher Zentralverlag,
19550, p. 90.
*In millions of DM, 1950 prices

There was a significant decrease in growth of
private production in 1952 and an absolute decline in
1953, reflecting the policy of constructing socialism.
The drop in 1953, however, is attributable not only to
the campaign against private ownership but also to the
unrest in the summer of that year. The trend toward
diminishing private ownership in the East German economy is seen in the steadily declining percentage of
overall production. Nonetheless, private production
continued to provide a surprisingly large share of
gross production, dropping from 43 percent in 1950 to
32 percent in 1955.(94) The figures for net production
are even higher: 47 percent in 1950 and 34 percent in
1955.

Land reform was perhaps the most popular Soviet
measure carried out in the SBZ. In 1945, the Red Army

confiscated all estates larger than 250 acres plus land
owned by former Nazis or Junkers.   The land was redis-
tributed   to landless peasants,   owners of small   farms
and German refugees from East Europe.   Over 2   million
people   benefitted.(95)   This created,   temporarily,   a
new   constituency of support for   the   occupiers.   The
parcels   distributed,   however,   were   too small to   be
economically viable.(96)   Collectivization,   following
the   model   of the Soviet kolkhoz,   marked   the   second
phase   of   agricultural reform.   Most new land   owners
created by the 1945-1946 land reform were collectivized
in 1952.   Nonetheless,   a substantial private agriculture survived until the late 1950s despite a policy   of
discrimination   against private farmers to entice   them
into collectives.   By the spring of 1960,   practically
all   peasants were collectivized.(97)   Gross production
figures based on 1936 prices show a significant drop in
1953 and again in 1956.   In 1958 agricultural   production was still considerably below 1936 levels.(98)

        The   system of planning and organization which was
created   during those years was characterized   by   centrally planned production,   centrally fixed prices, and
state   monopoly on foreign trade: the hallmarks of   a
Soviet   type economy.   That side of Soviet policy   was
one   factor   which   induced large numbers of   the   East
German work force to flee to the West.   As   previously
noted,   migration   from the SBZ in 1947 is estimated at
130,000;   in 1948 ,   at 150,000.(99)   Between 1949, when
the   West Germans began keeping official   records,   and
1961,   when the Wall was built,   almost two and   three-
quarter million East Germans fled to West Germany.(100)
Most of those were the young,   able-bodied, and skilled
workers.   These figures represented over 15 percent of
the   total   population and had a devastating impact   on
the labor force.(101)

Economic Recovery

        The   early postwar years saw a sharp reduction   in
the   national wealth in the area that became   the   GDR.
However,   in spite of the heavy dismantling and reparations burden,   the SBZ initially was able to recover at
a   faster   rate than the Western Zones.(102)   This   reflected not only the more balanced character of the SBZ
but   also the active efforts on the part of the   Soviet
occupiers   to enlist the cooperation of the Germans   in
organizing the economy.   Unlike the Americans and British,   the   Soviets relied on the KPD   and   anti-fascist

Germans for the work of political and economic reconstruction. The Soviets remained in the background as
much as possible.(103) Early nationalization of basic
industry is also credited with contributing to impressive recovery in the early period.(104) By contrast,
economic recovery in the Western Zones was thwarted by
lagging coal production in the Ruhr and by delayed
implementation of monetary reform.(105)

There was notable reduction in the rate of recovery in 1947, attributable to a hard winter and summer
drought. Resulting food shortages and the disruption
of patterns of production due to industrial reorganization lowered labor productivity. Distribution problems
also contributed to economic difficulties.(106) In
1948 divisive actions by the Allies in Germany added to
the deteriorating economic position of the SBZ vis-à-
vis the Western Zones. The separate currency reforms
plus the Berlin blockade and Western counterblockade
essentially severed economic contact between the SBZ
and the Western Zones and enhanced cooperation among
the Western Zones. In addition, the effects of differing occupation policies were becoming visible. In mid
1948 the production curve of the Western Zones overtook
that of the SBZ. The volume of production in the
Soviet Zone, measured on the 1936 index, then remained
15 to 20 percent behind the other zones through the mid
1950s.(107)

The large loss of capital through dismantling in
the early postwar years explains in part the resultant
backwardness of the SBZ economy compared with that of
West Germany. The loss amounted to almost five times
East German investment and roughly double West German
investment until 1950.(108) Until 1950, capital expansion in the SBZ was quite small. In the late 1940s and
early 1950s, reparations demands made East Germany a
net exporter not only of value-added manufactures but
also of raw materials which were in short supply.
Soviet demand for a large portion of current production
was concentrated in investment goods industries. At
the same time, pressure was added to an already over-
burdened economy to improve living conditions in the
zone in competition with the West. The uncompensated
outflow of goods, coupled with efforts to improve the
living standard, produced a low rate of investment in
the GDR in the early 1950s. It was low not only by
comparison with East European rates of investment but
by West European standards as well. Gross fixed investment amounted to less than 15 percent of the GNP in

the early 1950s, compared with more than 20 percent in
Bulgaria, Czechoslovakia, Hungary, and Poland.(109)
After 1955, the rate of investment in the GDR began to
increase rapidly and approached 24 percent of GNP in
the 1960-1963 period, as shown in Table 8. The termination of reparations payments was an important factor
allowing for increased investment.

Table 8
Gross Fixed Investment in East Germany

	1950-54	1955-59	1960-63
As percentage of GNP			
Total	14.5	19.4	23.6
Industry	5.8	8.3	11.4
Agriculture	1.8	2.2	2.9
Services	6.9	8.9	9.3
As percentage of total Investment			
Industry	40	43	48
Agriculture	12	11	13
Services	48	46	39

Source: Maurice Ernst, "Postwar Economic Growth in
Eastern Europe," in New Directions in the Soviet Economy (Washington, D.C.: Government Printing Office,
1966), p. 890.

Investment rates in West Germany were considerably
higher than in the GDR, but per capita fixed capital
remained comparable due to the decline in East German
population.(110) In allocation of investment, the
tendency of Soviet type economies is to invest more
heavily in industry and agriculture at the expense of
services than is the norm in Western societies.(111)
The effect is illustrated by the difference in standard
of living between East and West.

Reduction in capital stock from dismantling, the
very low rate of investment, disruption of production
patterns, and the flight of labor all contributed to
the slow rate of economic recovery in the GDR after
initial impressive gains. Gross national product did
not reach the 1936 level until sometime between 1953
and 1954. Industry, transportation, and communications
recovered somewhat earlier. By contrast, construction
and trade recovered two years after the GNP, while
agriculture had not reached its 1936 level by
1958.(112)

    Within industry, emphasis was on basic industry
and metalworking, as previously noted. The relative
performance of the major industrial groups is most
easily seen in a comparison of recovery rates based on
the 1936 index presented in Table 9.   All industrial
groups reached their 1936 levels before the gross national product, with the exception of manufactured
consumer goods.

Table 9
Production of Major Industry Groups Compared with GNP

	Mining & gas	Producer goods	Invest. ind.	Consumer goods	Food ind.	GNP*
1936	100	100	100	100	100	100
1950	132	96	67	44	66	75
1951	146	110	78	54	85	84
1952	150	118	86	59	92	93
1953	160	133	116	65	102	99
1954	170	141	129	72	110	106
1955	187	153	136	73	115	112

Source: Stolper, Structure of the East German Economy,
pp. 247-51, 418.
*East German coverage

In the distribution of GNP, consumption grew more rapidly than investment.(113) East Germany was the only
country in the East bloc in which that happened.(114)
It was also the only country in East Europe in which
consumption grew much faster than the GNP in the early
1950s.(115) Nonetheless, by 1958 consumption still had
not reached the 1936 percentage share of GNP. This was
due in large part to the notable shift in emphasis from
consumption to investment which began in 1955.   The
percentage distribution of GNP is seen in Table 10.

```
--------------------------------------------------------
                         Table 10
        Percentage Distribution of GNP, 1936 Prices
--------------------------------------------------------
```

	1936	1950	1951	1952	1953
Individual consumption*	60.5	32.7	38.6	44.4	47.7
Gross investment	18.7	18.7	22.1	21.6	23.7
Gross fixed investment	-	11.6	13.0	13.0	16.0
Inventory accumulation	-	7.1	9.1	8.6	7.7
Other**	20.8	48.6	39.4	34.0	28.5

	1954	1955	1956	1957	1958
Individual consumption*	52.9	54.5	53.1	51.5	53.1
Gross investment	18.0	21.6	26.2	30.3	39.0
Gross fixed investment	16.6	19.1	23.2	25.9	27.7
Inventory accumulation	1.4	2.5	2.9	4.4	11.2
Other**	23.9	23.9	20.8	18.3	7.9

```
--------------------------------------------------------
```

Source: Stolper, Structure of the East German Economy,
p. 437.
*Consumption is deflated by the retail price index.
**"Other" denotes government and the export balance,
which until 1954 included substantial reparations deliveries. This accounts for the extraordinarily high
share of GNP in this category between 1950 and 1954.

Consumption as a percentage of GNP, if deflated by
the cost of living index, surpassed the 1936 level in
1952.(116)   Due to the slow rate of economic recovery,
however, only in 1955 can real consumption be said to
reach 1936 levels, despite its impressive rise as a
percentage of GNP.(117)

Standard of Living

Soviet economic aid, emphasis on consumption over
investment, and enlistment of German energies and tal-
ents in the reconstruction of the economy were all part
of an early focus on improving the standard of living
in the SBZ. This effort was intended to translate into
a positive Soviet image throughout Germany and to
strengthen the appeal of the Soviet position on reunification in the Council of Foreign Ministers. The
economic policies which were beneficial to the East
German population should be understood as a critical
aspect of Soviet ambivalence toward Germany and as
substantive measures taken to pursue the possibility of
extending Soviet influence throughout Germany.

During the early postwar period of rapid economic
recovery in the Eastern Zone, the SBZ was better fed
than the other zones.(118) The Western currency reform
in 1948 worsened the consumer's situation in the SBZ
relative to his counterpart's in the Western Zones. In
1949-1950 the situation in the Soviet Zone was alleviated somewhat by imports of meat and by moderation of
Soviet demands on current production for the army and
for reparations. Table 11 compares daily calorie intake by ration group in the occupation zones.

Table 11
Postwar Rations in Calories per Day

	Normal consumer	Heavy worker	Miner
Soviet Zone			
March 1946	1,100 (1,200)*	1,903	3,023
Nov. 1947	1,325 (1,517)	2,053	3,911
March 1948	1,336 (1,552)	2,369 (2,614)	3,991
Dec. 1948	1,526 (1,587)	2,525 (2,733)	3,990
June 1949	1,526 (1,587)	2,525 (2,733)	3,990
Jan. 1950	2,200 -	- -	-
Western Zones			
March 1946	1,025 (1,330)	2,230	2,495
Nov. 1947	1,100 (1,394)	2,302	3,100
March 1948	1,190 (1,410)	2,335 (2,555)	2,910 (3,130)
Dec. 1948	1,549	2,162	3,653
June 1949	1,569	2,182	4,329
Jan. 1950	-	-	-

Source: Nettl, Eastern Zone, p. 182.
*parentheses denote ration scale in large towns.

The Soviet occupiers used special rations to attract technicians and engineers from the Western Zones
as well as to retain those living in the SBZ. Valentin
Sokolov, sent to Germany in May 1945 by the Soviet
Commissariat for the Aviation Industry to take part in
dismantling, recounts that a "full ration" was the
privilege of those special groups, senior skilled workers, and a reward bestowed upon leading workers.   A
full ration consisted of twenty pounds of meat, a few
pounds of fat, thirty packs of cigarettes, seventy-two
eggs, and large quantities of flour, sugar, fresh vege-
tables, tea and other goods.(119) During the lean
years of 1945 to 1946, this was an abundance unknown
elsewhere in Germany.(120) According to Sokolov, a
large number of Germans with desired skills were driven

by hunger to work in the Soviet Zone.(121)   Ordinary
workers did not receive such bounty: skilled workers
received up to one-quarter of a ration; foremen, up to
one-half; supplementary rations were awarded workers
for particularly noteworthy performance.

This picture contradicts the commonly held perception that conditions in the Soviet Zone were much worse
than in the Western Zones in every way. Early economic
recovery data and consumption statistics are important
refutations of stereotyped images of Germany under
Soviet occupation.   To keep the matter in perspective,
however, the German population as a whole was much
worse off than before the war.   Data comparing per
capita consumption of basic foodstuffs in 1936 with
1950-1956 in Table 12 show in concrete terms sharply
reduced consumption of meat, butter, eggs and milk in
the early 1950s; the decline being made up by increased
consumption of bread and potatoes.(122)

Table 12
Per Capita Consumption of Basic Foodstuffs

	Meat kg	Butter kg	Fats kg	Eggs piece	Milk liter	Sugar kg	Flour kg	Potatoes kg
1936	46.8	8.5	-	117.0	127.0	22.9	103.4	170.8
1950	22.1	5.4	11.5	63.1	74.0	20.2	120.4	219.3
1951	27.7	7.7	16.2	70.1	78.0	23.9	120.7	210.6
1952	36.0	8.4	18.2	87.5	89.9	31.8	120.5	182.6
1953	40.6	9.2	20.3	107.6	78.8	31.0	120.3	197.3
1954	43.6	10.3	23.9	113.5	78.6	30.5	115.8	176.5
1955	43.2	9.7	24.9	116.2	84.5	27.8	114.8	169.6
1956	43.2	9.9	25.4	144.0	89.1	28.2	-	170.3

Source: Statistisches Jahrbuch der DDR, 1956, p. 203.

Such a diet reflects shortages as well as poverty.   The
quickest recovery and improvement beyond 1936 levels of
consumption is noted in sugar, butter, and eggs.   Meat
consumption improved more slowly, and milk intake remained significantly below 1936 levels.   The absolute
reduction in, and slow recovery of, nourishment standards for the SBZ population comes as no surprise.
Production figures show that by 1958 agriculture was
still far below 1936 levels in absolute terms.(123)   As
a percentage of GNP, agriculture declined overall from
18 percent of GNP in 1950 to 11 percent in 1958.   Food
industries did not reach 1936 levels of production in

absolute terms until 1953, somewhat before GNP recovery.(124)   The combination of agricultural and food
industries' production indicates the depressed consumption   levels   shown above.   Surely the loss of   the
agriculturally rich territory east of the Oder-Neisse
to Poland adversly affected the diet of the East Germans as well, not to mention the depletion of livestock
and poultry by the Soviets in the immediate postwar
period. The initial influx of German refugees from the
East contributed to lower consumption levels in 1945
and 1946, but this was more than offset by the loss of
population in later years.

As would be expected in economically depressed
conditions, providing food required a greater share of
a family's budget. Statistics on the average monthly
expenditures of a four-person industrial household of
middle income in 1955 and the comparative costs of the
same purchases in other years show the highly inflated
economy compared with 1936.   Only in housing, heating,
and lighting did costs either remain constant with or
actually decline below 1936 levels.   Reduced costs of
food and clothing in 1956 were still more than double
those in 1936.(125) Cost comparisons, of course, do
not reflect the quality of goods available, which is
generally regarded as below 1936 standards. Nor do the
figures compare actual living standards in 1936 and
1955.   Calculations of the average monthly wage deflated by the cost of living index and by the retail
price index in Table 13 illustrate the severely reduced
real income of the average German worker.

Table 13

Average Monthly Wages of Industrial Workers

	Gross monthly wage DM-O*	Cost of living index 1936=100	Real monthly wage DM-O	Retail price index 1936=100	Real monthly wage DM-O*
1950	265	306.9	86.3	418.6	63.3
1951	298	242.2	123.0	368.8	80.8
1952	318	222.1	143.2	329.9	96.4
1953	344	211.3	162.8	307.9	111.7
1954	376	196.4	191.1	284.1	132.3
1955	386	191.9	201.1	274.0	140.9
1956	396	191.0	207.3	272.9	145.1
1957	409	187.9	217.6	270.0	151.5
1958	421	184.6	228.1	263.6	159.7

Source: Stolper, Structure of the East German Economy, p. 431.
* DM-O = East German Mark

A breakdown of average monthly income according to economic sector shows that workers in transportation enjoyed the highest average monthly wage from 1950 through 1958. Industrial and construction workers were paid comparable wages and came next in the income hierarchy. The poorest workers were those in agriculture, forestry, and water resources. Their earnings averaged less than two-thirds of their counterparts in industry from 1950 through 1956 but showed significant gains in 1957 and 1958.(126)

When grouped into sector according to ownership, workers in the socialist sector were paid substantially better than their counterparts in the private sector. The divergence in wages between socialist and private sectors increased with the years in certain areas of employment, especially in agriculture and forestry but also in industry and trade. The overall wage differential between socialist and private sectors, however, remained roughly constant.(127)

Data on the average monthly income of industrial workers broken down according to position in the production process show that technical personnel consistently earned significantly higher wages than any other group.(128) The wage differential between production workers and technical personnel grew substantially from 1950 to 1953, the latter at times earning almost double

the former group.   The gap appeared to stabilize after
that.   At the same time, technical personnel steadily
increased a smaller wage advantage over economists   and
administrative personnel throughout the period 1950 to
1955.   The hierarchy of favored positions is   readily
apparent in the wage structure.   Nonetheless, all
groups steadily increased their wages,   thereby improving their standards of living.

      Data presented on wages, the cost of living index,
average monthly household expenditures,   and individual
consumption of basic foods,   coupled with production
figures in agriculture,   food industries,   and manufactured consumer goods industries,   create a picture of
improving but still very low standard of living.   Thus,
despite the emphasis on improving consumption in the
GDR, every measure indicates that the average worker
remained worse off in the 1950s than he was in   1936.
The impact of Soviet reparations policy on the economy
was too severe to be overcome by temporarily favoring
consumption over investment.(129)   In fairness it must
also be noted that despite the depressed standard of
living in the SBZ,   the East Germans lived better than
their Soviet counterparts in the USSR.   From the Soviet
point of view,   it would no doubt seem unjust for   the
defeated Germans to enjoy a higher standard of living
than the victorious Soviet peoples.   Recall also   that
Roosevelt agreed with that assessment at Yalta.   From
that perspective,   the Soviets' total economic policy
toward East Germany might be judged differently.

Reorientation of Trade

      Structural changes in the East German economy went
hand in hand with reorientation of trade toward   the
East.   Reorientation of trade served the dual   purpose
of ensuring the viability of the SBZ economy   independent of West Germany and,   at the same time,   providing
industrial goods and equipment necessary for Soviet
economic recovery and industrial development in many of
the East bloc countries. The first years after the war
did not show immediate realignment with the East in
trade,   reflecting Soviet interest in keeping open the
possibility of economic and political access to   the
West.   The Soviet Military Administration controlled
foreign trade until 1949 and tolerated private enterprise.   Most trade was with West Germany until   1948,
when the currency reform and Berlin blockade interrup-
ted the flow of goods between them.   Overwhelming hos-

tility toward anything German on the part of many East European countries served further to severely restrict trade between the SBZ and the bloc until the 1948 turning point.(130)   Trade statistics show a shift in trade orientation from an almost negligable involvement (4 percent) before the war to roughly 75 percent of trade with the East bloc in 1948.(131) The new trade pattern continued throughout the 1950s.   The formation of an East European economic bloc was institutionalized by the creation of the Council for Mutual Economic Assistance (CMEA) in January 1949.   It was established to counter the Economic Recovery Program in Western Europe.   The GDR was admitted to the organization as a full and equal member in September 1950.(132)   This step was symbolic of the move toward economic integra- tion of the GDR into the East bloc and provided a framework for still closer ties with the Soviet Union and the other allied countries.(133) The creation of the CMEA was a significant indicator of the deepening entrenchment of the postwar world into two opposing blocs.

After the GDR joined CMEA, Soviet-East German economic cooperation continued under the auspices of Wissenschaftlich-technische Zusammenarbeit (WTZ) agree- ments.   Under these agreements the Soviets had free access to scientific/technical research and documents from the GDR.   They also legitimized the placement of Soviet economic experts in key positions in administra- tions of large enterprises and centers for scientific research and technical development.(134)

In conjunction with the reorientation of trade, the volume of East Germany's trade dropped significant- ly.   By the mid 1960s, trade with the East bloc had scarcely reached the volume of external trade of the region in 1936.   In 1955, imports were only 27 percent of 1936 levels, while exports were just over one-half of that base year.(135) In April 1950 the first trade agreement between the GDR and the Soviet Union was signed in Moscow.(136) The Soviets traded primarily raw materials and produce for finished goods, a pattern that would characterize Soviet-East German trade in succeeding years.   A supplementary protocol provided additional deliveries of foodstuffs from the Soviet Union on credit to help relieve the difficult economic conditions in the GDR.   The first long-term trade agreement between the USSR and the GDR was concluded in September 1951, covering the period 1952-1955.(137) From this time, trade relations between the two coun-

tries were based on long-term agreements.   Trade agreements with other bloc countries followed.

     Reorientation of trade toward the East affected
not only the trading partners but composition of goods
traded as well.   Before World War II, East Germany
enjoyed a comfortable equilibrium in food trade, whereas after the war the area had a significant and consistent   trade   deficit   in   this   sector.(138)   The
export/import structure of the GDR and its changes
between 1950 and 1955 are evident in Table 14.

Table 14
GDR Trade with the East Bloc
(in percentages)

	1950	1951	1952	1953	1954	1955
Exports						
Basic industries	41	28	27	19	19	20
Metalworking ind.	37	55	60	74	74	73
Food & light ind.	18	14	12	5	6	5
Agriculture & forestry	2	2	-	-	-	-
Imports						
Basic industries	42	43	39	38	40	42
Metalworking ind.	4	3	4	4	3	2
Food & light ind.	37	35	35	36	36	33
Agriculture & forestry	15	18	20	21	19	21

Source: Calculated from Statistisches Jahrbuch der
DDR, 1955, p. 243.
- means negligible

The dramatic increase in the metalworking industries'
share of total exports came at the expense of basic and
light industries.(139) The area has traditionally been
primarily an exporter of finished industrial goods.
The change between pre-World War II and postwar exports
has been from manufactured consumer goods, precision
instruments and optics, and processed food to machinery, equipment, and chemicals. In exchange East Germany
received raw materials and food from her new East
European trading partners.(140) The GDR became the
primary capital goods supplier to the East bloc.   The
change in trade composition reflected the major changes
in the GDR's economic structure previously discussed.
The First Five Year Plan had been designed to broaden
the industrial base and to increase production in re-

sponse to East bloc needs as well as to compensate for
the loss of economic ties to West Germany. The strik-
ing decline in export of basic industries reflected the
growing industrial capabilities of the USSR and the
other bloc countries. The concurrent shift away from
the initial postwar emphasis on building up basic industry reflected the extent to which the GDR economy
was intentionally molded to meet Soviet and East European needs.(141)

Long-term changes have arisen from the reorientation of trade. The GDR has become dependent upon the
Soviet Union as the primary supplier of raw materials
and food vital to the industrialized economy. At the
same time, the GDR enjoys access to a huge, virtually
guaranteed market in the CMEA. A negative side to this
change has been the opportunity costs to the GDR economy. As a result of being a supplier of development
assistance and investment goods to less-developed CMEA
members, the GDR was unable to modernize her own industry satisfactorily for a considerable period of time.
Whole branches of industry worked preponderantly for
the Soviet market; some industries, like shipbuilding
and uranium, were created solely for Soviet benefit.
In turn, development of traditional sectors of the
economy was blocked. In addition, due to lack of
specialization and inability to reach economies of
scale, the GDR was unable to compete effectively in the
world market in many areas.

Another cost generally attributed by Western
scholars to East Germany's trade reorientation is that
of unfavorable terms of trade, which amounted to significant sums of indirect reparations paid by the GDR
to the Soviet Union.(142) Price discrimination against
the GDR was facilitated by the political and economic
dominance enjoyed by the USSR as the postwar occupying
power. This fit a pattern of price discrimination
against all bloc countries. The Soviet Union generally
paid low prices for East European goods and benefitted
substantially by re-exporting these goods. Conversely,
the East Europeans generally paid higher than market
prices for imports from the Soviet Union.(143) This
abuse appears to have been most blatant up to the mid
1950s, when a qualitative change in Soviet-East European relations began.

It should be noted that the East Europeans suffered even less favorable terms of trade from the West,
initially due to the economic warfare waged against the

Soviet Union and her allies during the Cold War and later to uncompetitive products, unresponsive foreign trade bureaucracies, and other incompatibilities which hampered profitable trade with the West. The GDR's trade balance showed regular deficits with nonbloc countries until the early 1960s.(144) The deficits were made possible mainly by Soviet hard-currency credits.

In trade with the Soviets, the GDR registered a small deficit for the years 1948 to 1953. This was due to the importation of much-needed foodstuffs and raw materials. See Table 15.

Table 15
GDR Balance of Trade with the Soviet Union
(millions of current dollars f.o.b.)

1948	1949	1950	1951	1952	1953
- 8	+ 23	- 40	+ 58	- 27	- 25

1954	1955	1956	1957	1958	1959
+130	+100	+ 12	+74	+146	+ 17

Source: Calculations made from trade data in Paul Marer, Soviet and East European Foreign Trade, 1946-1969: Statistical Compendium and Guide (Bloomington: Indiana University Press, 1972), pp. 27, 37.

If reparations are included, which provides a more accurate picture of the transfer of wealth, even at deflated prices, the GDR had substantial but declining surpluses, as seen in Table 16.

Table 16
Trade and Reparations Balance of the GDR with the USSR
(millions of current dollars)

	1951	1952	1953
Reparations	+566	+530	+466
Trade balance	+ 58	- 27	- 25
Total	+624	+503	+441

Source: Calculations made from compatible data in Erick Klinkmöller, Die gegenwärtige Aussenhandelsverflectung der sowjetischen Besazungszone Deutschlands (Berlin: Duncker & Humblot, 1959), p. 99, and from Table 15.

From 1954 until the end of the decade, the GDR had
constant surpluses in trade with the USSR despite the
termination of the bulk of reparations payments which
became effective on 1 January 1954.   The total surplus
registered for this period amounted to $479.3 million
at current prices. (The 1959 trade surplus was $17
million.)   Those export surpluses represented an in-
credible burden on the already strained and dismembered
economy.   Trade surpluses are generally considered
positive, but for East Germany in the postwar years a
trade surplus meant an outflow of goods in an economy
already strained by shortages.   Under those circumstances a trade deficit would have been more beneficial
to the domestic economy for the short term.

    GDR balance of trade with the bloc as a whole
paralleled that with the Soviet Union.   This is to be
expected, because the USSR was and remains the primary
trading partner of the GDR.   The GDR did, however,
register a modest surplus in trade with all bloc countries from 1948 through 1953, despite the deficit with
the USSR for that period.   A substantial surplus--
$1.016 billion--was accumulated from 1954 though 1959,
exceeding that with the Soviet Union.   The largest
export surplus with the bloc was registered in 1951 at
$684.7 million if reparations are included.   Surpluses
fell in succeeding years to the 1956 level of $80.5
million.(145)

    The extraordinary burden of reparations deliveries
led to a situation in 1952 in which the GDR could not
preserve a balance of payments equilibrium.(146)   The
payments crisis sharpened in 1953 and fused with other
growing problems to create the explosive events which
took place in the summer of that year.

CONCLUSIONS

The issue of exploitation is more subtle and complex than at first glance when the full range of Soviet
economic policy in East Germany is assessed against
varying, appropriate criteria: the Yalta and Potsdam
agreements, the Soviet reparations proposal, Soviet
losses, and German ability to pay.   The guarantee of an
absolute value of reparations from Germany to help
restore the devastated Soviet economy was a core element of Soviet policy toward Germany.   Soviet expecta-
tions of a favorable agreement on the reparations issue
based on Yalta were disappointed at Potsdam.   The compromise reached at the postwar conference bore only the
slightest resemblance to the more comprehensive Yalta
Protocol on German Reparations.   Even assuming the
Soviet position of complementarity of the two agreements, there was no mention of an agreed-upon value of
reparations Germany was to pay.   While this was not
unreasonable in view of the loss of German territory to
Poland and the need to evaluate Germany's postwar industrial capacity, from the Soviet perspective, given
its unequal burden in the war effort and the sympathetic position of the Roosevelt administration, the final
agreement could be interpreted as a duplicitous attempt
to deny the USSR its legitimate claims.   Seen in that
light and taking into account the uncertain nature of
prolonged occupation, the Soviet policy of removing as
much as possible as fast as possible from the SBZ could
be judged as harsh but not exploitive.   The exaction of
reparations from current production and the use of
German labor, pointed to as elements of exploitation in
violation of the Allied reparations agreement, were
approved by the United States, Great Britain, and the
USSR as legitimate forms of reparations at Yalta.
Thus, based on the Soviet perspective of the two agreements, this charge is not valid.

Assessed against German treatment of the Soviets
during their occupation during World War II and Germany's ability to pay, Soviet reparations policy was
not exploitive.   Soviet loss of life and damage to the
economy, despite relocation of important industrial
installations and construction of new ones beyond the
Urals, was compensated for only in small part by reparations.   Soviets estimate the damage done by the Nazi
occupation at $485 billion.   Thus, Soviet reparations
came to less than 4 percent of the total.(147)   In
fact, compared to the utter depravity of Nazi policy in

occupied Russia and the Ukraine, Soviet actions in Germany, brutal as they were in some cases, were understandable. In addition, East Germany was proven capable of meeting Soviet reparations demands without breaking the economy. There was new, albeit limited, investment and a steady growth in the GNP, although at a retarded rate--indications of economic strength despite the heavy reparations burden.

Judged against the Soviets' own reparations proposal, however, their policy as implemented appears exploitive. According to the best estimates, the Soviets exacted from their zone , in a much shorter period of time, twice the amount they requested from all Germany over a twenty-year period. This nearly equalled the amount recommended to be paid by all Germany to all the Allies. This does not account for aid received from the Soviets, nor does it take into account that the circumstances under which the Soviets presented their original proposal, seeking $10 billion, had changed substantially. It was made at a time when Stalin may well have counted on reconstruction aid from the United States. When this aid, promised by Roosevelt, was later denied by Truman, the Soviets may have compensated by extracting more reparations from East Germany.(148) In addition, deteriorating East-West relations and the unparalleled power of the United States made rapid economic reconstruction an urgent necessity for the Kremlin.

It has been shown that the Soviets sent economic aid to East Germany, essentially foodstuffs and raw materials, despite the hardship this imposed on their already extremely difficult economic conditions. The economic aid sent between 1945 and 1960 is valued at $9.4 billion.(149) When subtracted from the reparations figure, the net transfer of wealth from the GDR to the USSR comes to $9.6 billion, or somewhat less than the original Soviet request. Seen in this light, Soviet policy implemented the proposal made at Yalta which has been shown by other criteria to have been nonexploitive. It must be noted, however, that aid and reparations were not evenly distributed over this period of time. Additional ameliorating elements of Soviet policy, i.e., the emphasis on improving the standard of living and toleration of private enterprise, were attributable to the unique situation in Germany which offered opportunities as well as risks. They also served the goal of ensuring reparations deliveries by strengthening the economy. In this way,

even apparently contradictory policies complemented the
reparations policy and its ramifications, such as restructuring the economy and reorientation of trade.

In sum, the total of Soviet economic policy in
implementation and effect can be seen as dominated by
short-term concern for reparations, which represented a
certain and legitimate partial compensation for the
costs of World War II. In turn, the cumulative impact
of the reparations policy was one which went beyond the
direct transfer of wealth.

The conflict between political and economic goals
was apparent in the contrast between direct reparations
policies and those directed toward alleviating economic
hardship. The latter were elicited in large part by
the existence of an open border through Berlin and the
question of Germany's future. The Soviets did not want
to lose their skilled labor and management, nor did
they want to limit their options for gaining influence
in West Germany. At the same time, interest in reparations combined with the desire to extend Soviet influence in West Germany to retard sovietization of East
Germany. The resulting mixed picture of Soviet policy
torn between exploitation and moderation reflects the
ambiguity of the German situation and competing Soviet
goals.

NOTES

1.   Maurice Ernst, "Postwar Economic Growth in Eastern Europe," New Directions in the Soviet Economy (Washington, D.C.: Government Printing Office, 1966), p. 877; Heinz Köhler, Economic Integration in the Soviet Bloc with an East German Case Study (New York: Frederick A. Praeger, 1965), p. 12; Gert Leptin, Die deutsche Wirtschaft nach 1945: Ein Ost-West Vergleich (Opladen: Leske Verlag, 1971), p. 49; Edwin M. Snell and Marilyn Harper, "Postwar Economic Growth in East Germany: A Comparison with West Germany," Economic Developments in Countries of Eastern Europe (Washington, D.C.: Government Printing Office, 1970), pp. 559-60.

2.   Werner Bröll, Die Wirtschaft der DDR: Lage und Aussichten (Munich: Günter Olzog Verlag, 1972), p. 10.

3.   Köhler, Economic Integration, p. 12. Köhler states that in 1936, 24 percent of the population produced 28 percent of national industrial output. This area excludes East Berlin and territory transferred to Poland. Horst Duhnke, Stalinismus in Deutschland (Cologne: Verlag für Politik und Wirtschaft, 1955), p. 86. Duhnke says 26 percent of the population produced its equal in net industrial production in 1936. He specifies only the exclusion of territory transferred to Poland. The percentages are of national production in Germany's 1936 boundaries.

4.   Köhler, Economic Integration, p. 12.

5.   Ibid.

6.   Snell and Harper, "Economic Growth in East Germany," p. 559.

7.   Eastern Germany referred to here does not include the agriculturally rich territories east of the Oder-Neisse.

8.   Hans Liebe, "Agrarstruktur und Ernährungspotential der Zonen," in Wirtschaftsprobleme der Besatzungszonen, Deutsches Institut für Wirtschaftsforschung (Berlin: Duncker & Humblot, 1948), p. 23.

9.   Ibid., p. 24.

10.   Köhler, Economic Integration, p. 12.

11.   Wolfgang F. Stolper, The Structure of the
East German Economy (Cambridge: Harvard University
Press, 1960), p. 278.

12.   Leptin, Deutsche Wirtschaft, p. 50; Bruno
Gleitze, Ostdeutsche Wirtschaft (Berlin: Duncker &
Humblot, 1956), p. 11.

13.   Köhler, Economic Integration, p. 40.

14.   The United States Strategic Bombing Survey,
The Effects of Strategic Bombing on German Transporta-
tion, no. 200, (Washington, D.C.: Government Printing
Office, 20 November 1945), p. 3.

15.   Ibid.; J.P. Nettl, The Eastern Zone and Soviet Policy in Germany, 1945-1950 (London: Oxford University Press, 1951), p. 145.

16.   U.S. Strategic Bombing Survey, Effects on
German Transportation; U.S. Strategic Bombing Survey,
Overall Report: European War no. 2, 30 (Washington,
D.C.: Government Printing Office, September 1945), p.
38.

17.   U.S. Strategic Bombing Survey, Overall Report, no. 2, p. 38.

18.   Nettl, Eastern Zone, p. 147; Köhler, Economic
Integration, p. 13.

19.   Köhler, Economic Integration, p. 13. The
official East German position holds that war damage in
East Germany was much greater than in the West, with
industrial capacity suffering about 45 percent destruction compared with only about 20 percent in the West.
Politische Ökonomie des Sozialismus und ihre Anwendung
in der DDR (Berlin: Dietz Verlag, 1969), p. 132; also
A.B. Nikolaeva, Ekonomicheskoye Sotrydnichestvo GDR s
SSSR (Moscow: Izdatelstva Nayka, 1968), p. 7.

20. U.S. Department of State, Foreign Relations of
the United States: Diplomatic Papers: The Conference of
Berlin (Potsdam) (Washington, D.C.: Government Printing
Office, 1960), p. 473 (hereafter cited as Potsdam Documents. The exchange took place during a private meet-

ing between Truman and Molotov.

21.   Liebe,   "Agrarstruktur   und   Ernährungspotential," pp. 26, 28.

22.   Ibid., p. 25.

23.   Ibid., p. 31.

24.   Wilhelm Bauer, "Der allgemeine wirtschaftliche Charakter der Zonen" in Wirtschaftsprobleme der
Besatzungszonen, p. 11.

25.   Stolper,   Structure of the East German
Economy, p. 22.

26.   Ibid., pp. 23-4.

27.   Ibid., p. 23.

28.   Ibid., p. 27.

29.   Ibid., p. 37.

30.   See page 72 for explanation of trophy campaigns.

31.   Bröll, Die Wirtschaft der DDR, p. 14. Another source estimates over 50 percent of 1936 capacity
was lost.   Rudolf Meimberg, Die wirtschaftliche Entwicklung in Westberlin und in der sowjetischen Zone
(Berlin: Duncker & Humblot, 1952), p. 55.

32.   Duhnke, Stalinismus in Deutschland, p. 86.
In 1936, hard coal production in the area accounted for
only 3.9 percent of total production in Potsdam Ger-
many.   Production of crude steel was about 6 percent.
Bröll, Die Wirtschaft der DDR, pp. 10-2.   See also
Appendix C.

33.   John H. Backer, The Decision to Divide Germany (Durham, N.C.: Duke University Press, 1978),
p. 67. German anger at the extremely harsh reparations
terms of the Versailles Treaty was one of the factors
which served to promote Hitler. This reason, a well as
fear of Soviet expansion, made Churchill particularly
skittish about imposing harsh reparations on a defeated
Germany.

34.   See Chapter 2.

35.   Vassily Yershov, "Confiscation and Plunder by the Army of Occupation," in <u>Soviet Economic Policy in Postwar Germany</u>, ed. by Robert M. Slusser (New York: Research Program on the USSR, 1953), pp. 1-3.

36.   Konstantin Pritzel, <u>Die wirtschafliche Integration der sowjetischen Besatzungszone Deutschlands in den Ostblock und ihre politischen Aspekte</u> (Bonn: Deutscher Bundes-Verlag, 1962), p. 15.

37.   It will be recalled that Western soldiers also carried out booty campaigns, although not on the same scale.

38.   Köhler, <u>Economic Integration</u>, p. 11.

39.   Paul Marer, "Soviet Economic Policy in Eastern Europe," in <u>Reorientation and Commerical Relations of the Economies of Eastern Europe</u> (Washington, D.C.: Government Printing Office, 1974), p. 139. These figures do not include the value of goods removed in the trophy campaign.

40.   Köhler, <u>Economic Integration</u>, pp. 15-16; Snell and Harper, "Economic Growth in East Germany," p. 567.

41.   Erich W. Gniffke, <u>Jahre mit Ulbricht</u> (Cologne: Verlag Wissenschaft und Politik, 1966), p. 194.

42.   Leptin, <u>Deutsche Wirtschaft</u>, p. 51.

43.   There were often battles over whether to dismantle a plant or to leave it in Germany to produce for the reparations account. A classic case was the Zeiss optical works. Grigorii Petrovich Klimov, <u>Berliner Kreml</u> (Cologne: Kiepenheuer und Witsch, 1951), p. 368.

44.   The SMAD issued the order to create the SAGs on 5 June 1946. Beate Ruhm von Oppen, ed., <u>Documents on Germany under Occupation, 1945-54</u> (London: Oxford University Press, 1955), p. 141 (hereafter cited as<u>Documents on Germany</u>). The Soviets and the SED tried to create a political plus from the fact that these important enterprises were allowed to remain in Germany. The change in policy was attributed to the Soviet desire to create employment and a portion of the output for the German economy.

45.   Franz L. Neumann, "Soviet Policy in Germany," American Academy of Political and Social Science Annals (May 1949), p. 177. Neumann supports the higher estimate.

46.   Pritzel, Die wirtschaftliche Integration, p. 16; Marer, "Soviet Economic Policy in Eastern Europe," p. 141; Gniffke, Jahre mit Ulbricht, p. 199.

47.   Die sowietische Hand in der deutschen Wirtschaft (Bonn: Bonner Berichte aus Mittel-und Ostdeutschland, 1952), p. 52. At the end of April 1952, approximately one-fourth of the work force worked for the SAGs, this after the return of more than one-half of the SAGs to German ownership (p. 15).

48.   Neues Deutschland (8 January 1954).

49.   P.J.D. Wiles, Communist International Economics (New York: Frederick A. Praeger, 1969), p. 490; Vladimir Rudolph, "The Administrative Organization of Soviet Control," in Soviet Economic Policy in Postwar Germany, p. 56.

50.   Marer, "Soviet Economic Policy in Eastern Europe," p. 142.

51.   Ibid.; Die sowietische Hand, pp. 15-16.

52.   Franz Rupp, Die Reparationen der sowietischen Besatzungszone in den Jahren 1945 bis Ende 1953 (Bonn: Bonner Berichte aus Mittel-und Ostdeutschland, 1954), p. 15.

53.   Snell and Harper, "Economic Growth in East Germany," p. 560; Die sowietische Hand, p. 87.

54.   Nettl, Eastern Zone, pp. 208-9, 302.

55.   Ibid.; Die sowietische Hand, p.. 69; Rupp, Reparationen, pp. 8-9. Sources disagree as to whether 1936 or 1944 prices were used by the Soviets to place a value on deliveries.

56.   Documents on Germany, pp. 486, 488.

57.   Poland was to receive 15 percent of reparations delivered to the USSR, although it is generally agreed the Poles received only a small fraction of their due. It is unlikely the Poles had any voice in

the decision to reduce reparations claims.

58.   Documents on Germany, p. 489.

59.   Franklyn D. Holzman, International Trade under Communism: Politics and Economics (New York: Basic Books, 1976), p. 76; Rupp, Reparationen, pp. 8-9.

60.   Studiengesellschaft für Zeitprobleme, Die sowjetische Deutschlandpolitik, 4 parts (Duisdorf bei Bonn: Studiengesellschaft für Zeitprobleme, 1962-1963) 3:120.

61.   Holzman, International Trade under Communism, p. 76.

62.   Beziehungen DDR-UdSSR: 1949 bis 1955, 2 vols. (Berlin: Staatsverlag der Deutschen Demokratischen Republik, 1975), 1:164-65.

63.   Köhler, Economic Integration, p. 20.

64.   Ibid., p. 29; Marer, "Soviet Economic Policy in Eastern Europe," p. 139.

65.   Marer, "Soviet Economic Policy in Eastern Europe," p. 139; Stolper, Structure of the East German Economy, p. 5; Snell and Harper, "Economic Growth in East Germany," p. 568.   For a breakdown of payments according to type and year, see Appendix D.

66.   Welles Hangen, The Muted Revolution: East Germany's Challenge to Russia and the West (London: Victor Gollancz Ltd., 1967), p. 15.

67.   V.L. Sokolov, Soviet Use of German Science and Technology (New York: Research Program on the USSR, 1955), pp. 26-30; Pritzel, Die wirtschafliche Integration, p. 17; Gniffke, Jahre mit Ulbricht, p. 215; Köhler, Economic Integration, p. 23.

68.   Sokolov, Soviet Use of German Science and Technology, p. 27.

69.   David O. Childs, The GDR: Moscow's German Ally (London: George Allen & Unwin Ltd., 1983), p. 14.

70.   Percy Stulz and Siegfried Thomas, eds., Die Deutsche Demokratische Republik auf dem Wege zum Sozialismus: Dokumente und Materialien, 2 vols. (Ber-

108 Soviet Policy Toward East Germany Reconsidered

lin: Volk und Wissen Volkseigener Verlag, 1959-61),
1:156.

71. N.S. Khrushchev, Khrushchev Remembers (Boston: Little, Brown and Co., 1970), p. 233. Khrushchev
says there was even cannibalism in the Ukraine.
Klimov, Berliner Kreml, p. 328; Yershov, "Confiscation
and Plunder," p. 9.

72. Khrushchev, Khrushchev Remembers, p. 233.

73. Jurij L. Vasjanin, "Die Entwicklung der öko-
nomishcen Zusammenarbeit zwischen der DDR und der
UdSSR," Deutsche Aussenpolitik 18 (October 1973):1075.

74. Documents on Germany, pp. 143, 148.

75. Stulz and Thomas, Dokumente und Materialien,
1:156-57.

76. Vasjanin, "Ökonomische Zusammenarbeit," p.
1075; Stefan Doernberg, Kurze Geschichte der DDR (Berlin: Dietz Verlag, 1968), p. 131.

77. Marshall D. Shulman, Stalin's Foreign Policy
Reappraised (Cambridge: Harvard University Press,
1963), pp. 43, 65-66.

78. N.A. Baturin, "Trade of the Soviet Union with
the German Democratic Republic," in Foreign Trade of
the USSR with the Socialist Countries (New York: U.S.
Joint Publications Research Service, 1959) p. 114;
Köhler, Economic Integration, p. 309.

79. Otto Hofmann and Gerhard Scharschmidt, DDR:
Aussenhandel Gestern und Heute (Berlin: Verlag die
Wirtschaft, 1975), p. 57; Beziehungen DDR-UdSSR, pp.
229-30; Baturin, "Trade of the Soviet Union," p. 115.

80. Stolper, Structure of the East German
Economy, p. 417.

81. Köhler, Economic Integration, p. 40.

82. Ibid., pp. 41-42.

83. Karl C. Thalheim and Peter D. Propp, Die
Entwicklungsziele für die gewerbliche Wirtschaft der
sowjetischen Besatzungszone in der zweiten Fünfjahr-
planperiode (Bonn: Bundesministerium für Gesamtdeutsche

Fragen, 1957), p. 8.

    84.   Snell   and Harper,   "Economic Growth in East
Germany," p.   571; Fritz Schenk,   Magie der   Planwirtschaft (Cologne: Kiepenheuer & Witsch,   1960), pp. 68-
69; Jan Wszelaki, Communist Economic Strategy: The Role
of   East-Central   Europe   (Washington,   D.C.:   National
Planning Association, 1959), p. 52.

    85.   Duhnke,   Stalinismus in Deutschland, pp. 92-
93; Thalheim, "Die sowjetische Besatzungszone Deutschlands," in Die Sowjetisierung Ost-Mitteleuropa,   ed. by
Ernst Birke (Frankfurt am Main: Alfred Metzner Verlag,
1959) p. 346; Manuel Gottlieb, The German Peace Settlement   and the Berlin Crisis (New   York: Paine-Whitman,
1960), p. 58.

    86.   Nettl, Eastern Zone, pp. 114-25.

    87.   Stulz and Thomas, Dokumente und Materialien,
1:95-97.   Of those who voted, 77.7 percent approved the
nationalization.   Gregory W.   Sandford, From Hitler to
Ulbricht: The Communist Reconstruction of East Germany,
1945-46 (Princeton,   N.J.:   Princeton University Press,
1983),   p.   215.   The United States and Great   Britain
disregarded   similar   votes in Hessen and   North   Rhine
Westfalia,   according to Dietrich Staritz.   Sozialismus
in   einem halben Land (Berlin: Verlag Klaus Wagenbach,
1976), p. 100

    88.   Gottlieb, German Peace Settlement, pp. 61-62;
Richard   Lukas,   Zehn Jahre sowjetische   Besatzungszone
(Mainz: Deutscher Fachschriften-Verlag, 1955), p. 166;
Peter   Mitzscherling,   System und Entwicklung der   DDR-
Wirtschaft (Berlin: Duncker & Humblot,   1974),   p. 16;
Duhnke, Stalinismus in Deutschland, p. 102.

    89.   The central administrative organs   mentioned
before   were primarily advisory organs of Soviet   head-
quarters.   Gottlieb,   German Peace Settlement, pp. 65-
66.

    90.   Duhnke, Stalinismus in Deutschland, pp. 100-
2; Pritzel, Die wirtschaftliche Integration, pp 24-25.

    91.   Nettl, Eastern Zone, p. 65.

    92.   Heinz Krause, Economic Structure of East
Germany and Its Position within the Soviet Bloc (Washington,   D.C.:   Council   for Economic and Industry   Re-

search, 1955), part 2, p. 98; Gniffke, _Jahre_ _mit_ _Ulbricht_, p. 281; _DDR:_ _Werden_ _und_ _Wachsen_ (Berlin: Dietz Verlag, 1975), p. 128; Vlas. Leskov, "The Administration of Foreign Trade, 1946-1949," in _Soviet_ _Economic_ _Policy_ _in_ _Postwar_ _Germany_, p. 66.

93. Duhnke, _Stalinismus_ _in_ _Deutschland_, pp. 88-89; Pritzel, _Die_ _wirtschaftliche_ _Integration_, p. 26.

94. Snell and Harper data taken from the 1968 _Statistisches_ _Jahrbuch_ show a smaller share of gross production by the private sector: 38 percent in 1950 and 27 percent in 1955. Even these figures represent a much larger private sector than found in other East European countries at the same time. "Economic Growth in East Germany," p. 576.

95. Gottlieb, _German_ _Peace_ _Settlement_, pp. 54-55; Hangen, _The_ _Muted_ _Revolution_, p. 102; Nettl, _Eastern_ _Zone_, p. 85; Childs, _Moscow's_ _German_ _Ally_, pp. 14-15.

96. Thalheim, "Die sowjetische Besatzungszone Deutschlands," p. 345.

97. Snell and Harper, "Economic Growth in East Germany," pp. 576-77, 582.

98. Stolper, _Structure_ _of_ _the_ _East_ _German_ _Economy_, p. 417.

99. Ibid., p. 23.

100. Hermann Weber, _Von_ _der_ _SBZ_ _zur_ _"DDR"_ (Hannover: Verlag für Literatur und Zeitgeschehen, 1966-67) vols. 1 & 2, chronologies.

101. Stolper, _Structure_ _of_ _the_ _East_ _German_ _Economy_, p. 24.

102. Bröll, _Die_ _Wirtschaft_ _der_ _DDR_, p. 14; Nettl, _Eastern_ _Zone_, pp. 162-66; Duhnke, _Stalinismus_ _in_ _Deutschland_, p. 88

103. Backer, _Decision_ _to_ _Divide_ _Germany_, pp. 98-99; Sandford, _From_ _Hitler_ _to_ _Ulbricht_, p. 66.

104. Gottlieb, _German_ _Peace_ _Settlement_, p. 63.

105. Ibid., pp. 79-80; Backer, _Decision_ _to_ _Divide_ _Germany_, pp. 121-22.

106. Werden und Wachsen, pp. 103-4; Nettl, Eastern Zone, p. 241.

107. Duhnke, Stalinismus in Deutschland, p. 88.

108. Bröll, Die Wirtschaft der DDR, p. 15.

109. Ernst, "Economic Growth in Eastern Europe," p. 890; United Nations, Economic Survey of Europe (Geneva: Economic Commission for Europe), 1956, ch. II, pp. 2-3.

110. Snell and Harper, "Economic Growth in East Germany," pp. 553-54.

111. For comparative figures on East and West European investment, see Ernst, "Economic Growth in Eastern Europe," p. 890.

112. Stolper, Structure of the East German Economy, p. 417.

113. Investment goods in the GDR are underpriced in relation to consumer goods because turnover taxes and profits on capital and sales of investment goods are lower. Michael Keren, "The GDR's Economic Miracle," Problems of Communism, (January-February 1976), p. 88. Despite this, the statement above still stands, but in real terms the distribution between consumption and investment would look different.

114. Snell and Harper, "Economic Growth in East Germany," p. 576.

115. Ernst, "Economic Growth in Eastern Europe," pp. 885-86.

116. Stolper, Structure of the East Germany Economy, p. 434.

117. Ibid.

118. Liebe, "Agrarstrukstur und Ernährungspotential," p. 31; Nettl, Eastern Zone, pp. 181-83.

119. Sokolov, Soviet Use of German Science and Technology, p. 24.

120. Special rations plus other goods such as furs and stockings were rarities to many of the engineers

arriving from the Soviet Union, where a famine was beginning at the end of the war.

121. Sokolov, Soviet Use of German Science and Technology, p. 30. By contrast, Klimov contends that all top German scientists and technicians went over to the Western Allies. The SMAD represented third-rate scientists who stayed as important and first-class. Berliner Kreml, pp. 138-39.

122. Meat, fats, sugar, milk, and potatoes were still rationed at the end of 1953. It was often difficult to meet ration allowances. "Eastern Germany since the Risings of June 1953," World Today 10 (February 1954):67. It is not clear whether the consumption table presents ration allotments or amounts actually consumed.

123. Stolper, Structure of the East German Economy, pp. 247-51, 418.

124. See Table 9.

125. Statistisches Jahrbuch der DDR, 1956, (Berlin: VEB Deutscher Zentralverlag, 1957), p. 201.

126. Ibid., 1958, p. 312. The substantial differentiation in income was not unlike Stalin's policy adopted in the 1930s to stimulate production.

127. Ibid.

128. Ibid., 1955, p. 98.

129. By contrast, data on West German GNP, distribution of GNP, and average monthly wages show that by 1950 the West German standard of living was substantially higher than in 1936. Consumption as a percentage of GNP has remained quite consistent at 60 percent, which means steady improvement in the standard of living as the GNP has grown. Stolper, Structure of the East German Economy, pp. 419, 431, 436-67.

130. Köhler, Economic Integration, p. 71.

131. Frederic L. Pryor, The Communist Foreign Trade System (Cambridge: MIT Press, 1963), p. 165; United Nations, Economic Commission for Europe, Economic Survey of Europe, 1957 (Geneva: Economic Commission for Europe, 1958), p. A-64. Marer and Köhler show

a more gradual reorientation of GDR trade.   Each presents modestly different calculations, both of which
show East German trade with the bloc at 45 percent in
1948, not reaching 75 percent until 1950 and 1951
respectively. Köhler, *Economic Integration*, p. 72;
Marer, "Soviet Economic Policy in Eastern Europe,"
pp. 27, 37.

132. Some see the GDR's belated membership as the
culmination of the process of binding her to the bloc.
Boris Meissner, *Russland, die Westmächte und Deutschland: die sowjetische Deutschlandpolitik, 1943-1953*
(Hamburg: H.H. Nölke Verlag, 1953), p. 236. Others see
this as the beginning of a new stage of integration.
Studiengesellschaft, *Deutschlandpolitik*, 3:118.

133. Not until the 1960s did the Soviets attempt
to use the CMEA as an instrument for supranational
economic planning. Much attention was given to enhanced coordination of national plans from the mid
1950s, although little of substance was accomplished.

134. The WTZ began, in one assessment, one of the
most sinister aspects of exploitation in the postwar
period. Pritzel, *Die wirtschaftliche Integration*,
p. 50.

135. Snell and Harper, "Economic Growth of East
Germany," p. 569.

136. Bröll, *Die Wirtschaft der DDR*, p. 17;
Baturin, "Trade of the Soviet Union," p. 114.

137. Baturin, "Trade of the Soviet Union," p. 116;
Pritzel, *Die wirtschaftliche Integration*, p 47.

138. Alfred Zauberman, *Industrial Progress in
Poland, Czechoslovakia and East Germany, 1937-1962*
(London: Oxford University Press, 1964), p. 294.

139. Other sources present parallel, although not
such extreme, shifts in the export structure. See
Pritzel, *Die wirtschaftliche Integration*, p. 68; Erich
Klinkmüller and Maria Elisabeth Ruban, *Die wirtschaftliche Zusammenarbeit der Ostblockstaaten* (Berlin:
Duncker & Humblot, 1960), p. 219. The *Economic Survey
of Europe* uses a different breakdown of commodity
groups which makes comparison difficult. *ESE*, 1957,
p. A-62.

140. Zauberman, Industrial Progress, pp. 282, 289; Köhler, Economic Integration. p. 283; Klinkmüller, Die gegenwärtige Aussenhandelsverflectung der sowjetischen Besatzungszone Deutschlands (Berlin: Duncker & Humblot, 1959), p. 54.

141. See industrial production data in Table 6.

142. Ernst, "Economic Growth in Eastern Europe," p. 902; Wszelaki, Communist Economic Strategy, p. 60; Krause, Economic Structure of East Germany, 1:102-3; Pritzel, Die wirtschaftliche Integration, p. 67. Notable exceptions are Wiles, Communist International Economics, p. 240; Bröll, Die Wirtschaft der DDR, p. 120. Somewhere between the two are Marer, "Soviet Economic Policy in Eastern Europe," pp. 145-48, and Köhler, Economic Integration, pp. 357-59.

143. Ernst, "Economic Growth in Eastern Europe," p. 902; Wszelaki, Communist Economic Strategy, pp. 60-61; Leskov, "Administration of Foreign Trade," p. 71.

144. Klinkmüller, Aussenhandelsverflechtung, p. 23.

145. Calculated from Marer, Statistical Compendium, pp. 27, 37.

146. Ibid., p. 27.

147. Telegram from Berlin to the Secretary of State, 13 May 1950, National Archives documents.

148. Thomas G. Paterson, "American Expansionism and Power" in Major Problems in American Foreign Policy, ed. by Paterson, Vol. II (Lexingon, Mass.: D.C. Heath and Co., 1978) p. 316.

149. Marer, "Soviet Economic Policy in Eastern Europe," p. 145.

4
Building to a Crisis

The early 1950s was a period of growing difficulty
within the Soviet bloc. The indirect Soviet conflict
with the United States in Korea and the open break
between Stalin and Tito caused Stalin to tighten his
hold on the Eastern bloc. Purges of the communist
parties which began throughout East Europe in 1949 led
to uncertainty and fear which paralyzed virtually every
facet of society. This underlying, pervasive tension,
coupled with the cumulative effects of exploitive elements of Soviet economic policy in East Europe, especially in East Germany, undermined economic well-being
everywhere. Stalin's sudden death in March 1953 raised
anew the question of East Germany's future. The unsettled nature of leadership succession compounded economic hardships imposed by the Construction of Socialism
Program and unleashed pent-up tension and resentment
culminating in the June uprising, a turning point in
Soviet-East German relations.

INTERNATIONAL SETTING

In the beginning of the 1950s, direct confrontation between the United States and the USSR in Europe
over Germany had eased with the negotiated settlement
of the Berlin blockade. The focus of competition
shifted to Asia, where Soviet prospects looked considerably better. The Chinese Communist victory on the
mainland not only strengthened the forces of socialism
but also demonstrated that American interests could be
defeated. Anti-colonial unrest throughout the area
provided ample opportunity for the Soviet Union to
expand her influence at the expense of the West at
seemingly little risk.

There can be little doubt of Stalin's genuine
surprise at the American response to North Korea's
aggression to reunify the country in 1950. Korea had
never been considered an area of vital strategic interest to the United States. In a speech in January 1950,
Secretary of State Dean Acheson outlined those areas
vital to American national security, and Korea was not
mentioned.(1) Furthermore, the United States had accepted the loss of China, unquestionably more important
to American national interest. Therefore, there was no
indication or logical reason to suggest that the Americans would make a direct military commitment to check
communist expansion in Korea.

The extent to which the Soviet Union directed the
Korean initiative to reunify the country remains hotly
debated.(2) Those who assert the North Korean attack
was orchestrated in Moscow see the benefits to the
Soviets as an opportunity not only to expand their
influence but also to test the reliability of the
Chinese and to undermine the American-Japanese relationship.(3) The controversy over the scope of Soviet
involvement in initiating the conflict is beyond this
study. Needless to say, the U.S. government did not
doubt Soviet responsibility at the time. Whatever
Soviet intentions or involvement, the Korean conflict
proved to be very costly to Soviet interests. The
conflict stimulated U.S. rearmament, which only widened
the gap between the superpowers' military capabilities.(4) It strengthened America's anti-communist
resolve and the cohesion of the Western alliance while
reducing resistance to West German rearmament.(5) In
addition, American presence in Japan was perpetuated by

a security pact concluded shortly after the countries
signed a peace treaty.(6)

      Soviet awareness of their vulnerability to the
U.S. monopoly on nuclear weapons is attested to by the
concentration on research and development in this field
in the late Stalin years.(7)   This contrasted with
Stalin's apparent indifference to the capability of
such weaponry when advised by President Truman at Potsdam that a bomb had been successfully tested.(8)   At
the time, it was estimated in U.S. circles that the
Soviets were at least a decade behind in development of
nuclear weapons, but in just four years they exploded
their first atomic bomb.   In August 1953 the Soviet
leadership announced the successful testing of a ther-
monuclear weapon and delivery system which produced a
"favorable shift in the correlation of forces."(9)
Until that time, military vulnerability was a key element in Soviet foreign policy. Stalin was consistently
very cautious in his foreign policy initiatives in the
interest of preserving and strengthening the Soviet
Union during a period of absolute vulnerability.   He
limited the extension of the Soviet sphere of influence
to those areas with borders contiguous to the USSR and
proceeded cautiously to consolidate control, always
testing the reaction of the Western powers.   Stalin
restrained his more militant proteges in East Europe,
who pressed for rapid socialist transformation of their
societies in the aftermath of the war. He also checked
similar sympathies in West European communist parties.
The Korean gambit can more justly be attributed to the
failure of the United States to make known its strategic interest in the area than to Stalin's recklessness.
It was not until after Stalin's death that the Soviet
Union attempted to project her power worldwide.(10)

      Stalin presented a comprehensive analysis of the
world situation in Economic Problems of Socialism,
published just before the Nineteenth Party Congress of
the CPSU convened in October 1952, the first party
congress in thirteen years.   Stalin subscribed to the
two-camp theory championed by Zhdanov at the 1947
Warsaw Conference but his prescription for relations
between the two camps was directly opposite.   Zhdanov
had called for heightened struggle between the two
camps, whereas Stalin prescribed a general relaxation
of tensions.   According to Stalin's analysis, capitalism had entered a deepening general crisis due to the
shrinking markets brought about by the disintegration
of the unified world market.   The shrinking markets in

turn meant increased struggle for markets and raw materials, which would eventually lead to war among the
capitalists.   Under those circumstances, war was more
likely among the capitalists than between the capitalists and the Soviet Union.   The main theatre of conflict within the capitalist camp was calculated to
exist between the United States and Great Britain.
Secondary contradictions were between the United States
and the defeated capitalist states: Germany, Italy, and
Japan.(11)   The socialist camp, therefore, was to follow a policy of reducing international tensions in
order to exacerbate intra-capitalist contradictions.
In this spirit the Soviet Union initiated a major
effort to resolve the German and Austrian questions.
Proposals for mutual disarmament and troop reductions
were also proffered.(12)

Stalin's unexpected death in March 1953 did not
alter the general policy of peaceful coexistence.   His
successors took advantage of the open situation to
expand Soviet overtures to the West.   They moved quickly to negotiate an end to the Korean war and made other
conciliatory gestures to the West.(13)   The timing
could hardly have been less propitious.   McCarthyism
was in full swing in the United States which soured any
prospects for accommodation with the USSR.   A purge of
the State Department was underway.   In international
politics, the U.S. posture became increasingly aggressive.   The new Eisenhower-Dulles administration adopted
a confrontational policy which called for the liberation of East Europe and massive retaliation against the
USSR in response to conflict anywhere in the world.
The CIA had been active in East Europe, stirring up
unrest through sabotage and espionage, which contributed to the purges which swept the entire area.(14)
U.S. propaganda urged the East Europeans to revolt
against Soviet enslavement and intimated U.S. support
in the struggle.

The Soviet desire to reduce tensions between the
great powers was enhanced by the need of the party
leadership for a breathing space to solidify its position and control.   Stalin's death was a momentous event
which created a vacuum of uncertainty in the USSR.   The
ensuing power struggle within the leadership also added
to the need to pursue accommodation abroad.

It is important to reiterate that Stalin's death
did not mark the significant change in Soviet foreign
policy that is popularly assumed.   The evolution toward

a policy of accommodation and detente with the West in
Europe had been apparent since the end of the Berlin
blockade.   The post-Stalin leadership was more active
and broad-range in its initiatives for rapprochement
with the West than Stalin had been, contributing to the
appearance of a major policy change at that time.

COMPETITION OVER GERMANY

     Negotiations between the Allies over Germany had
come to a standstill.   There were no meetings of the
Council of Foreign Ministers from June 1949 until January 1954.(15) Nonetheless, the struggle over Germany's future continued unabated despite the formation
of two separate German states in 1949.   In October
1950, a Foreign Ministers' conference of East bloc
states met in Prague to devise a strategy for hindering
West German integration into the Western defense system
and into the proposed European Coal and Steel Community.   The East bloc communique criticized the three
Western powers' move toward expanding the authority of
the West German government and revising the limitation
on German industry.(16) The Western governments also
had agreed to begin the steps necessary to end the
state of war with Germany.(17) The Prague statement
denounced these actions as inimical to the reunification of Germany and renewed the call for creation of an
all-German constituent council, on a parity basis,
which would prepare for the creation of an all-German
provisional government.(18)   The statement also proposed conclusion of a peace treaty with a reunited
Germany and a renewed four-power commitment to prohibit
Germany's remilitarization.

     In Germany, meanwhile, the SED pursued a National
Front policy domestically, designed to win support in
West Germany.   Stalin's telegram of congratulation to
Wilhelm Pieck and Otto Grotewohl upon the founding of
the GDR included a statement of his intention of winning the GDR and the German people for the peace policy
of the Soviet bloc.(19) He noted that Soviets and
Germans had suffered most in the war.   This reference
to Soviet-German cooperation continued favorable discussion of a return to the Rapallo policy of the 1920s
in both the Soviet and East German press.(20) At the
Third Party Congress of the SED in 1950, Otto Grotewohl
outlined the central tasks of the Program of the

National Front: "Improvement of living conditions, construction of a united German state, negotiation of a peace treaty and withdrawal of all occupation for- ces."(21)   The West German middle class, however, showed no indication of working with the SED for national unity.   Therefore, a year later the SED adopt- ed a new strategy of "national struggle from below." At the sixth meeting of the SED Central Committee in July 1951, Ulbricht presented two major changes from the previous National Front Program.   First, the main enemy of the national movement was the reappearance of German imperialism in the Federal Republic in alliance with American imperialism.   Second, those serving the interests of imperialism included not only the conser- vative governing coalition in Bonn but also the leader- ships of the Social Democratic Party and the West German labor unions.   Therefore, the SED should concen- trate on winning the allegiance of the West German working class while isolating their leaders.(22)   In the fall, the SED renewed efforts for German reunifica- tion under the slogan "Deutsche an einen Tisch!" (Ger- mans at one table!) The East German formula called for negotiations between the two Germanies as equals to initiate the preparation for all-German elections.(23)

Despite these overtures, integration of the Feder- al Republic into the Western bloc proceeded, acceler- ated by Western fears of Soviet expansion generated by the Korean conflict.   In April 1951 West Germany became a founding member of the European Coal and Steel Com- munity.(24)   At the same time, restrictions on indus- trial production were considerably loosened, an action denounced by the Soviets as a violation of the Potsdam Agreements and as a step toward rebuilding the FRG's military potential.   In July the Western powers termi- nated the state of war with Germany, while discussions on granting sovereignty to West Germany and including it in a proposed European defense community contin- ued.(25)   In addition, the U.S. Senate approved sending additional troops to Europe as a symbol of American commitment to the integrity of Western Europe.(26)

Reports were circulating among U.S. intelligence circles at that time indicating a major Soviet policy change toward Germany, allegedly based on Soviet recog- nition of SED failure to attract wide support.   A shift to a Rapallo policy by the Kremlin was interpreted to mean an alliance with the German military and indus- trial circles which had concluded the Rapallo pact in 1922 and the Molotov-Ribbentrop pact in 1939.   The

Soviets were believed to be willing to allow free
elections as the basis for reunification. A transi-
tional government excluding all prominent SED people,
composed of representatives from the FRG and prominent
German conservatives favorably disposed toward the
USSR, would oversee the transition. In exchange for
reunification the Soviets were expected to want recognition of the Oder-Neisse border, renunciation of rearmament, and a long-term nonaggression pact from the
new German government.(27) Specific aspects of the
anticipated Soviet policy shift proved to be overly
optimistic, but an important Soviet overture on Germany
was in the offing.

The Soviet leadership apparently felt most threatened by the possibility of a rearmed West Germany
integrated into an anti-Soviet military alliance. In a
significant effort to prevent that and to resolve the
German question on terms compatible with Soviet interests, the Kremlin sent a note to the three Western
powers on 10 March 1952 calling for a peace treaty with
a reunified Germany. This marked a return in Soviet
policy to Rapallo, which had been briefly abandoned
during the "national struggle from below" campaign.
The Soviet proposal included provisions for the withdrawal of all occupation troops, recognition of the
Oder-Neisse border, and the observance of strict German
neutrality but did not specify the means by which
reunification was to occur. Two other provisions, new
to Soviet discussion of the German question, called for
the establishment of a national defense force and a
guarantee of civil and political rights to former members of the German military, including officers and
former Nazis, with the exception of those under indict-
ment for war crimes.(28)

In the ensuing exchange of notes between the Soviets and the Western governments, major differences
focused on the process of reunification. The Western
powers wanted free elections to be held first in order
to form a national government with which a peace treaty
could be signed. The Soviets and East Germans, on the
other hand, proposed the formation of a provisional
government, appointed from the existing German governments on a parity basis, with which a peace treaty
could be signed, to be followed by free elections.(29)
Although both sides agreed on the need for free elections, the difference in conditions proposed for con-
ducting the elections made each unwilling to compromise. The Western powers did not recognize the legiti-

macy of the GDR government and were therefore unwilling
to negotiate with its representatives in a provisional,
all-German government. Furthermore, the demand for
parity representation in a provisional government
seemed presumptuous, considering the difference in size
of population and territory under the jurisdiction of
each, although that seems to have been the only formula
by which the Soviets could have protected their interests. The parties also disagreed on monitoring elections. The West wanted an independent United Nations
commission to guarantee the process, while the Soviets
favored a commission of the four occupying powers.(30)
The failure of negotiations on the reunification of
Korea made the West particularly cautious in negotiating the reunification of Germany, and, perhaps as
important, McCarthyism was gaining momentum in the
United States, creating a difficult atmosphere for
accommodation with the USSR.(31)

The Soviets renewed their overture in April and
sweetened the offer with the announced return of sixty-
six SAGs to the East Germans at the end of the month.
The timing of the return was no doubt designed to
influence West German opinion in favor of the Soviet
proposal.(32) The political offensive was stepped up
through the Soviet press in East Germany, which por-
trayed Germany at a historical turning point: Two
paths lay before Germany: Either a peace treaty,
reunification, "and building an all German democratic
government or . . . perpetuation of the division and
with it the danger of a new war in Europe.(33)

The issues of neutrality and Germany's eastern
border were other points of contention between the
former Allies. The Soviets contended that the border
issue had been settled at Potsdam, whereas the West
reaffirmed the position that only the final peace settlement could determine the border.(34) The neutrality
disagreement, however, was more pressing. The Western
position held that a reunited Germany should be free to
enter into alliances which embody the principles and
goals of the United Nations (which meant NATO). The
Soviets, on the other hand, wanted Germany to be pro-
hibited from entering into any coalition or military
alliance which was directed against any former enemy of
Germany (which also meant NATO).(35) The Kremlin was
clearly worried about continuing momentum toward rearm-
ing and integrating West Germany into the Western military alliance.

Just days before the Bonn and Paris treaties were signed, the Soviets sent a third note to the Western powers on the urgency of resolving the German question. The note criticized the forthcoming treaties not only for deepening the division between the two Germanies but for setting the two in direct conflict with each other.(36) Despite Soviet protest, the General Treaty, granting sovereignty to West Germany, was signed in Bonn on 26 May 1952.(37) The following day the European Defense Community (EDC) Treaty was signed in Paris, which provided for a West German military to be integrated into a European armed force.(38) To the Soviets, the EDC represented a realization of one of their worst fears. Soviet critics compared the Bonn and Paris treaties to those of Locarno and Munich, whose infamous purpose was to turn German expansionist forces against the East.(39) West Germany had strong irredentist claims against the USSR which included not only the parts of East Prussia incorporated into Poland and the USSR but all of East Germany.

Despite Western rejection of the reunification proposal and the signing of the Bonn and Paris treaties, the Kremlin pursued its initiative in an effort to prevent ratification of the treaties. In July the World Peace Council met in special session in East Berlin to support the Soviet peace treaty proposal for Germany as well as to condemn the U.S. treaty with Japan and the use the germ warfare in Korea.(40) In late August, the Soviets sent a fourth unfruitful note on Germany to the Western allies which reiterated the general terms of the previous proposal and called for a four-power conference to discuss the matter. The Soviets were dogged in their efforts to derail West German integration into the anti-Soviet alliance. Should those efforts fail, they no doubt wanted to ensure that the onus for the division of Germany rested squarely with the Western powers.

The West German Bundestag approved the Bonn and Paris treaties in March 1953.(41) The European Defense Community was effectively scuttled, however, when the French National Assembly refused to ratify the treaty in August 1954.(42) The collapse of the EDC can be counted a temporary success for the Soviet campaign, which played upon sentiment favoring a comprehensive European security system as well as French fears of a rearmed Germany. Ultimately, fears of Soviet intentions generated by the Korean conflict outweighed fears of Germany and led to German rearmament. After reject-

ing the EDC, the French approved West German membership
in NATO, which they had delayed five years. The Paris
Treaties, signed by the Atlantic Council and West Germany on 22 October 1954, announced the entry of the FRG
into NATO and also recognized the end of the occupation
regime in West Germany.(43) A primary objection to the
EDC within Europe had been the proposed creation of an
integrated European military force. NATO structure, on
the other hand, maintained the national military forces
while providing coordination of the individual commands.(44)

      Debate over the possibilities for Germany's future
in the 1952 Soviet reunification proposal persists.
There is no disagreement on the link between the proposal and the Soviet goal of keeping West Germany out
of a Western military alliance, but there is debate as
to whether Stalin feared that development enough to
sacrifice the GDR to prevent it. Those who see nothing
new in the proposal characterize it as merely a ploy to
create dissension among the Western allies and sufficient hope among the West Germans to scuttle their
negotiations.(45) This was understood as a direct
application of the strategy outlined by Stalin in his
Economic Problems of Socialism.   The credibility of
the initiative was undermined, critics argue, by the
adoption of the program for the Construction of Socialism in the GDR by the Second Party Conference of the
SED in the summer of 1952.(46) At the same time,
measures were taken to reduce contact between the two
Germanies. Residents were evacuated from a "belt"
along the border with West Germany which was widened to
five kilometers, and access between East and West Germany was increasingly restricted.(47) East German
officials claimed the intensified Absperrung (demarca-
tion) was necessary to protect the GDR from counter-
revolutionary activities of agents headquartered in
Berlin.(48) Skeptics also point out that the Soviet
proposal would require two major concessions from the
West--shelving the EDC and implicitly recognizing the
GDR--while requiring no comparable concessions from the
Kremlin.(49) Furthermore, the formula which granted
parity representation to East and West Germany in the
provisional government was designed to give East Germany, and therefore the Soviets, authority unrelated to
the relative strength of the two countries. GDR membership in the CMEA was interpreted as formalizing a
process of integration into the Soviet bloc which
showed the hollowness of Soviet diplomatic gestures
favoring reunification on any terms remotely acceptable

to the West. The upgrading of diplomatic missions exchanged between the GDR and other socialist countries to embassies between 1953 and 1955 is cited as further evidence of the integration and commitment of the Kremlin to maintaining the East German regime, even though these occurred after the West's rejection of Soviet diplomatic initiatives.

Those who counter that the West missed an opportunity for reunification argue that the willingness to accept a rearmed but still neutral Germany was a substantial concession from the Soviets who had consistently regarded that prospect as anathema.(50) In support, it is pointed out that only after the Federal Republic joined NATO was the Warsaw Pact formed, indicating that the Kremlin did not consider NATO a real threat until that time.(51) Advocates of this perspective note further that the Construction of Socialism program was adopted only after the West had rejected the Soviet proposal. Fritz Schenk, a high official in the State Planning Commission, lends credence to that connection by his assertion that the new program was totally unexpected. The surprise shift in policy led to intense activity throughout the party and the government to change economic plans and party policy in accordance with the new direction in policy.(52) Stalin's analysis of the world situation set forth in Economic Problems of Socialism is cited as additional support for the credibility of the March 1952 proposal. A major change in Soviet German policy was signalled by Stalin's expectation of the restoration of a capitalist Germany which would later turn against the United States as the contradictions within the capitalist camp intensified.(53) The contradictions among the capitalist countries would serve to prohibit a united capitalist front against the USSR. Stalin wrote of the revival of Germany and Japan as great powers without mentioning the GDR. From this it is extrapolated that Stalin had come to expect a reunited Germany and that a reunited, neutral Germany better suited Soviet interest than having a major part of Germany allied with the West.(54) This argument rests on the advantages to the Soviet Union of resuming the Rapallo Politik. Contrary to arguments based on GDR integration into the Soviet bloc, the relatively late participation of the GDR in bloc affairs is pointed to as evidence of the tenuousness of East Germany's status. The Conference of East bloc Foreign Ministers in Prague in October 1950 was the first time the GDR participated as an equal partner. East Germany was not included as a member of the

CMEA until one year after its founding.   The Construction of Socialism was not proclaimed until the   summer
of 1952, and the country remained without treaty protection until the mid 1950s.(55)   By the time of
Stalin's death, it was the only country in the Soviet
sphere not considered a people's republic.   Additional
evidence that the Kremlin might have been willing to
relinquish the GDR is found in the East German government's obligatory recognition of the Oder-Neisse as its
eastern frontier.(56) This was most unpopular throughout Germany and was not designed to enhance the popularity or appeal of the GDR regime.   In addition, after
Potsdam Stalin consistently called for the reunification of Germany and pursued negotiations on the issue.
The uncertainty cast on the GDR's continued existence
impeded its consolidation.   A noted scholar of Soviet
foreign policy considered it "inexcusable that the West
did not understand that the Soviets primary aim was a
resolution of the German problem as a whole and preven-
tion of the establishment of a rearmed West German
state."(57) Furthermore, according to Ulam, the Berlin
blockade and every other Berlin crisis should be understood in this light.   The goal was not to force the
West out of Berlin but to bring the Allies to the
negotiating table.(58)   Additional support for this
position can be found in the later resolution of the
Austrian problem, which allowed the restoration of an
independent, neutral, and democratic state.(59)

DETERIORATING CONDITIONS IN THE GDR

In the early 1950s, those trends in the GDR toward
the creation of a Soviet type society and its integration into the Soviet bloc were accelerated as West
German integration into the Western bloc proceeded.
After the Third Party Congress in July 1950, a purge of
the party was begun.(60) This served the historical
task of transforming the SED into a party of the New
Type.(61)   It also followed a pattern in East Europe,
begun in 1949, of thoroughgoing party purges following
the Soviet break with Tito and in response to U.S.
efforts to destabilize the region.   The main focus of
the purges was to eliminate those who had emigrated to
the West during the Hitler period or who had family in
the West.(62)   They were undertaken later in the GDR
than in other East bloc countries, possibly to allow
some time for the tensions resulting from the blockade

to subside. At the same time, the accelerated campaign
to integrate the FRG into the Western alliance no doubt
pressed the need to strengthen the "Muscovite" faction
of the SED.   In addition, defections of top-ranking
party people such as Erich Gniffke and Wolfgang
Leonhard may well have contributed to the perceived
necessity to "cleanse" the party.   Thus, the transformation of the SED into a party of the New Type, discussion of which had already begun in 1946, may be understood   both as a response to changed external conditions and as a minimal guarantee for continued Soviet
influence in East Germany should more favorable opportunities for the USSR in Germany not materialize.

     Elections in the GDR assumed the same function as
in the USSR.   On 15 October the first national elections for the parliament (Volkskammer) and provincial
assemblies (Landtage), as well as regional and local
elections (Kreis und Gemeindewahlen), were held.   A
unity list agreed upon in advance by all parties in the
GDR garnered 99.7 percent of the vote.(63) There were
no opposition candidates.   It should not be concluded
from this, however, that homogeneity had been achieved
among the three parties; in fact, despite the purges,
the SED continued to include differing voices.   Nonetheless, the maintenance of a multiparty system in the
GDR did assume a high degree of cooperation which
excluded competitive elections.

     At the time, the GDR's initiation into the Soviet
bloc was signalled by entry into the CMEA and an invitation to Prague for bloc diplomatic consultations.
Furthermore, the SED discarded the previously official
policy of German neutrality and restoration of Rapallo
as the best hope for peace between East and West.(64)
This position, however, was subject to change as directed by Moscow; for example, German neutrality was
championed once again in 1952 in conjunction with the
Soviet reunification initiative.   State Secretary of
the Foreign Ministry Anton Ackermann wrote in Tägliche
Rundschau that the Rapallo Treaty had been a "major
blow against the shameful Versailles system and an
incalculable act of friendship from the Soviet to the
German people.   Germans can look to the same alliance
to help secure peace, freedom and independence."(65)
The new signs of GDR integration into the Soviet bloc
and the shifts on neutrality represent the larger ambivalence of the USSR in defining her interests in
Germany and assessing opportunities and/or threats to
Soviet national security.

The year 1952 was a critical one in the Ulbricht regime's commitment to the sovietization of the GDR. After the West's rejection of the Soviet proposal for German reunification in March and the signing of the Bonn and Paris treaties in May, the SED adopted a program for the Construction of Socialism at the Second Party Conference in July.   The main task was to create the economic basis for socialism through further devel- opment of socialized industry and the collectivization of agriculture.   The state had to break the resistance of the capitalists and landowners, organize all working people around the working class, and create a national military to defend the GDR.(66)   The transformation of the SED into a party of the New Type according to the CPSU model was a necessary precondition for the con- struction of socialism.(67)

Administrative   reform   was   undertaken   directly after the Second Party Conference to provide the mecha- nism needed for executing the new program.   The five Länder were replaced by fourteen districts to strength- en unified, central direction of the economy.(68)   The districts were drawn up to correspond to economic re- quirements.(69)   New district councils (Bezirkstage and Bezirksräte) were an integral part of the state admin- istration.   Centralization prevailed over federalism; the Länder governments had been seen as a barrier to the execution of policy.(70) The new order also re- quired the further revolutionary transformation of the justice system.   A socialist legal code was to replace the bourgeois one.   In addition, the Volkspolizei (People's police) was expanded and measures were insti- tuted to minimize unauthorized contact with West Ger- many to protect the country against counterrevolu- tion.(71)

Administrative centralization paralleled further economic centralization.   An important socialized in- dustrial base had already been created through the expropriation of Nazi holdings and the transformation of the most important German industries into SAGs by the Soviet Union.   The Soviets had returned most of the least important SAGs to German ownership by this time. The agricultural sector, however, was made up of pre- dominantly small holdings as a result of the land reform instituted after the war.   A campaign was begun for the collectivization of agriculture because "so- cialism cannot stand on one leg."(72)

Major   economic difficulties arose soon after   the
adoption of the new program.   Peasant   resistance   to
collectivization led to food shortages.   Emphasis   on
heavy industry and shortfalls in production led   to
shortages of consumer goods, which in turn contributed
to a reduction in productivity in many sectors of the
economy.(73)   A shortage of labor and material was
pervasive.(74)   Many private businessmen and farmers
fled to the West after the Second Party Conference.
Domestic production problems were compounded by ongoing
balance-of-payments difficulties tied to reparations
deliveries and the Western trade embargo instituted at
the start of the Korean war, which left plants operating below capacity due to the inability to get necessary parts.   Production quotas set in the 1952 plan
were met, but wages rose beyond levels anticipated for
the period, creating further economic strains.(75)
Before the end of the year, Ulbricht sent Stalin a plea
for economic assistance.(76)

At the same time, a purge of the top echelons of
the party was being prepared by the Central Committee.
A December 20 resolution on the "Lessons from the Trial
of the Conspirator Slansky" justified the coming purge.
Victims could also be blamed for the bad economic
situation.   The focus was once again on those party
members who had emigrated to the West during the Hitler
period and particularly on Jews.(77) Further impetus
for the purge was provided by the discovery of the
"Doctors' plot" in the Kremlin in January 1953.   Fear
generated by the political climate contributed to growing paralysis in all facets of life.   Unwillingness to
take responsibility and make decisions exacerbated
economic difficulties. The result was a vicious circle
caught in a downward spiral.   Unlike most other East
European countries, however, there were no "show
trials" in the GDR and no top SED functionaries were
executed.   Stalin's death stopped what appeared to be
preparation for a massive purge of the Soviet Communist
Party and curtailed the purge of the SED.

Stalin's death on 6 March 1953 created new opportunities and enhanced Soviet maneuverability in foreign
and domestic policy.   Decision-making in the Kremlin
shifted to a collective leadership in which Beria and
Malenkov, as moderates and reformers, struggled for
power against Molotov, heir to the Stalinist tradition.
The uncertainty of the period and the temporary influence of Beria and Malenkov led the Soviet Union to
soften its image both at home and abroad.   An end to

the Korean conflict was negotiated, which contributed
to the reduction of international tensions. Other
measures were taken to improve East-West relations.
Domestically, the powers of the secret police were
curbed and fears of a massive purge were reduced,
easing the political climate. In addition, economic
reform to improve living conditions was begun under the
auspices of the New Course. The heart of the New
Course called for a shift in traditional concentration
on heavy industry to increased production of consumer
goods. Malenkov is considered the author of the New
Course, whereas Beria's stamp is seen in Soviet-East
European relations. East European ruling parties were
urged to institute collective leaderships and to embark
on domestic reform programs similar to the Soviets' New
Course.(78)

A representative of the Soviet Planning Chief came
to East Berlin in April and relayed the Soviet leadership's plan for the New Course. Because all Soviet
reserves were needed to initiate the new policy domestically, SED requests for economic aid could not be met
and the East Germans were urged to slow the pace of
socialist construction.(79) U.S. intelligence began
looking for a change in East German leadership in
conjunction with the new Soviet policy of conciliation.(80)

The unresolved leadership struggle in the Soviet
Union enhanced Ulbricht's maneuverability and independence. Opposition by the Stalinist faction in the USSR
headed by Molotov to the plans for the New Course
provided Ulbricht the opportunity to ignore the latest
advice coming from the Kremlin. West German integration into the Western alliance was proceeding apace, so
Ulbricht apparently saw the uncertainty in the Kremlin
as an opportunity to tie East Germany securely to the
Soviet bloc. Instead of moderating policy, he actually
stepped up socialist transformation. All self-employed
persons forfeited their ration cards and were then
forced to buy goods from the much higher priced state
stores. Subsidies on foods were eliminated or reduced,
and special priced travel fares for workers were all
but abolished. Pressure was increased to hasten collectivization of agriculture.(81) A final measure
adopted at the Thirteenth Plenum in May 1953 decreed
that workers' production norms would be raised a minimum of 10 percent, effective 1 June 1953, to solve the
economic crisis. This increase in norms meant a real
reduction in salary and, therefore, a decline in stan-

dard of living.(82)   At the same time, the plenum
confirmed the recent purge of Franz Dahlem, which enhanced Ulbricht's control of the party.   Dahlem was a
member of the Politburo and Secretariat and Ulbricht's
chief rival.   He was expelled for alleged blindness to
efforts by imperialist agents to infiltrate the party.
He had emigrated to France during World War II and was
purged for the "security of the leadership."(83)
Ulbricht was able to maintain his hard line until June.

In late April Semyonov, political advisor to the
Soviet Control Commission and advocate of Beria's policy toward Germany, was recalled to Moscow.   He returned
to Germany in a strengthened position as High Commissioner on 5 June with an ultimatum from the CPSU Politburo that the SED work out a plan for a New Course
within one week.(84)   Semyonov reportedly brought with
him the text of a plan which the East German Politburo
adopted verbatim on 9 June.   The resolutions of the New
Course reversed many earlier decisions which promoted
the construction of socialism.   Expropriation of private property was halted, forced collectivization was
stopped, some farms and businesses were returned to
their former owners, ration cards were to be issued to
all citizens, and subsidized food prices were restored,
as were special travel fares for workers.   The economic
plan was to be altered to reduce the emphasis on heavy
industry in favor of increased production of consumer
goods.   Trade was to expand through credits to socialized and private business.   The need to improve the
living standard of all classes of the population was
publicly acknowledged.(85)

The Politburo communique also contained some overtures to West Germany.   It stated that the resolutions
were taken with the restoration of German unity in
mind.   The measures would facilitate the rapprochement
of the two Germanies.   Those who had fled to West
Berlin or West Germany were invited to return, reclaim
their property or its equivalent, and enjoy full citi-
zenship rights.   Restrictions on traffic between East
and West Germany were to be eased and trade was to be
encouraged.(86)

The New Course was a repudiation of Ulbricht's
hard-line policy, which was, through radical transformation of East German society, intended to stake East
Germany's future on the USSR and to extinguish the
possibility of German reunification on terms unfavorable to the SED--something Ulbricht feared as a real

possibility.   All   slogans and banners related to   the
Second Party Conference were to be discreetly   removed.
All reference to the Construction of Socialism and even
the word "socialism" was ordered deleted from all party
materials.(87)   Semyonov   is reported to have   harshly
criticized   the Ulbricht group and sought a   change   in
party leadership.(88)   In a well known story,   Semyonov
advised   Ulbricht   to celebrate his   upcoming   sixtieth
birthday   as Lenin had his fiftieth: he had invited   a
few close friends for dinner.   Ulbricht's birthday, by
contrast,   was   to have been a national celebration   in
the   tradition of the cult of personality which he   had
promoted   following Stalin's example.(89)   At the   same
time,   Paul   Strassenberger,   a colleague of   Schenk's,
reported   a conversation with Soviets at Karlshorst   in
which   he   was   asked   if the   people   would   welcome
Ulbricht's resignation.   Strassenberger interpreted the
question   to mean the Soviets were planning   Ulbricht's
replacement.(90)   In accordance with the Soviet   shift
to   collective leadership and internal reform,   it   appears an old-line Stalinist such as Ulbricht no   longer
served the Kremlin's purposes.   Rudolph Herrnstadt and
Wilhelm   Zaisser   formed the core of an   opposition   to
Ulbricht   within   the   SED   apparently   supported   by
Semyonov   with Beria's blessing.(91)   Zaisser had   been
Minister for State Security since the Ministry's establishment in 1950 and a member of the Politburo.   He was
also an agent of the Soviet Secret Police and confidant
of   Beria.   Herrnstadt   was   chief   editor   of   **Neues
Deutschland**,   the official party paper, an agent of the
Soviet GPU,   and candidate member of the Politburo.(92)
Herrnstadt   had   spent time before the war   in   Moscow.
The   groundwork   for a shift in leadership was laid   in
the communique announcing the New Course.   The   Politburo   acknowledged   past   mistakes on the part of   the
party   and   government which had created the   need   for
change.(93)   Semyonov also placed   some   responsiblity
for   past mistakes on the former Soviet Control Commission   in   an article in **Tägliche** **Rundschau** of   13   June
which heralded the New Course as a "significant, qualitative   change .   .   .   in the economic   and   political
development of the GDR."

The   criticism   of the Soviet Control   Commission,
heretofore   unheard of,   implied criticism of   Stalin's
German policy.   The new policy and prospective   change
in   SED leadership conformed with Beria's position that
a reunited Germany was in the Soviet Union's   long-term
interest.(94)

It is ironic that the New Course, which signalled
an end to Stalinist type control, was imposed in Germany in consummate Stalinist fashion.   The new policy
was announced without even formal approval of the Central Committee.   According to party rules, a Party
Congress must be convened to initiate such a major
policy change.   Instead, <u>Neues</u> <u>Deutschland</u> simply published the Politburo communique announcing the New
Course on 10 June.(95)

THE BREAKING POINT

Growing economic difficulties and increasing discontent within East Europe were dramatized by the
strikes and riots in Pilsen, Czechoslovakia, in 1952.
This unrest was contained by Czech police but, nonetheless, underscored the need for change in Soviet-East
European relations as well as in domestic programs and
practices.   The changes deemed necessary were grouped
under the umbrella of the New Course.

Because of its extraordinarily precarious situation, the GDR was the first country in which the New
Course was introduced.   However, due to Ulbricht's
opposition, whose hand was strengthened by the ongoing
power struggle in the USSR, the policy was not implemented in any thorough or consistent manner.   The intransigence of Ulbricht shows an independence designed
to flout Moscow's new policy yet cement Soviet-East
German ties.   In addition, the failure to explain and
solicit the support of the populace for the new policy
limited its effectiveness.   Ulbricht succeeded in pre-
venting the revocation of the increased work norms in
the process of shifting to the New Course.   The new
work quotas met with enormous resistance because they
meant a real decline in wages during a time of deteriorating economic conditions, made particularly acute by
food shortages.(96)   Increased work norms became the
critical issue which galvanized worker opposition to
the regime.(97)

By 12 June 1953, work stoppages and threats of
strikes were commonplace. The uncertainty of party and
government officials in dealing with the growing unrest
exacerbated the problems.   Construction workers in the
Stalinallee in Berlin walked off the job on 16 June and
mobilized others to join them.   That afternoon it was

announced that the Council of Ministers had withdrawn the higher production norms. But this was no longer enough to satisfy the crowds. As unrest grew and spread beyond Berlin on the 17th, demands escalated to encompass economic and political grievances. The government was called upon to account for past mistakes. Pent-up resentments against the regime and the system exploded spontaneously. Spontaneity, however, proved to be a serious weakness. There was no leadership to channel the strength of the assembled masses. There was no focus to sustain their outrage. The situation, nonetheless, paralyzed the SED leadership, and the German police were unable to control the demonstrations. Soviet troops were called upon the afternoon of the 17 June, after the rising had spread throughout the GDR. But the crowds had already begun to disperse of their own accord. By the time Soviet troops appeared on the scene, unrest was already waning. U.S. reports gave Soviet troops high marks for their restrained behavior in restoring order thoughout East Germany.(98) This is reflected in the casualty figures: 25 killed, including 4 security police; 378 wounded, including 191 police.(99)

The inability of indigenous forces to overthrow the East German authorities was never in question; twenty Soviet divisions deployed throughout the GDR precluded the possibility. Widespread public opposition seemed to melt away under the realization of its own limited potential.(100)

The irony is that the upheaval occurred as the New Course promised an improvement in conditions and as the Soviet leadership chose to exercise a lighter hand. The tragedy is that the June uprising ultimately served to maintain Ulbricht in power against growing internal and Soviet opposition and eliminate Beria, who seemed to have represented the best hope for German reunification.

CONCLUSIONS

The apparent contradiction of the major policy innovations of 1952 and 1953 reflects the continuing fundamental ambiguity of Soviet policy toward Germany. The March reunification proposal and the New Course promised moderation, reform, and rapprochement while the Construction of Socialism Program represented the radicalization of GDR domestic and foreign policy nec- essary to transform the country according to the East European pattern. The entire issue of ambiguity is futher complicated during this period by Ulbricht's growing assertion of independence, noted most clearly in his intransigence in implementing the New Course.

The Soviet proposal to the Western allies in March 1952 on the reunification of Germany, presented in conjunction with the revival of the spirit of Rapallo, was without doubt an attempt to preempt West German integration into the Western military alliance, which had been hastened, in part, by Soviet policy in Korea. The radicalization of East German policy was not under- taken until after the West had rejected the Soviet initiative and after the signing of the Bonn and Paris treaties. It is arguable that following Allied rejec- tion of the Soviet proposal, Stalin resolved to consol- idate his position in the GDR because he could hardly count on a successful campaign to halt ratification and because he wanted to preclude the eventuality of a reunited Germany in an anti-Soviet alliance. This meant that at this point there were two feasible and acceptable solutions to the German question from the Soviet perspective: a reunited, neutral Germany or a divided Germany. The transformation of the GDR along East European lines indicates a new focus on the latter option, which certainly enjoyed strong support among the Ulbricht faction of the SED. Testimony to the totally unexpected nature of the adoption of the 1952 Construction of Socialism Program supports the conten- tion that this represented a major departure in Soviet policy and was not the most desirable option. The shift in focus from reunification to consolidation of the GDR illustrates the interplay of Soviet and Western policy and the priority for each side of securing influence in postwar Germany.

Stalin's death reopened the question of Germany's future and the status of the GDR. The new moderation in Soviet domestic and foreign policy went hand in hand with the dictated retreat from sovietization of the GDR. The imposition of the New Course in East Germany served two distinct Soviet purposes. First, the retreat from socialist transformation of the GDR and accompanying measures to improve relations between the two Germanies fit a pattern of easing tensions between East and West, the most notable example of which was the settlement of the Korean conflict. The New Course in all its aspects represented a spirit of moderation and accommodation, necessitated by a period of uncertainty caused by leadership struggles and engendered by a general recognition of the need for reform. Second, the New Course potentially served to eliminate a serious economic burden on Soviet resources at a time when the Soviets were turning their attention to improving the standard of living of the general populace. Deteriorating economic conditions in the GDR under the Construction of Socialism Program portended a reversal of the heretofore advantageous economic relationship for the Soviets. Thus, the shift to the New Course was a response to the Soviets' new political and economic interests and conditions which might potentially have led to a retreat from Stalin's recent commitment to the GDR.

The June uprising, which challenged the East German leadership and, therefore, Soviet policy, forced the Soviets' hand. East Germany's only chance of being united with the rest of Germany in an independent state would have been through negotiations in which the Soviets could guarantee their security and protect their interests. The threat posed by East German unrest was not to the survival of the SED regime under Soviet sponsorship but rather to the strength of the Soviet position in German affairs.

Changing and uncertain political and economic conditions fomented East German rebellion. Political tension was generated by public criticism of past government and party policy and the uncertainty of Soviet intentions. The abrupt change from the socialist transformation to the New Course, juxtaposed with retention of increased work quotas, sparked worker opposition. The political climate was free enough and the SED leadership sufficiently insecure and divided to allow disaffections to boil over into the first major unrest in East Europe since the war.

NOTES

1.   Adam B. Ulam, Expansion and Coexistence: The History of Soviet Foreign Policy, 1917-1967 (New York: Praeger, 1968), p. 579.

2.   See Barton J. Bernstein, "American Military Intervention in the Korean Civil War," in Major Problems in American Foreign Policy, Vol. II, 2nd edition, ed. by Thomas G. Paterson, (Lexington, Mass.: D.C. Heath and Co., 1984), pp. 440-58; David F. Trask, "The Korean War and the Cold War," in Major Problems in American Foreign Policy, Vol. II, 1st edition, ed. by Paterson, pp. 337-44; Robert R. Simmons, "The Korean Civil War," in Major Problems in American Foreign Policy, Vol. II, 1st edition, ed. by Paterson, pp. 344-62.

3.   Boris Meissner, Russland, die Westmächte und Deutschland: Die sowjetische Deutschlandpolitik, 1943-1953 (Hamburg: H.H. Nölke Verlag, 1953), pp. 230-31.

4.   Ulam, Expansion and Coexistence, p. 527; Marshall D. Shulman, Stalin's Foreign Policy Reappraised (Cambridge: Harvard University Press, 1963), p. 145.   U.S. military expenditures increased during the Korean conflict from $13.2 billion in FY 1950 to $48.2 billion in FY 1951 to more than $60 billion in FY 1952.

5.   General Eisenhower's campaign rhetoric promoted a shift in U.S. policy from containment to "roll back."

6.   U.S. Department of State, Treaty of Peace with Japan (monograph, 1952)

7.   Shulman, Stalin Reappraised, pp. 269-70.

8.   U.S. Department of State, Foreign Relations of the United States: Diplomatic Papers: The Conference of Berlin (Potsdam) (Washington, D.C.: Government Printing Office, 1960), pp. 378-79 (hereafter cited as Potsdam Documents).

9.   DDR: Werden und Wachsen (Berlin: Dietz Verlag, 1975), p. 255; Werner Erfurt, Die sowjetrussische Deutschland-Politik (Esslingen: Bechtel Verlag, 1959), p. 78; Shulman, Stalin Reappraised, pp. 197-98; Raymond

L. Garthoff, _Soviet Strategy in the Nuclear Age_ (New York: Frederick A. Praeger, 1958), p. 76.

10.   Credit assistance to Argentina in 1953 marked the beginning of the Soviet economic offensive among the less developed countries. Konstantin Pritzel, _Die wirtschaftliche Integration der sowjetischen Besatzungszone Deutschlands in den Ostblock und ihre politischen Aspekte_ (Bonn: Deutscher Bundes Verlag, 1962), p. 55. In 1954, the Soviets allegedly sent military supplies to nationalist forces in Guatemala, the first foray of its kind into the politics of Latin America. Soviet involvement in Guatemala is now being questioned. Revisionists suggest it may have been manufactured by the U.S. to justify her own involvement in the coup which toppled Arbenz.

11.   Iosif Stalin, _Ekonomicheskie Problemy Sotsializma v SSSR_ (Gosydarstvenoe Uzdatelstvo Politicheskoy Literatyri, 1952), pp. 30-6.

12.   Meissner, _Russland, die Westmächte und Deutschland_, pp. 329-30.

13.   The Soviet leadership withdrew objection to Dag Hammerskjold becoming the new Secretary General of the United Nations and renounced territorial claims against Turkey, moved toward reconciliation with Tito, and proposed a three- power conference to discuss the issue of air safety in German airspace. Ulam, _Expansion and Coexistence_, p. 546; Arnulf Baring, _Uprising in East Germany: June 17, 1953_ (Ithaca: Cornell University Press, 1972), p. 23.

14.   Leonard Moseley, _Dulles_ (New York: Dial Press, 1978), p. 288.

15.   Discussions over Germany continued at lower diplomatic levels but failed to make progress on major differences.

16.   Beate Ruhm von Oppen, _Documents on Germany under Occupation, 1945-54_ (London: Oxford University Press, 1955), pp. 517-20 (hereafter cited as _Documents on Germany_). The Foreign Ministers of Great Britain, the United States, and France met in New York in September to review the German situation in general and the Allied relationship with the Federal Republic.

17.   Ibid., p. 518.

18.   Ibid., pp. 522-27.

19.   Die sowjetische Besatzungszone Deutschlands in den Jahren 1945 bis 1954 (Bonn: Bundesministerium für Gesamtdeutsche Fragen, 1956), p. 112 (hereafter cited as SBZ, 1945-1954.

20.   Tägliche Rundschau (11 March 1949); Berliner Zeitung (16 October 1949).

21.   Protokoll des III Parteitages, Band I (Berlin: Dietz Verlag, 1951), p. 237. At the same time, Grotewohl expressed the Party's adherence to Marxism-Leninism and the need for the transformation of the SED into a party of the New Type. It was at this Congress that the SED adopted new party statutes modelled on the CPSU.

22.   Walter Ulbricht, "Das Wiedererstehen des deutschen Imperialismus," Einheit (June 1961), pp. 602-32; SBZ, 1945-1954, p. 154.

23.   Studiengesellschaft für Zeitprobleme, Die sowjetische Deutschlandpolitik, 4 parts (Duisdorf bei Bonn: Studiengesellschaft für Zeitprobleme, 1962-1963) 3:104.

24.   Johannes Hohlfeld, ed., Dokumente der Deutschen Politik und Geschichte (Berlin: Dokumenten Verlag, 1951-1956), 7:36.

25.   Ibid., pp. 99-100. The idea of a defense community was born the summer of 1950. pp. 150-55. The Bundestag voted in favor of joining the security pact in July 1950. p. 153. Documents on Germany, pp. 576-78.

26.   Europa Archiv (January 1952), pp. 4626-27.

27.   "Will Russia's Policy Concerning Germany Be Changed?" Tages Anzeiger (5 February 1951). Translation sent to Department of State from Bern marked secret. National Archives documents. Views of former German officer on Soviet aims in Germany from B.R. Shute, Frankfurt, to Department of State 19 April 1951, National Archives documents.

28.   Deutsches Institut für Zeitgeschichte, Dokumente zur Deutschlandpolitik der Sowjetunion, 3 vols, (Berlin: VEB Deutscher Verlag der Wissenschaften, 1957-1968), 1:289-93.

29.   Dokumente der Deutschen Politik und Geschichte, 7:172-83, 382-90.

30.   Ibid., 7:174-75, 178-79, 382-83.

31.   Meissner, Russland, die Westmächte und Deutschland, p. 319; Studiengesellschaft, Deutschlandpolitik, 3:75.

32.   Beziehungen DDR-UdSSR, 1949 bis 1955: Dokumentensammlung, 2 vols. (Berlin: Staatenverlag der Deutschen Demokratischen Republik, 1975), 1:354-57.

33.   N. Orlov, "Deutschland an einem geschichtlichen Wendepunkt," Tägliche Rundschau (1 May 1952).

34.   Dokumente der Deutschen Politik und Geschichte, 7:171, 173.

35.   Ibid., pp. 173, 175, 177.

36.   Ibid., pp. 181-82.

37.   Ibid., text, pp. 190-311.

38.   Ibid., text, pp. 311-50.

39.   E. Tarle, "The Possible and the Impossible," New Times 21 (21 May 1952); A. Yerusalimsky, "The Bonn Compact and the Lessons of German History," New Times 23 (4 June 1952):8; Frederick H. Hartmann, "Soviet Russia and the German Problem," The Yale Review (Summer 1954), p. 519.

40.   Die Beschlüsse des Weltfriedensrates auf seiner Ausserordentlichen Tagung in Berlin vom 1-6 Juni 1952 (Berlin: Union Verlag, 1952), pp. 6-8, 12.

41.   Dokumente der Deutschen Politik und Geschichte, 8:59n.

42.   Werner Weber and Richter W. Jahn, Synopse zur Deutschlandpolitik, 1941 bis 1973 (Göttingen: Verlag Otto Schartz & Co., 1973), p. 204. This action also nullified the Bonn Treaty since both treaties were considered a unit. After the French action, the West German government stated it did not want limited sovereignty on the basis of one-sided declaration by the occupying powers, but full sovereignty achieved by negotiation and contractual agreement. pp. 204-5. The

Bonn   Treaty   represented the former,   while the   Paris
Treaty represented the latter.

43.   Dokumente   der   Deutschen   Politik   und
Geschichte,   8:468-70.   The   Paris Protocol issued the
following day officially ended the occupation regime.

44.   Ulam, Expansion and Coexistence, p. 558.

45.   Victor Baras, "Stalin's German Policy after
Stalin," Slavic Review (June 1978),   pp. 259-67; Melvin
Croan,   "Reality   and Illusion in   Soviet-German   Relations,"   Survey   (October   1962),   p.   308;   Studiengesellschaft,   Deutschlandpolitik,   3:124-43,   4:129-32,
151.

46.   Baras,   "Stalin's German Policy," p.   266;
Meissner,   Russland, die Westmächte und Deutschland, p.
308.   It   should be noted,   however,   that the   Second
Party Conference occurred after the signing of the Bonn
and Paris treaties.   According to Gerhard Wettig,   the
Soviet failure to prevent the treaties led them to   the
Construction   of   Socialism   Program in   the   GDR.   Die
Parole   der   nationalen   Einheit   in   der   sowjetischen
Deutschlandpolitik, 1942-1967 (Cologne: Berichte   des
Bundesinstituts   für   Ostwissenschaftliche   und   Inter-
nationale Studien, 1967), p. 11.

47.   Dokumente   der   Deutschen   Politik   und
Geschichte, 7:353-37; Studiengesellschaft, Deutschlandpolitik, 3:151.

48.   These actions were taken after the Bonn and
Paris   treaties were signed but during the period   when
the Soviet pursued their initiative.

49.   Baras, "Stalin's German Policy," pp. 262-64.

50.   Hermann Achminov,   Warum Ändern die Sowjets
Ihren Kurs? (Cologne: Rote Weissbächer, 1953), pp. 10-
13; Erfurt, Sowjetrussische Deutschland-Politik, p. 72;
Walter Laqueur,   Russia and Germany: A Century of Conflict (Boston: Little, Brown and Co., 1965),   pp. 277-
78;   Walter Osten,   "Deutschlandpolitik der Sowjetunion
in   den   Jahren   1952-53," Osteuropa   (January   1964),
pp.   2-3; Ulam,   The Rivals: America and Russia Since
World War II (New York: viking Press,   1971),   p. 148;
Ulam,   Expansion and Coexistence,   pp.   504-6;   Paul R.
Willging,   "Soviet   Foreign Policy in the German   Question: 1950-1955" (Ph.D.   diss.,   Columbia University,

1973), pp. 123-49.

51.   Ulam, Expansion and Coexistence, p. 505.
The Warsaw Pact was not really that significant in
military terms since the Soviet Union controlled bloc
military forces and had long had bilateral military
pacts with Czechoslovakia, Poland, Bulgaria, Hungary,
and Rumania. It was more significant in political
imagery as an institutional adversary or counterweight
to a NATO newly strengthened by the inclusion of West
Germany. The fact that the East German military was
not included in the Warsaw Pact until 1956 lends credence to Soviet hostility toward rearmed Germans of any
stripe. The Warsaw Pact also provided legitimacy for
continued stationing of Soviet troops in Hungary and
Rumania once the Austrian Treaty was signed.

52.   Fritz Schenk, Im Vorzimmer der Diktatur
(Cologne: Kiepenheuer & Witsch, 1962), pp. 142-46.

53.   Stalin, Economicheskie Problemy, pp. 34-5.

54.   Achminov, Warum Andern die Sowjets Ihren
Kurs? pp. 9-13; Osten, "Deutschlandpolitik der Sowjetunion," pp. 2-3; Klaus Erdmenger, Das folgenschwere
Missverständnis (Freiburg i. Br.: Verlag Rombach,
1967), pp. 138-39.

55.   Peter Bender, East Europe in Search of
Security (Baltimore: Johns Hopkins University Press,
1972), pp. 12-13; Melvin Croan and Clark J. Friedrich,
"The East German Regime and Soviet Policy in Germany,"
Journal of Politics 20 (1958):48-49.

56.   Documents on Germany, pp. 497-500; Ulam,
Expansion and Coexistence, p. 508.

57.   Ulam, The Rivals, p. 148.

58.   Ibid. Inclusion of Greater Berlin into the
GDR may well have been a second, less desirable, option.

59.   William Lloyd Stearman, The Soviet Union and
the Occupation of Austria (Bonn: Verlag für Zeitarchive, 1961), pp. 164-65. The relevance of the
Austrian settlement to the potential reunification of
Germany will be discussed in Chapter 5.

60.   Protokoll der II Parteikonferenz der Sozialistischen Einheitspartei Deutschlands (Berlin: Dietz

Verlag, 1952), p. 14. All members were required to turn in their party cards. Those no longer considered suitable were not reissued cards. More than 150,000 were stricken from the party list of just over 600,000 members. Carola Stern, Porträt einer bolschewistischen Partei (Cologne: Verlag für Politik und Wirtschaft, 1957), p. 134; Dokumente der Sozialistischen Einheitspartei Deutschlands (Berlin: Dietz Verlag, 1952), band 3, pp. 589-91.

61.   Protokoll des III Parteitages, band 1, p. 21. New party statutes, band 2, pp. 307-21.

62.   Stern, Porträt, pp. 118-19.

63.   Weber and Jahn, Synopse, p. 105; Meissner, Russland, die Westmächte und Deutschland, p. 240; Richard Lukas, Zehn Jahre Sowjetische Besatzungszone (Mainz-Gonsenheim: Deutscher Fachschriften Verlag, 1955), pp. 35-36.

64.   Meissner, Russland, die Westmächte und Deutschland, p. 223; SBZ, 1945-1954, p. 124.

65.   Tägliche Rundschau (16 April 1952).

66.   Protokoll der II Parteikonferenz, pp. 58-61.

67.   Werden und Wachsen, p. 220.

68.   Ibid., p. 223. Even after the creation of the VVBs, some enterprises remained under Länder authority.

69.   Dokumente der Deutschen Politik und Geschichte, 7:392-97; Werden und Wachsen, pp. 223-24.

70.   Felix E. Hirsch, "The Crisis of East Germany," International Journal 9 (Winter 1954):12; Meissner, Russland, die Westmächte und Deutschland, p. 314.

71.   Werden und Wachsen, pp. 224-25.

72.   Ibid., pp. 227-28.

73.   Official East German data on productivity covers only socialized industry, and the figures are based on gross production, which economists agree are meaningless. See Statistisches Jahrbuch der DDR, 1955

(Berlin: VEB Deutscher Zentralverlag, 1956), p. 119 and Wolfgang F. Stolper, The Structure of the East German Economy (Cambridge: Harvard University Press, 1960), p. 267.

74.   Baring, Uprising in East Germany, p. 7; Schenk, Im Vorzimmer der Diktatur, p. 165. Schenk, as personal advisor to the Chairman of the State Planning Commission of the GDR, Bruno Leuschner, had access to accurate information on the state of the economy as far as such information existed.   He notes the shortage of labor in the increasingly chaotic economic situation, while official statistics record a high level of unemployment during this period. Statistisches Jahrbuch der DDR, 1955, p. 119. See also Stolper, Structure of the East Germany Economy, p. 416.

75.   Baring, Ibid.

76.   Schenk, Im Vorzimmer der Diktatur, pp. 165-66, 183; Victor Baras, "Beria's Fall and Ulbricht's Survival," Soviet Studies 27 (July 1975):381.

77.   Baras, "Beria's Fall and Ulbricht's Survival," p. 382; Dokumente der Sozialistischen Einheitspartei Deutschlands, band 4, pp. 199-219; Stern, Porträt, p. 124; Heinz Brandt, The Search for a Third Way (Garden City, N.Y.: Doubleday & Co., 1970), pp. 166-71. Brandt was a member of the SED and administrator for the district of Berlin.   He had personal contact with many of the top SED officials. Schenk, Im Vorzimmer der Diktatur, p. 167; Pritzel, Die wirtschaftliche Integration, p. 53.
Rudolph Slansky was the General Secretary of the Czech Communist Party.   Other show trials of Rajk in Hungary and Kostov in Bulgaria had set the pattern, but Slansky was accused of being a Zionist agent working for American imperialism. He was executed in 1952.

78.   It may seem suspect that Beria, head of the notorious Soviet secret police, should promote policies of moderation and reform.   Beria was, however, consistently a moderate on the nationalities question.   He had opposed Zhdanov's policy of Great Russian chauvinism and had taken the side of minority nationalities at the Nineteenth Party Congress. This posture is consistent with support for a policy easing controls on East Europe. Charles H. Fairbanks, Jr., "National Cadres as a Force in the Soviet System: The Evidence of Beria's Career, 1949-53," in Soviet Nationality Policies and

Practices, ed. by Jeremy Azrael (New York: Praeger, 1978), pp. 148-52.

79. Baring, Uprising in East Germany, p. 20; Osten, "Deutschlandpolitik der Sowjetunion," p. 6; Schenk, Im Vorzimmer der Diktatur, p. 185; Stern, Porträt, p. 154. Despite these corroborating accounts that the Soviets refused the SED requests for additional aid, a trade agreement between the USSR and the GDR was signed on 27 April providing for increased deliveries of foodstuffs, raw materials, and other machinery beyond those agreed to in the long-term trade agreement signed 27 September 1951. Beziehungen DDR-UdSSR, 1:429-30. Brandt notes that because the Kremlin was disturbed by the growing discontent in the GDR extensive food deliveries were promised but they were unreliable. Brandt, Search for a Third Way, p. 176.

80. To the Department of State from N. Spencer Barnes, Chief Eastern Affairs Division, Berlin, 28 April 1953. National Archives documents.

81. Baring, Uprising in East Germany, p. 20; Schenk, Im Vorzimmer der Diktatur, p. 185; Brandt, Search for a Third Way, p. 174.

82. Dokumente der Sozialistischen Einheitspartei Deutschlands, band 4, pp. 410-14. A campaign to raise quotas had begun in January 1953.

83. Ibid., pp. 405-8. Dahlem was fully rehabilitated in July 1956 and rejoined the Central Committee in February 1957. Stern, Porträt, pp. 129-30; Brandt, Search for a Third Way, pp. 180-81.

84. Brandt, Search for a Third Way, p. 186; Osten, "Deutschlandpolitik der Sowjetunion," p. 6. Semyonov was a protege of Beria. At the end of May, the Soviet Council of Ministers dissolved the Soviet Control Commission, as the Western Allies had done, and eliminated the control functions of the Commander of the Soviet Armed Forces in Germany. An Office of the High Commissioner was created to represent Soviet interests in Germany. I.I. Iljutchov, a protege of Semyonov, replaced Pushkin as Soviet Ambassador to the GDR, further strengthening Semyonov's position. Meissner, Russland, die Westmächte und Deutschland, p. 333.

85.   Dokumente der Sozialistischen Einheitspartei Deutschlands, band 4, pp. 428-31.

86.   Ibid.

87.   Brandt, Search for a Third Way, pp. 199-200. Brandt, as propaganda secretary, was ordered by Hermann Axen to carry out this directive without commentary or explanation.

88.   Ibid., pp. 185-86; Baras, "Beria and Ulbricht," p. 384; Schenk, Im Vorzimmer der Diktatur, p. 192.

89.   Brandt, Search for a Third Way, pp. 181, 191; Carola Stern, Ulbricht: Eine politische Biographie (Cologne: Kiepenheuer & Witsch, 1963), p. 167.

90.   Schenk, Im Vorzimmer der Diktatur, p. 192.

91.   Brandt, Search for a Third Way, pp. 181, 191; Harold Laeuen, "Berijas Deutschlandpolitik," Osteuropa (April 1964), p. 258; Osten, "Deutschlandpolitik der Sowjetunion," p. 7; Stern, Porträt, p. 166; "Berija gab Auftrag an Zaisser-Herrnstadt: Sturz Ulbrichts," Die Neue Zeitung (23 August 1953); Erdmenger, Das folgenschwere Missverständnis, p. 142.

92.   Stern, Porträt, pp. 163-64; Studiengesellschaft, Deutschlandpolitik, 3:115; Osten, "Deutschlandpolitik der Sowjetunion," p. 7.

93.   Dokumente der Sozialistischen Einheitspartei Deutschlands, 4:428.

94.   Brandt, Search for a Third Way, p. 187; Osten, "Deutschlandpolitik der Sowjetunion," p. 4.

95.   Brandt, Search for a Third Way, p. 193.

96.   Arnulf Baring, Uprising in East Germany: June 17, 1953 (Ithaca, N.Y.: Cornell University Press, 1972), p. 17; Brandt, Search for a Third Way, pp. 200-2. It should be noted that the increased work norms were not as unjust as they appeared in light of reduced productivity and increased wages in the early 1950s. They were, however, perceived as a clear affront in the context of the New Course, which was seen as favoring the middle class.

97.   An excellent firsthand account of the events
leading up to the uprising and the handling of those
events by East German officials is presented in Brandt,
Search for a Third Way, pp. 183-220. See also Baring,
Uprising in East Germany; Stefan Brant, The East German
Rising (New York: Frederick A. Praeger, 1957); Schenk,
Im Vorzimmer der Diktatur, pp. 187-208.

98.   Intelligence report from Berlin to Bonn, 30
June 1953. National Archives documents.

99.   SBZ, 1945-1954, p. 257.

100.   There had been no effort to take over the
communications or other focal points essential to making a bid for power. Baring, Uprising in East Germany,
p. 78.

5
Transition to Support

The June uprising reportedly took the Soviet and East German leaderships by surprise. The need to use Soviet troops to restore order was a major embarrassment to the unsettled Soviet leadership and its efforts to improve East-West relations. It was certainly a significant setback to fading Soviet hopes of wooing the West German population.

The events precipitated a qualitative revision of Soviet policy toward East Germany. The new policy included three major elements: support for the Ulbricht faction of the SED in the face of a serious leadership challenge, elevation of the GDR's political status, and transformation of economic relations between the two countries. These policy changes occurred within the broader context of the ever present German question.

THE AFTERMATH

One of the first tasks of the East German and Soviet leaderships was to explain the workers' uprising. The press in both countries attributed the June events to Western agents and fascist provocateurs who exploited legitimate worker dissatisfaction in an effort to overthrow the East German government. The SED Central Committee, meeting 21 June 1953, charged that the introduction of the New Course had forced the hand of hostile forces in West Germany. The new policy promised such an improvement in the East German standard of living, so the argument went, that the West German regime felt threatened.(1)   Because the New Course had not had time to remedy or even improve the economic situation, worker discontent was rife and an easy target for hostile manipulation. It was later emphasized that only about 5 percent of the working class had taken part in the strikes, underlining the lack of popular support for the anti-state action.(2)

Zaisser and Herrnstadt were accused of taking advantage of the policy change to the New Course and the June uprising in order to assert their own control over the party. Zaisser allegedly proposed that Herrnstadt be elected First Secretary of the Central Committee.(3)   Herrnstadt, editor of Neues Deutschland, had published a number of articles critical of party errors and proposed a renewal (Erneuerung) of the party. The renewal was interpreted by opponents as advocating a transformation of the SED into a people's party of all classes--a decidedly un-Marxist position. An article appearing 14 June which was cited as particularly treacherous accused the SED of misusing the trust of the working class. The Zaisser-Herrnstadt faction was charged with promoting a policy which sacrificed the interests of the working class, created confusion, and thereby contributed to the uprising.(4)

The initial uncertainty within the party following the uprising was reflected in the failure to take immediate action against the opposition or the demonstrators. Official Central Committee greetings to Zaisser on his sixtieth birthday appeared in Neues Deutschland on 20 June. Max Fechner, Minister of Justice, stated in an interview which appeared in Neues Deutschland and Tägliche Rundschau that the right to strike was guaranteed by the constitution and, therefore, the activities of 17 June were not punishable.(5)

The SED was clearly divided over an appropriate response to the demonstrators and weakened by the leadership challenge which had been encouraged by the
Soviets.

The challenge to Ulbricht's leadership in the SED,
however, was soon thwarted.   At the Fifteenth Central
Committee Plenum at the end of July, Ulbricht succeeded
in purging his opposition.   He accused Zaisser and
Herrnstadt of intending to restore capitalism and
transform the SED, the consequences of which would be
the reunification of Germany as a bourgeois society in
which the SED would be an opposition party.(6)
Ulbricht stated that German reunification might only
occur far in the future, after a social revolution had
altered the West German system.(7)   Zaisser and
Herrnstadt were expelled from the Central Committee and
the Politburo.   Anton Ackermann, Hans Jendretzky, and
Elly Schmidt were also removed from the Politburo
(Jendretzky was a candidate member) as members of the
anti-party faction.   Fechner received the harshest
treatment; he was expelled from the SED as an enemy of
the party and the state.(8)   However, no criminal charges were brought against any of the purge victims and
no one was executed, despite their link with Beria.

Zaisser and Herrnstadt had been backed by Beria in
the SED power struggle.(9)   Beria himself was engaged
in a power struggle within the CPSU after Stalin's
death.   The East German rising was seen as an indict-
ment of Beria's proposed moderation of policy toward
East Europe in general and accommodation with the West
over Germany in particular.   Beria's fall from power
was linked to the East German rising, although the fear
inspired in his colleagues by his position as head of
internal security was undoubtedly of more immediate
import.(10)   At the end of June, Beria was removed from
office and arrested, and he was later executed for
treason.(11)   According to Soviet sources, he was accused of planning to deliver the GDR to the West.
Khrushchev never altered his accusation that Beria
planned to give up the GDR.(12)   Khrushchev also makes
clear in his memoirs his long-standing animosity toward
Beria and his efforts to thwart his rival in the power
struggle that ensued following Stalin's death.(13)   The
purge of Beria set the stage for the removal of the
Zaisser-Herrnstadt faction in the SED.   No direct evidence proves that Beria, Zaisser, and Herrnstadt coor-
dinated a leadership challenge to Ulbricht, but circum-
stantial evidence lends credence to such an assumption.

Public charges in the Soviet and East German press linked the men. The three shared a common demise, accused of similar malevolent acts. It also seems logical that Zaisser and Herrnstadt would seek to garner support from appropriate Soviet authorities in their attempt to assume leadership of the SED, particularly since Soviet disenchantment with Ulbricht stemmed in large part from Ulbricht's recent obstinacy in pursuing his perception of SED interests in opposition to CPSU directives. The continued succession struggle in the USSR provided the opportunity for such a challenge.

Ironically, then, the June uprising actually saved Ulbricht. The Kremlin could not allow him to be removed in the wake of the unrest because it would not only underline the weakness of the GDR regime but also reflect a weakness of the Soviet position in East Europe as a whole.(14) Despite the Soviet move to consolidate Ulbricht's position, the Kremlin did not abandon its commitment to the New Course. The events in Czechoslovakia and especially in East Germany served to convince the Soviet leadership that a retreat from Stalinist policies in East Europe as well as in the Soviet Union was necessary to provide some relief for the populations, which had been strained to the breaking point.(15) Prime Minister Malenkov, the main proponent of the New Course, proclaimed the beginning of this policy in the Soviet Union to the Supreme Soviet in August, after the Fourteenth SED Central Committee Plenum had affirmed East Germany's continuing adherence to the New Course. The SED took steps to correct flaws in implementation of the policy. Measures were adopted to increase pensions, salaries, and assistance to the disadvantaged beyond the initial proclamation of the New Course. The party also specifically promised to increase the housing supply and to improve working conditions in state enterprises. An additional 30 million deutsche Mark (DM) for the remainder of 1953 was appropriated for those and other measures to improve the benefits and living standard of working people.(16)

The Fifteenth Plenum of the Central Committee at the end of July reconfirmed the party's intention of pursuing the New Course but at the same time affirmed the Second Party Conference policy which had ushered in the Construction of Socialism Program.(17) To quote the party resolution:

The essence of the New Course is found
in the diligent improvement in the economic
situation and the political relationships in
the GDR, to be achieved promptly, and on this
basis, to significantly improve the standard
of living of the working class and all working people. Improvement in the material position of the population will be achieved
through increased production of food, consumer goods and light industry at the expense of
heavy industry, through the development of
initiative of private trade and private industry as well as the advancement of agriculture. (18)

The same document stated the following: "It was also
correct, that our party led Germany on the road to
socialism and began the establishment of the basis for
socialism in the GDR.   This general policy was and
remains correct."(19) The apparent incompatibility of
these two sections from the resolution clearly illustrates the contradictory nature of the situation which
simultanously preserved Ulbricht's leadership position
and the program he opposed.   The result was a prevailing tension between the two.(20)

The New Course can be interpreted as a tactical
withdrawal from the pursuit of socialist construction
dictated by objective conditions present in the summer
of 1953, much as the New Economic Policy introduced by
Lenin in 1921 represented a retreat from the ambitious
but disastrous policy of War Communism.(21) Seen from
this perspective, there was no contradiction in assert-
ing the validity of both the Construction of Socialism
Program and the New Course.(22)

A WATERSHED IN SOVIET-EAST GERMAN RELATIONS

Political Status of the GDR

As a result of the June uprising, the Kremlin began a policy designed to consolidate the SED regime and elevate the GDR's political status internationally, a focus which continued through 1955. In August 1953 a large East German delegation, headed by Grotewohl and Ulbricht, travelled to Moscow at Soviet invitation to discuss the situation in the GDR, relations between the two countries, and the German question as a whole. At the conclusion of the meetings on 22 August, measures were announced to upgrade the political stature of the GDR. In response to a request from the East German delegation, it was agreed that steps would be taken to suspend the sentences of those German prisoners of war who had been convicted of war crimes, excepting those whose crimes had been particularly heinous. Further, it was agreed that their respective diplomatic missions should be upgraded to embassies and that ambassadors would be exchanged.(23) In October, the elevation of missions to embassy status took place. Semyonov, who had been Soviet High Commissioner in Germany, was appointed the first Soviet Ambassador to the GDR. Semyonov, it will be recalled, had long been involved in German politics and was an advocate of Beria's policy of moderation in Germany.(24) His appointment over others allied with Ulbricht's position showed the Soviet leadership's commitment to reform despite the perceived necessity of maintaining Ulbricht in power for security reasons. The other East bloc countries rapidly followed suit in upgrading their missions to ambassadorial level.(25)

The GDR was recognized by the Soviet Union as a sovereign state on 25 March 1954 in a Soviet declaration on the relations between the two countries. The declaration contained three points: first, the Soviet Union would maintain the same relations with the GDR as with other sovereign states, which meant that the GDR was henceforth free to control domestic and foreign affairs, including the question of its relations with West Germany; second, the Soviet Union retained those functions necessitated by the Potsdam Agreements, which included continued stationing of Soviet troops on German soil; and finally, the High Commissioner's oversight of the business of the East German government would be curtailed to matters of security and relations

with   the other occupying powers.(26)   Schenk   asserts
that   this   change in relations was more   formal   than
substantive.   He notes that the East German leadership
still   consulted with the Soviets on all major   issues.
He also observed, however, that the Soviets became less
intrusive   in East German affairs after   Stalin's
death.(27)   The Soviet High Commission moved from
Karlshorst,   which   had   been the home of   the Soviet
Military Administration and the Soviet Control Commission,   signalling the end of a conventional   occupation
regime.(28)   In accordance with the GDR's sovereign
status,   the High Commission was reorganized and the
number of workers reduced by about two-thirds.(29)
Many Russians left Germany in the summer of 1954, and
their office space and living quarters were turned over
to the GDR.

On 25 January 1955,   the Praesidium of the Supreme
Soviet declared an end to the state of war existing
between the Soviet Union and Germany.   Therefore, all
legal limitations on the rights of Germans as citizens
of an enemy state were to be lifted.   Termination of
the state of war,   however, did not alter Germany's
international obligations or the rights and obligations
of the Soviet Union conferred by the Potsdam Agreements.(30)   This policy was promoted as a step   toward
the peaceful reunification of Germany.(31)

The   GDR was included as a founding member of the
Warsaw Treaty Organization,   which was formed on 14 May
1955 following the entry of the Federal Republic into
NATO.   According to the official Soviet   explanation,
the threat of West German remilitarization and the
danger this posed to peace and security in Europe
impelled the East bloc to form a military alliance.(32)
Although an original signatory of the treaty,   the GDR
was not a member of equal standing in the organization.
In the agreement on creation of a united military
command,   the question of East German participation was
postponed,   apparently because of strong Czech and
Polish objections.(33)   East Germany's armed forces
were not included in the Warsaw Pact forces until
1956.(34)   Thus,   the GDR's inclusion in the formation
of the Warsaw Pact was a boost in status,   but a qualified one.   It was also probably deemed necessary in the
wake of West Germany's entry into NATO to maintain some
sense of parity between the two Germanies.

The   first treaty governing the relations   between
the Soviet Union and the GDR was negotiated in   Septem-

ber 1955.   This treaty formally ended the occupation regime.   Relations were to be on a basis of complete equality, mutual respect for sovereignty, and noninter- ference in internal affairs.   The same elements in the Soviet declaration of March 1954 were reconfirmed.(35) In addition, the treaty transferred control of the borders to the GDR, with the exception of military traffic, and nullified all directives of the Allied Control Council (from 1945-1948) in East German terri- tory.(36)   Furthermore, in accordance with the GDR's sovereign status, the Soviet government abolished the Soviet High Commission and entrusted all matters per- taining to Germany to its Ambassador.(37)   Consulta- tions between the Soviet Union and the GDR on interna- tional questions and the development of economic, tech- nical, and cultural ties were promised.   Continued stationing of Soviet troops in the GDR was also pro- vided for, with the stipulation that the troops not mix into the country's internal affairs.(38)   The treaty was ratified in October 1955.

The issue of German prisoners of war in the Soviet Union, discussed in August 1953, was finally acted upon on 29 September, days after the signing of the state treaty.   According to Soviet figures, there were 9,626 Germans incarcerated in the USSR.(39)   In light of the fact that the war had ended more than a decade ago, the Praesidium of the Supreme Soviet ordered their repatri- ation: 8,877 were to be relieved of further imprison- ment and returned to their homes in either East or West Germany; the remaining 749 were to be turned over to the appropriate German government as war criminals, due to the severity of their crimes.(40)

The GDR had rapidly enhanced its political status and political future in the period between August 1953 and September 1955 , but East Germany cannot be said to have attained full and equal status in the bloc until June 1964, when the Treaty of Friendship, Mutual Assis- tance, and Cooperation was concluded with the Soviet Union.   This treaty guaranteed for the first time the inviolability of East German territory.(41)   This marked a new quality in Soviet-East German relations, the basis for which had been laid in the state treaty of September 1955.

Soviet Economic Aid to the GDR

     The Soviet Union moved quickly to provide emergen-
cy economic aid to the GDR, which Ulbricht had been
seeking since before Stalin's death.(42) Moscow newly
offered "every assistance" to the foundering East German economy.(43) In July, the Soviet government promised to deliver the following goods during the remainder of the year over and above the trade agreement for
1953:

Butter	27,000	tons
Animal fat	8,500	"
Vegetable oil	11,000	"
Oil seeds	15,000	"
Meat	20,000	"
Cheese	1,500	"
Cotton	7,000	"

These goods, valued at 231 million rubles, were to be
delivered on credit.(44) The total delivery of goods
from the Soviet Union to the GDR in 1953, valued at
1,130 million rubles, or $280 million, included the
following:(45)

Grains	935,000	tons
Butter	57,000	"
Animal fat	9,500	"
Vegetable oil	29,500	"
Meat	25,000	"
Cotton	69,000	"
Wool	5,200	"

The first special delivery of foods from the USSR
arrived at the end of July.   In addition, foreign
currency to buy needed goods from the West was provided.(46)

     The August meeting between Soviet and East German
delegations in Moscow, discussed previously, initiated
a series of changes not only to upgrade the GDR politi-
cally but also to transform the economic relations
between the two countries.   The Soviets and Germans
issued a communique on 23 August on the results of the
three-day negotiations.   Both parties agreed to various
measures designed to further economic development and
improve the standard of living in the GDR.(47)   The
communique specified additional deliveries from the
Soviet Union to the GDR of food, coal, rolled ferrous
metals, copper, lead, aluminum, cotton, and other goods

beyond those in the 1953 trade agreement, valued at 590
million rubles.(48) In addition, the Soviets granted
credits of 485 million rubles to the GDR, of which 135
million was in convertible currency for the purchase of
goods in the West. The other portion was to finance in
part the additional deliveries from the Soviet Union
agreed to in July and in the August meeting. The
credit was to be repaid in two years, beginning in
1955, at 2 percent interest.(49)

Soviet aid is reflected in the composition of East
German trade during this period, presented in Table 17.
Note the large jump in imports of food and tobacco, raw
materials, and semifinished goods in 1953 and continued
high levels in 1954. By contrast, exports of same
remained steady or dropped between 1952 and 1953.

Table 17
GDR Trade with the East Bloc
(millions of current dollars)

	1950	1951	1952	1953	1954	1955
Exports						
Engineering products	105	308	333	564	743	690
Other manufactures	33	60	45	36	47	43
Raw materials & semifinished goods	127	169	161	160	200	200
Food and tobacco	12	25	16	3	13	7
Imports						
Engineering products	17	14	25	30	28	22
Other manufactures	42	76	112	113	145	161
Raw material & semifinished goods	167	197	241	302	341	367
Food and tobacco	130	157	202	305	294	278

Source: United Nations, Economic Commission for Europe,
Economic Survey of Europe, 1957 (Geneva: Economic Commission for Europe, 1958), p. A-62.

Although the figures are for trade with the entire
bloc, since the USSR was and remains by far the most
important trading partner of the GDR, the data primarily represent shifts in Soviet policy.

The year 1953 marked the beginning of one-sided
receipt of credits from the Soviet Union, although the
GDR had received some emergency credits prior to the
August agreement.(50) The next large infusion of credit did not occur until 1957, when the Soviets extended

700 million rubles of credit for purchase of commodities in the USSR plus 300 million rubles in convertible
currency.   In January 1956, the GDR received a credit
of 80 million rubles for purchase of commodities in the
Soviet Union.(51)   By the end of the First Five Year
Plan,   the GDR had a huge debt burden which it was
unable to finance.   At the same time, the economy
needed new credits to finance the Second Five Year
Plan.   The Soviet Union liquidated East German's accumulated debt by revaluing the uranium deliveries from
Wismut,   thereby creating a balance in GDR-Soviet
trade.(52)

     The most important result of the August 1953 meet-
ing was an agreement on the termination of German
reparations and other measures: reparations payments
were ended as of 1 January 1954, remaining SAGs were to
be returned as of 1 January 1954, cost to the GDR for
maintenance of Soviet troops was to be reduced to 5
percent of the state's budget, and accumulated debt for
occupation costs since 1945 was forgiven.(53)   East
German reparations payments were terminated by an
agreement of the Soviet and Polish governments (the
Polish government had been receiving a portion of reparations since the end of the war).   According to Soviet
calculations, the East Germans were spared payment of
$2.54 billion at 1938 world prices, which would have
been due after 1 January 1954.   The figure took into
account Soviet reductions in reparations in May 1950.

     A Soviet-German commission was provided by the
August protocol to carry out the transfer of the remaining thirty-three SAGs to German ownership.   The
Soviets had retained the most important enterprises.
An article in Neues Deutschland on the day of the
transfer stated that the last SAGs "are of decisive
significance for the economic strength of the GDR.   The
result of the transfer of these enterprises will mean .
. . more food, more textiles, more consumer goods for
the daily needs of every citizen."   The SAGs, valued at
2.7 million DM, were to be returned without charge.(54)
The return meant an additional savings of 200 million
DM in subsidies and 400 million DM in possible profits
which previously had gone to the Soviets.(55)   The GDR
debt of 430 million DM from the transfer of sixty-six
SAGs in 1952 was also forgiven.(56)   The only enterprise not turned over to the East Germans was the
uranium producing Wismut, A.G.   As of 1 January 1954,
it was transformed into a mixed German-Soviet company.
Total output of the plant was still shipped to the

USSR, but the GDR received compensation for deliveries.

Surprisingly, the exploitive character of the SAGs, or joint stock companies was conceded by the Soviet leadership. Even Stalin apparently stated that mixed companies were not for allied or friendly countries but were only good for satellites.(57) After Stalin's death, Mikoyan denounced the mixed companies in much stronger terms. He criticized them as a blatant form of Soviet interference in the internal affairs of the people's democracies and even as economic exploitation of weaker countries. He demanded their abolition.(58) All SAGs had been returned by this time. Abolition of mixed companies in East Europe followed.

The reduction in cost to the GDR for maintenance of Soviet occupation troops to 5 percent of the state budget, stipulated by the August protocol, was never to exceed the 1949 level of 2,182 million DM. Occupation costs for 1954 were calculated to run 1,600 million DM compared to 1,950 million in 1953.(59) The cost to the GDR for Soviet occupation troops was further reduced by an agreement reached on 17 July 1956, effective 1 January 1957, when annual support costs were reduced by one-half, accompanied by a reduction in Soviet military personnel.(60) As of 1 January 1959, the GDR was relieved of all occupation costs.(61) This eliminated the last remnants of direct reparations exacted by the Soviet Union from East Germany.

It will be recalled that total reparations actually paid to the Soviets are estimated by Western scholars to have been roughly $19 billion. This figure includes dismantling, occupation costs, and depletion of SAG stocks and equipment, as well as direct payments.(62) Total Soviet aid to the GDR from 1945 to 1960 is estimated to value $9.4 billion, including reparations cancellations.(63) The bulk of Soviet aid came between 1953 and 1958; the June uprising provided the shock which initiated the change. The effect was to reduce the net transfer of resources from East Germany to the USSR to roughly the amount initially requested for reparations, albeit from the whole of Germany.

Soviet commitment to improving conditions in the GDR continued. In 1955, Khrushchev pledged to turn the GDR into a showcase of the East bloc designed to attract the West. In his memoirs, Khrushchev wrote of his "dream to create conditions in the GDR [so] that it would become a showcase of moral, political and material achievement."(64) This policy was a significant expression of the new Soviet commitment, designed to reassure the East German leadership, while Khrushchev pursued the establishment of Soviet-West German diplomatic relations and reached agreement with the West on the Austrian State Treaty. It was also part of a general campaign initiated by Khrushchev to overtake the United States economically in an attempt to shift the focus of superpower competition.(65)

The August 1953 agreement marked the end of reparations as the dominant element of Soviet economic policy toward the GDR and ushered in a policy of economic support complemented by enhanced political status for East Germany. This is not to say that all remnants or indirect effects of the reparations policy in the Soviet-East German relationship were eliminated, just as it would be inaccurate to overlook Soviet economic assistance to the GDR prior to 1953. It has been argued that the policy change in 1953-1954 was merely a shift in exploitation to the commercial realm, as evidenced by preferential exports to the USSR and deterioration in East German terms of trade.(66) These elements resemble the relationships between dominant and dependent economies in the world market described by Albert Hirschman's theory of foreign trade and national power.(67) The dependency in Soviet-East German economic relations, however, is the obverse of traditional dependency as analyzed by Hirschman. The USSR was the supplier of raw materials, while the GDR supplied capital equipment and processed goods.

Some perceive exploitive elements built into the changes in the East German economy initiated at the end of the war. Significant economic costs are attributed to the postwar division of Germany and the restructuring of the East German economy to meet the needs of the Soviet and other East European economies at the expense of the area's traditional industries.(68) These factors in turn retarded technological advancement and added the opportunity costs of forgone investments to the legacy of Soviet occupation. Economic ties initially imposed by the Soviet Union were later reinforced by the extension of credits, upon which the East German economy became dependent. The dependency became self-perpetuating, strengthened by economic and political realities of the postwar world. The change in East German economic organizing principles toward the Soviet

economic model also resulted in additional economic
costs in terms of efficiency and quality of production.
These elements are perhaps best reflected in the well-
known discrepancy in standards of living between the
GDR and the Federal Republic, although the contributing
factors are much more complex than that. To put the
entire issue in perspective, it must be reiterated that
the opportunity costs of these postwar changes were
accompanied by access to a huge, guaranteed market in
the CMEA and secure supplies of raw materials from the
USSR. The value of these benefits is as difficult to
measure as the cost of forgone opportunities. It is
important to recognize that the net effect of the GDR's
economic reorientation included benefits as well as
costs.

Despite the enduring remnants of Soviet reparations policy which molded East German economic development, there was a qualitative shift in Soviet-East
German relations in 1953-1954. The termination of
reparations, the return of the most important enterprises to East German control, the infusion of economic
aid, and the upgraded political stature accorded the
GDR government all signalled a new Soviet policy of
support for East Germany. These measures were intended
to accelerate economic development and raise the populations' living standard, alleviating political tensions. They were also designed to bolster the prestige
of the Ulbricht leadership, badly damaged by the June
uprising.

CHANGES IN THE DOMESTIC ECONOMY

The impact of the shift in Soviet policy was
reflected in the economic policies in the GDR. The
government renewed its commitment to the New Course.
Public attention focused on measures to improve the
standard of living. Salary increases and price and tax
reductions, coupled with credits for farmers and others
privately employed, provided initial improvement.(69)
The fifteenth plenary session of the SED Central Committee in July 1953 promoted the development of private
initiative in trade and industry as well as in agriculture in order to raise the well-being of the population.(70) In the second hald of 1953, roughly 3,000
businesses were returned to private ownership. During
the same period, private trade increased 20 percent

over the first half of the year.(71) Collectivization
in agriculture was halted and partially reversed.   By
the end of 1953, 70 percent of agricultural land was in
private hands.(72) Other measures, such as increased
credits and reduced deliveries to the state, encouraged
agricultural production.(73) Table 7 (p. 83) illustrates the change in fortune of private producers under
the New Course. The year 1954 saw the largest increase
in the contribution of private producers to total production in the five-year period, following an absolute
decline in 1953.   In 1954, with the return of the last
SAGs, approximately 80 percent of total production was
nationalized. The New Course did not affect the status
of major producers but halted, and in some cases reversed, the expropriation of small businesses and
crafts.(74)

     At the Fourth Party Congress in the spring of
1954, Ulbricht described the essence of the New Course
as shifting resources from certain branches of heavy
industry and heavy machinery to the production of consumer goods.(75) (See Table 6, p. 81) He declared
that extraordinary measures would be taken to stimulate
food and luxury industries, the textile industry and
other branches of light industry, housing construction,
and agriculture.(76) Earlier salary increases, instituted in July 1953, had not been matched by increased
production of consumer goods and, therefore, had
created an imbalance in supply and demand.(77)   This
imbalance was to be rectified by a program for the
production of 1 billion DM worth of consumer goods
above that called for in the 1954 plan. The Zusatz-
programm (supplemental program), proposed by Ulbricht
at the Fourth Party Congress, remained outside the
economic plan, giving the progam a rather tenuous
quality.(78)

     The emphasis on consumption at the expense of
gross investment in response to the June rising was
particularly evident in 1954.   (See Table 10, p. 88)
The sharp drop in accumulation was due primarily to a
significant reduction in inventories in concert with
the general policy shift. In 1954, inventory accumulation dropped from high levels ranging from 7 to 9
percent of the GNP at 1936 prices to a low of 1.4
percent.   Relatively low levels were maintained until
1958, when inventories jumped to 11.2 percent.

     Reliable investment distribution data for this
period are difficult to find.   The East German statis-

tical yearbook, **Statistisches Jahrbuch der Deutschen Demokratischen Republik**, does not provide it.   Fritz Schenk, former East German State Planning Commission official, stated that the investment plan was altered to favor consumer goods over heavy industry, 52 percent to 48 percent, in accordance with the push to increase consumer goods production.   This cannot be verified directly.(79)   A set of figures presented by Köhler shows a significant increase in funds allocated to light industry and the production of food,drink, and tobacco in 1954, but not enough to support the shift noted by Schenk.   Furthermore, Köhler's data show in-creased investment in light industry and food, etc., at the expense of metalworking industries, while basic industries received a considerably higher share of investment.(80)   Such high investment in basic industry is unexplained by production figures as well as by policy statements.   Table 6 shows metalworking indus-tries steadily increasing their share of industrial production at the expense of basic industries.

Official focus on improving the standard of living in the GDR following the June 1953 events is reflected in the substantial improvement in the average real monthly wage in 1954, as seen in Table 13, p. 92. Also, per capita consumption of most major food groups increased between 1953 and 1954, with the exception of a significant decline in consumption of potatoes and flour, a standard indication of improved diet.   The emphasis on improving consumption did not eliminate all shortages, however, as is attested to by the continua-tion of food rationing until 1958.(81)   In September 1953, Ulbricht promised to lift rationing on all re-maining goods by the summer of 1954 and reduce prices. At the Fourth Party Congress, however, Ulbricht de-clared that rationing would continue in the interest of maintaining low prices for the working class.   He il-lustrated the advantages by comparing ration prices with prices for the same goods in West Germany, which in most cases were considerably higher.(82)

Expanded foreign trade was another element consid-ered essential to improving the standard of living in the GDR.   Ulbricht lauded the Soviet Union for the tremendous assistance the measures of the August 1953 protocol would contribute to this goal.(83)   The signi-ficant increase in trade volume in 1954, particularly in GDR exports, as seen in Table 17, was financed in large part by the Soviets and made possible by the termination of reparations.   A supplemental trade

agreement   between   the   Soviet   Union   and   the   GDR   signed
in   June   1954   also   contributed   to   the   increased   volume.(84)   Concurrently,   East   Germany's   imports   from   the
West   increased   significantly,   financed   by   hard-currency
loans   from   Moscow.(85)   The   GDR   also   enjoyed   a   dramatic
improvement   in   the   terms   of   trade   in   the   second   half   of
1953,   which   was   another   means   by   which   the   Soviets
aided   the   East   German   economy.(86)   This   advantage   was
short-lived,   however,   and   was   not   achieved   again   in   the
decade.

The   strong   emphasis   on   improving   consumption   was
particularly   noteworthy   against   the   background   of   generally   bleak   economic   performance.   Major,   abrupt
changes   in   economic   focus--from   the   Construction   of
Socialism   Program   in   1952   to   the   New   Course   in   1953--
were   detrimental   to   productivity   and   supplies.   Emigration   of   critically   needed   workers   and   farmers,   particularly   after   the   1952   program   and   the   June   uprising,
negatively   effected   economic   performance.   As   a   result,
the   First   Five   Year   Plan   fell   far   short   of   fulfillment.
The   GDR   finished   the   period   in   serious   debt   and   in   need
of   new   credits   to   embark   upon   the   Second   Five   Year
Plan.(87)   The   Soviet   Union,   as   previously   noted,   intervened   by   revaluing   past   uranium   deliveries,   thereby
balancing   the   GDR's   foreign   trade   ledger   and   clearing
the   way   for   extending   new   credits.(88)   This   action   not
only   alleviated   a   short-term   economic   crisis   but   served
to   strengthen   the   GDR's   ties   to   Moscow.

In   sum,   the   June   uprising   served   as   the   catalyst
for   a   transformation   of   Soviet-East   German   relations   in
which   the   Soviets   retained   decisive   influence   in   East
German   affairs.   The   Kremlin   dictated   the   renewed   commitment   of   the   SED   to   the   New   Course,   a   policy   which
became   meaningful   only   after   the   crisis.   At   the   same
time,   the   shift   in   Soviet   economic   policy   made   the
program   possible   by   releasing   the   GDR   from   reparations
obligations   and   by   providing   direct   aid   and   credits.
These   resources   enabled   the   expansion   of   consumer   goods
production,   development   of   trade,   and   increased   investment   vital   to   general   improvement   in   the   standard   of
living   and   to   the   functioning   of   the   economy   as   a
whole.

Retreat from the New Course

The fate of the New Course hung with that of Malenkov, its main proponent in the Kremlin, who was engaged in a power struggle with Khrushchev for leadership of the party and the country. The struggle involved economic policy: Khurshchev promoted a return to heavy industry, while Malenkov favored continuation of the New Course. According to the U.S. Ambassador to Moscow, Charles Bohlen, the debate was precipitated by imminent West German rearmament.(89) Khrushchev won that struggle, and on 8 February 1955 Malenkov "voluntarily" resigned as Chairman of the Council of Ministers.(90) A retreat from the New Course had already begun in the Soviet Union.   After Malenkov's resignation, the program was doomed throughout the bloc. Its demise was marked by a renewed emphasis on heavy industry, although without the extremes that had been evidenced in the First Five Year Plans in all bloc countries or in the Soviet Union during most of the Stalinist period.   The needs of consumer industry and agriculture were given more importance than in earlier years, certainly with an eye to internal stability.

The return to a conventional, albeit modified, structure of economic development served Khrushchev's intent to shift the focus of competition between the capitalist and socialist systems to the economic realm. The drive to catch up and overtake the West spread throughout East Europe.   In the GDR this effort was expressed in the campaign to make East Germany the showcase of the socialist bloc.

The retreat from the New Course in the GDR did not mean a reversion to the 1952 program for the Construction of Socialism, although the widely publicized emphasis on the production of consumer goods was significantly reduced.(91) Four months after Malenkov's resignation, Ulbricht declared the end of the New Course: "The most noteworthy aspect of (the New Course) was not that it was new, but that it was false . . . ."(92) This marked a savored victory for the East German leader who had consistently opposed the policy and had almost lost his position because of it.

The Second Five Year Plan, 1955-1960, illustrated the change in policy.(93) Ulbricht elaborated the main tasks of the plan at the Third Party Conference of the SED, 24-30 March 1956. In order of priority, they were (1) to development of basic industry and mechanical engineering through increased productivity, (2) to minimize disproportions in the economy, (3) to improve agriculture, and (4) to improve the material and cultural well-being through increased production of consumer goods, foodstuffs, construction of housing, etc.(94) Industrial production of capital goods again became the focus of the economy after the 1954-1955 lull, but growth targets were more modest than in the First Five Year Plan. Lowered growth targets reflected not only moderation on the part of leadership but also the reality that economic growth depended on increases in productivity rather than additions to labor force or capacity. Projected increases in national income, however, remained remarkably high.(95) Thus, expansion of production remained paramount, but not at any price.

Another key indicator of the shift in policy was the marked increase in investment to a level commensurate with the rest of the East bloc. It will be recalled that the share of GNP devoted to investment in the First Five Year Plan was considerably below that in the rest of East Europe or West Europe due to the emphasis on raising consumption and the loss of resources through reparations. In the Second Five Year Plan, investment was to more than double that in the First: 47.7 billion DM, of which 3.6 billion was declared for the national defense.(96) Investment did increase dramatically during the period 1955-1960. (See Table 8, p. 86 and Table 10, p. 88.)

The return of the East German Second Five Year Plan to the more orthodox socialist pattern of development reflected a new entrenchment of the GDR in the East bloc, reinforced by a conscious effort to coordinate the Second Five Year Plan with the economic plans of all the socialist countries.(97) This move paralleled the political consolidation of the status quo in Germany. The softened quality of the plan underlined the end of a harsher era for the population and the economy.

PEACEFUL COEXISTENCE AND THE GERMAN QUESTION

Peaceful coexistence had not been particularly
fruitful since the resolution of the Berlin blockades.
East-West tensions were heightened by the Korean conflict. The Eisenhower-Dulles foreign policy proclaimed
the "roll back" of communism, liberation of East Europe, and "massive retaliation" against the USSR as
primary goals and principles. The U.S. Secretary of
State, John Foster Dulles, reflected the spirit of the
times. He saw the USSR as the source of evil in the
world which had to be dealt with forcefully in order to
minimize and ultimately extinguish its influence.   At
the same time, Dulles felt the United States must
negotiate patiently with the Soviets to eventually
bring about fundamental change in the USSR.(98)   The
administration was reportedly optimistic that a power
struggle would ensue from Beria's arrest which would
topple the Soviet system.(99) The issues of right and
wrong were not clouded by ambiguity in Washington.

That U.S. actions to liberate East Europe extended
only to covert activities and moral support would not
be evident until 1956 , when the Hungarians waited in
vain for U.S. military assistance. In the meantime the
United States was active in East Europe, supported the
overthrow of Jacobo Arbenz Guzman in Guatemala, and
embarked upon a military buildup which included establishment of military bases and alliances worldwide. An
anti-communist witch-hunt hounded independent-thinking
individuals in the United States. The mood in Washington was not receptive to peaceful coexistence.

The West may well have been relieved when the East
German uprising and the use of Soviet troops contra-
vened the Soviet policy of peaceful coexistence initiated by Stalin and pursued by his successors. Washington saw peaceful coexistence as little more than a
decoy which capitalized on worldwide pacifist sentiment.   The West sought to take advantage of the East
German and Soviet weakness displayed by the June
events.   The Western Allies met in Washington in July
1953 to discuss, among other things, the East German
crisis and the German problem as a whole. In a note to
the Soviet Union dated 15 July, the three Western
powers proposed a four-power conference be held to
discuss free elections in all Germany and conditions
for creating an all-German government.(100) The Soviet
response on 4 August agreed in principle to a Four

Power Conference but rejected the proposed agenda as
unproductive. The Kremlin offered a more comprehensive
one which addressed the need for a general relaxation
of tensions. This marked the beginning of a significant attempt by the Soviet Union to shift the primary
focus from the German problem to problems of international security under which the German issue would be
subsumed. The Soviets pressed for the inclusion of the
People's Republic of China in any discussion of the
international situation as a nation equally responsible
as the World War II Allies for the maintenance of
peace. The new Soviet position also insisted on dis-
cussing the situation in Asia as well as in Europe in
conjunction with the issue of arms reduction.(101) The
German question, including the problems facing the
restoration of a united Germany and the conclusion of a
peace treaty, could be discussed within the comprehensive framework. At that time, the Soviets linked success in the solution of the German problem with a
solution to the Austrian question.(102) The events of
17 June should not be allowed to interfere with positive efforts to promote detente.(103) The new Soviet
approach to resolving the German question reflected the
extent to which the June uprising had altered conditions for reunification. The GDR had been seriously
weakened, while the FRG, by comparison, was in a much
better position due to Marshall aid and integration
into the Western alliance. At that time, a reunited
Germany would have meant absorption of the GDR due to
the accentuated inequalities. In order to preclude
that eventuality, which posed a fundamental threat to
Soviet national security, the Soviets had to first
strengthen the GDR by consolidating support for
Ulbricht and easing the economic crisis, which they
did. The new approach to resolving the German question
was designed to promote the relaxation of tensions
which the Soviets needed for domestic political reasons
and, at the same time, to underline that new conditions
had rendered the old formulae for Germany unwork-
able.(104)

     Before the West answered the note and the same day
a government delegation from the GDR was invited to
Moscow, the Kremlin sent another note to the Western
powers on the German question. The note of 15 August
stated that the conclusion of a peace treaty with
Germany was of primary importance for the settlement of
the German problem and for strengthening the peace in
Europe. The Soviets denounced the Bonn and Paris treaties of May 1952 for reawakening German militarism and

for integrating West Germany into an aggressive anti-Soviet military alliance in violation of the Potsdam Agreements.(105)   Ratification of the treaties would preclude German reunification.   The note again rejected the Western proposals for free, all-German elections as the basis from which to build an all German government. The Soviets based their criticism on the neutral commission proposed by the Western powers to supervise the elections, which, according to the Kremlin, reduced Germany to a colony without rights.   The Soviets then presented their standard recommendations.   First, a peace conference should be convened within six months to agree on a peace treaty with Germany which should include the participation of all interested states, and representatives of both German governments, in all stages of preparations of the peace treaty.   Second, a provisional all-German government should be created from representatives of the existing German parliaments with participation of democratic organizations.   Also included was the possibility that the two German governments would continue to exist parallel to the provisional all-German government for a given period of time.   This was a new wrinkle in the Soviet position which might have contributed to compromise in that it could have increased the willingness to experiment with a provisional government while protecting Western and Soviet interests.   It was, however, not given any particular consideration.   The main task of the provisional government would be to prepare for free, all-German elections to be held without interference from outside powers.   Finally, Germany should be freed from all reparations obligations as of 1 January 1954.(106) The terms for easing Germany's economic burden were precisely those which the Soviet Union presented to the GDR in August and which were the heart of the 22 August protocol.(107)   The issue of parity was not abandoned because proportional representation would essentially eliminate Soviet and SED interests.

The Soviets pursued their diplomatic offensive on the German question during the Soviet-East German meeting in August.   In a statement on the results of the negotiations, the Soviet proposals set forth in the 15 August note to the Western powers were reiterated with East German support.(108)

An exchange of notes between the Soviet Union and the Western powers ensued; each side repeated the main elements of their respective positions.(109)   Despite the lack of progress toward a compromise, the four

powers finally agreed to a meeting of the Council of
Foreign Ministers to be held in Berlin in early 1954.

        The Foreign Ministers met from 25 January to 18
February, the first time such a meeting had taken place
in five years. Once again, the standard positions were
presented.   The critical issue of disagreement was the
role of free elections in the procedure of German
reunification.   Implicit in this disagreement was the
fundamental incompatibility of each side's understanding of the concept. Molotov argued that elections such
as the West proposed had made possible Hitler's rise to
power and that a repetition of such a travesty must be
prevented.(110)   Dulles recognized that there was no
rule or international law whereby national unifications
or reunifications had to be accomplished by elections.
The reunification of the United States following the
Civil War was adequate proof of that.   Dulles also said
that the United States should be flexible on the method
for German reunification.   But support for free elections as the only means for German reunification acceptable to the West was a decided propaganda advantage.   Hence the West refused to consider alternative
methods.(111)   Faced with Western intractability, the
Soviet Foreign Minister modified his position in the
third week of negotiations.   Molotov introduced the
"Two State Thesis," which recognized the continuation
of the status quo in Germany for the time being.   This
concept is a key departure from the Kremlin's German
policy and signalled a new Soviet expectation that the
division of Germany would be maintained.   As part of
this new approach, Molotov recommended the withdrawal
of most occupation forces, plus increased economic,
cultural, and other ties, in order to alleviate tension
between the two Germanies.(112)   He also mentioned the
possibility of the Soviet Union's establishing diplomatic relations with West Germany.   Most important to
the Soviets, however, was the proposal for a treaty on
the collective security of Europe which would include
East and West Europe, obviating the rationale for the
European Defense Treaty, which was still under consideration.(113)   The Berlin Conference ended without
agreement or significant progress toward resolving the
issues dividing the major powers on the German problem
or the Austrian question.(114)

        After the failure of the Berlin Conference, the
Soviet Union issued the statement recognizing the sov-
ereignty of the GDR. The declaration not only enhanced
East Germany's political stature but also specifically

recognized East German authority in handling inter-
German relations.   In an address before the SED Fourth
Party Congress just days later, Mikoyan reiterated the
significance of the new relationship between the USSR
and the GDR.   He also renewed the Soviet suggestion
made at the Berlin Conference for the development of
economic, cultural, and other ties between the two
Germanies which would lead to a true rapprochement.(115)   Ulbricht followed with harsh criticism of
the West German government in his lengthy report to the
congress but echoed SED support for the measures sug-
gested to bring about closer ties between the GDR and
the Federal Republic, something that Ulbricht clearly
did not favor.(116)   His public support was a nod to
continuing Soviet dominance in SED __Deutschlandpolitik__
despite the recognition of sovereignty.

It has been argued that Soviet recognition of East
German sovereignty is irreconcilable with any credible
interest in German reunification.(117)   It is important
to note, however, that the Western Allies initially
recognized the Federal Republic as a sovereign state as
early as 1952, although it did not become official
until May 1955, while they continued to press for a
unified German state.   The Soviets apparently saw the
need to equalize the political status of East and West
Germany as a prerequisite to begin the reunification
process on terms acceptable to the Kremlin.(118)   Continuing Soviet proposals for rapprochement between East
and West Germany indicate that Moscow had not yet
settled on the Two State Thesis and was still keeping
options open.

The Soviets were greatly heartened by the French
rejection of the European Defense Treaty in August
1954, a treaty they had campaigned against since its
inception.   They continued to promote their concept of
collective European security, which would eliminate
opposing military blocs in Europe.   Germany would be
included as a unified state and, until that time, in
its divided state.(119)   As a step toward realizing the
goal, Moscow offered again to join NATO.(120)   The
Soviet victory against the EDC was short-lived, however.   In October a treaty was signed in Paris by the
Atlantic Council and the West German government providing for West Germany's entry into NATO.(121)

The Kremlin immediately began efforts to thwart
the implementation of the Paris Treaty.   In a note to
the three Western powers, the Soviets proposed a con-

ference of Foreign Ministers be held in November to
discuss the urgent issues threatening the peace and
security of Europe.(122)   The Paris Treaty was denounced in the same terms as the European Defense
Community had been.(123)   The call for a conference on
European security was renewed in November, this time to
include all European states and the United States.   The
Soviets also requested that the People's Republic of
China be allowed to send observers to the conference,
recommended to be convened 29 November in either Moscow
or Paris.   The Kremlin pressed the urgency of the
conference, noting that in December some European countries would begin consideration of the Paris Treaty.(124)   Both Soviet proposals for convening a European security conference were rejected by the
West.(125)

A security conference was held in Moscow from 29
November to 2 December, with only the East European
states and observers from the People's Republic of
China participating.   The Declaration of the Conference
held out the possibility of German reunification if the
plans to remilitarize and integrate West Germany into
the Western military alliance were abandoned.(126)   The
same theme was reiterated in a note to the Western
powers dated 9 December and in the "Statement on the
Peaceful Solution of the German Question by the Soviet
Government," issued 15 January 1955.(127)   The 15 January statement did, however, contain some important
points of departure from earlier Soviet statements on
the subject.   First, it contained no mention of forming
a provisional all-German government as a first step
toward reunification.   Instead, free, all-German elections were presented in that place.   In assessing the
significance of this shift, it is important to recall
that free elections had been held in Austria, Czechoslovakia, and Hungary under Soviet military presence,
which means that Soviet presence does not by definition
preclude free elections.   Thus, this shift in the Soviet position was a major compromise.   The Kremlin
agreed with the general outline of the Western powers'
formula for reunification.(128)   Second, the urgency of
the Soviet appeal to the West Germans was stronger than
before.(129)   They threatened that should the West
German parliament ratify the Paris Treaty, it would
bear ". . . heavy responsibility for the continuation
of the division of Germany and for the inability of the
German people to assume their rightful position in the
international community for years to come."(130)   Finally, the Soviets made a more definite offer to nor-

malize relations with the Federal Republic.(131) The persistence with which Moscow pursued its initiative on the German issue in order to prevent the ratification of the Paris Treaty, as well as the modification of the Soviet position revealed by the offer to sanction free elections or to normalize relations with West Germany, indicated the seriousness with which the Soviet leadership viewed the imminent military integration of West Germany into the Western alliance. In an attempt to appeal to the West German populace and to revitalize the four-power negotiations over Germany, the USSR ended its state of war with Germany on 25 January 1955.

Despite the Kremlin's tenacious campaign, the West German Bundestag ratified the Paris Treaty on 27 February. The other participant countries did the same, and the treaty went into effect on 5 May 1955.(132) Why did the West not respond favorably to the Soviet initiative, particularly when the Kremlin appeared to accept Western demands for free, all-German elections? After years of fruitless negotiations and the recent failure of the Berlin Conference, this Soviet proposal was not received as genuine but rather as another tactical device to thwart the Western alliance.(133) The international climate was one of Cold War. The domestic climate in the United States was fervently anti-communist. The political leadership in the United States and the FRG saw any solution to the German question which was acceptable to the USSR as suspect and, almost by definition, unacceptable to the West. That the Soviets might not trust Washington appeared not to figure in Dulles's calculations, as would become clear in Geneva.

In response to these adverse developments, the "Second Conference of European Countries to Guarantee the Peace and Security of Europe" met in Warsaw from 11 to 14 May and established the Warsaw Treaty Organization (WTO).(134) It bears repeating that this was more a symbolic reaction to the Paris Treaty than an action of military significance. Another interpretation suggests that is was a response to the potentially disintegrative effect the Austrian State Treaty, signed at the same time, might have on bloc cohesion.(135) The WTO did legitimize the stationing of Soviet troops in Rumania and Hungary after the signing of the Austrian State Treaty.(136) In accordance with the Soviet campaign for a European security system, the Warsaw Pact was open to all European states, "independent of their social or state system, which are prepared, through participation in this treaty, to contribute to the unification of efforts of peaceloving states toward the goal of guaranteeing the peace and security of the people."(137)   Furthermore, Article 11 stated that in the event a system of collective security in Europe were created, the Warsaw Treaty would be terminated.(138) In this way, Moscow explained, the GDR's membership in the Warsaw Pact in no way precluded German reunification.   Thus, despite previous threats that ratification of the Paris Treaty cemented the division of Germany, the Kremlin once again offered the option of reunification in conjunction with an agreement on a European security system.

The Soviets also presented the successful negotiation of the Austrian State Treaty by the four powers, signed 15 May 1955, as a hope and model for German reunification. Negotiations had been long and arduous; the final, critical compromise had been made by the USSR.(139)   The result was the reunification of Austria, the withdrawal of all occupation forces, and the establishment of an independent, neutral state between East and West Europe. The Soviets specifically stated that Germany could follow the same course, and the East Germans echoed that pronouncement.(140)

The overture was not without effect on West German public opinion. The West German government moved quickly, however, to dash hopes for a solution to the German problem along those lines. Government spokesmen stated that the difference in "size, location, and status" between Austria and Germany precluded one serving as a model for the other. Another significant difference not mentioned was that, although divided into zones of occupation like Germany, Austria had had a single government since November 1945 with which to reach a settlement. The West German government also declared its opposition to neutrality for Germany.(141) The Western powers virtually simultaneously announced they would reject all Soviet proposals for a reunited, neutral Germany.(142)

The realistic possibility of Soviet agreement to a treaty with Germany similar to that with Austria will never be known because the West was unwilling to pursue that option. It is conceivable that the Soviet leadership saw it in the national interest to create a band of neutral states in Europe which would serve as a buffer between East and West; the buffer zone would include Yugoslavia, Austria, Germany, Switzerland,

Sweden, and Finland.(143) All of those states, with the important exception of Germany, are today either neutral or nonaligned. The Austrian Treaty was, on its own, of strategic advantage to the USSR because it split the Western alliance geographically, dividing Italy from West Germany.(144) More important, it was the first step in a new series of Soviet initiatives to promote peaceful coexistence and reduce international tensions. Khrushchev's attempt at rapprochement with Tito and Mao Zedong, development of ties with India, overtures to West Germany, the Geneva summit, and a general easing of domestic controls were all part of that leader's campaign to present a new image at home and abroad.(145)

The Geneva summit, 18-22 July 1955, was the first meeting of the heads of formerly allied states in ten years, and hopes were high among all peoples for some new understanding and accommodation among the great powers.(146) But the conditions for accommodation were not favorable. President Eisenhower had agreed to attend a summit over the objections of Dulles and largely in response to prodding by British Prime Minister Winston Churchill.(147) Dulles wanted President Eisenhower to have no part in according legitimacy to the Soviet leadership. Before going to Geneva, Eisenhower felt the need to state publicly that he would make no secret deals with the Soviets. Neither Eisenhower nor Dulles had been impressed by Khrushchev's efforts to reduce international tensions, with the exception of the Austrian Treaty.(148) Eisenhower saw little prospect for agreement on Germany but hoped for some progress toward disarmament.(149) The Soviets, of course, were well aware of the Eisenhower-Dulles goal of "rolling back communism" to the Soviet borders. Khrushchev noted that the U.S. leadership employed all possible techniques to isolate the USSR, including economic and cultural boycotts. Khrushchev's feeling of inferiority vis-à-vis the Western leaders was symbolized by his inferior airplane and dowdy clothes.(150) He was without doubt outflanked at the gathering. The British, French, and U.S. leaders conferred privately prior to their meeting with Khrushchev and Nikolai Bulganin.(151) Bulganin was officially head of the Soviet delegation by virtue of his position as Chairman of the Council of Ministers. Marshal Zhukov was included in the delegation in hopes that his wartime friendship with Eisenhower might break the ice.(152)

The attendant Foreign Ministers proposed the following agenda for the summit on 19 July: reunification
of Germany, European security, disarmament, and promo-
tion of contacts between East and West.(153)   The
United States wanted to talk about the "captive
nations" of East Europe and the international communist
conspiracy, but these were omitted from the agenda.(154)   The Soviet delegation pressed its position
that an agreement on European security was the key not
only to reducing international tensions but also to
resolving the German question.   The Soviets presented
their strongest statement of the Two State Thesis,
declaring that given this reality, reunification by
some technical formula was not possible.   They noted
that since World War II, two separate Germanies had
developed, different in economic and social structure.
Also, each had joined opposing military alliances.(155)
As a result, reduction of tensions in Europe through a
collective security system had become a prerequisite
for German reunification.   In reality, it appears the
inclusion of the FRG in NATO forced Soviet adoption of
the Two State Thesis as the only remaining acceptable
option.(156)   The Two State Thesis, first introduced
tentatively at the Berlin Conference, represented a
middle solution to the whole German question.   The
Soviets' maximum program of a united communist Germany
had clearly not been possible since the Berlin blockade, if ever.(157) The other extreme of a reunited
Germany in NATO was never acceptable, and the integration of West Germany into the Western alliance had
ended prospects for a reunited, neutral Germany.   The
Soviets called for the development of economic and
cultural ties between East and West as a basis for
future cooperation in Europe.   As the proponents of
collective security, the delegation from Moscow consistently presented themselves as the champion of German
reunification and as having been forced to accept the
division of Germany, while attributing the opposite
motivation to their Western counterparts, citing as
evidence the Paris Treaty and remilitarization of West
Germany.(158)

The Western delegates defended the Paris Treaty
and clung to their position, which considered free,
all-German elections the only means for German reunification.   The West expected that a reunified Germany
would freely choose to be a NATO partner.   President
Eisenhower stated the fundamental difference between
the Soviet and the Western approach to the issues:
whereas the Soviet Union was of the opinion that the

security problem must be resolved as the basis for resolving the German question, the United States saw just the opposite, i.e., reunification of Germany was the precondition to guaranteeing European security.(159) In truth, reunification could not be reached on terms acceptable to both the United States and the USSR. Eisenhower felt that a reunited neutral Germany would pave the way for eventual communist control.(160) By contrast, the United States thought it perfectly reasonable that the Soviets should accept a reunified Germany in alliance with the West as the only viable option. The West, in turn, would limit German rearmament and ensure through mutual security treaties that Germany would not attack the USSR.(161) The notion that U.S. assurances from an administration that pledged to roll back communism would in any way neutralize Soviet fears of a rearmed Western-allied Germany strains credulity, but by all appearances Dulles was unable to attribute any legitimacy to Soviet interests and fears. Khrushchev states in his memoirs that the Soviets wanted an agreement at Geneva which would recognize the two Germanies and allow each to develop its own system. By contrast, he assessed the Western goal to be liquidation of the GDR.(162) Thus, no progress was made on these issues.

In an effort to make progress toward disarmament, Eisenhower stunned the other heads of state with his unexpected Open Skies proposal. Then, as now, one of the major sticking points to effective arms control has been the issue of verification. Eisenhower proposed open surveillance by all the powers as the least intrusive accurate method of overcoming this problem. Bulganin indicated some interest, but Khrushchev scotched further consideration when he discarded it as merely a trick to aid U.S. espionage.(163) Ambassador Bohlen felt the Soviets did not want the United States to be able to calculate their military weakness with greater accuracy.(164)

The only agreement of the summit was that all divisive issues were resolvable through negotiations and that the Geneva summit was to be regarded as a starting point for further negotiations. This illustrates the desire on both sides to maintain an image of willingness to cooperate, while attesting to the lack of basis for cooperation. The Foreign Ministers were directed to hold a conference in October 1955 to further discuss the issues that were raised during the summit.(165) Thus, the "spirit of Geneva" was largely

an illusion created by the image of the four heads of
state sitting together, nurtured by the hopes such a
scene engendered. Khrushchev clearly wanted to prolong
the atmosphere, which lent credibility to his image as
a moderate and to his campaign for peaceful coexistence.

    After the Geneva summit, the Soviet delegation
stopped in Berlin to reassure officials that the Soviet
commitment to the GDR had not faltered.   Both East and
West German officials feared that the United States and
the USSR might reach an accommodation which would jeop-
ardize their opposing interests.   Khrushchev stated
that the "German question cannot be resolved at the
expense of the GDR." Unacceptable were the possibili-
ties that the GDR would be drawn into NATO or that the
workers would give up their political and social
achievements.(166)   This declaration represented a
further step toward acceptance of and commitment to the
status quo in Germany, which the Soviets had first
introduced at the Berlin Foreign Ministers Conference.
After West Germany's entry into NATO and Western refusal to accept the Austrian Treaty as a model for Germany, the new position was articulated more consistently, albeit accompanied by the assertion that the Kremlin supported the reunification of Germany as a "peaceloving, free, and democratic" state. Concrete evidence
for the shift in policy was provided by the Kremlin's
renewed overture to establish diplomatic relations with
West Germany.   The Soviet government sent a note directly to the West German government on 7 June 1955,
proposing the normalization of relations without de-
manding reciprocal recognition of the GDR.(167)   A
delegation to be headed by Chancellor Konrad Adenauer
was invited to Moscow.   In a further exchange of notes,
the West Germans accepted and agreement was reached to
begin discussions on 9 September.(168)

    During the course of negotiations, Khrushchev
declared that the Paris Treaty and West German membership in NATO were accomplished facts which defined the
German situation.   Based on that reality, the Soviet
Union proposed to establish diplomatic relations with
the Federal Republic and promote trade between their
two states.(169) The hosts asked nothing in exchange
for normalization of relations.(170) In fact, immediately following the conclusion of negotiations, Chancellor Adenauer specifically stated at a news conference that their agreement did not entail any changes in
his government's policy on German issues or its claim

to represent the interests of all the German people in international affairs.(171)   In truth, Adenauer had abandoned his demand for free, all-German elections as the price for establishing diplomatic relations.(172) Throughout the deliberations, the Soviets emphasized development of mutually advantageous economic relations, leaving the question of reunification for the Germans to resolve.(173) A communique issued 13 September announced agreement of both governments to establish diplomatic relations, set up embassies, and exchange Ambassadors.(174)

Within days, Soviet and East German delegations met in Moscow to negotiate their first treaty on relations between the two countries.(175) The resulting agreement served to confirm the sovereignty of the GDR, which had been recognized by the Soviet Union in the March 1954 declaration, and to eliminate any appearance of a special relationship between Moscow and Bonn. Although it appeared to strengthen the GDR's position within the socialist bloc, it was more accurately a minimum step necessary to proclaim the Soviet commitment to their ally.   Negotiations had not been entered into until after the ratification of the Paris Treaty and after the Moscow-Bonn agreement.   Furthermore, a treaty was imperative to formalize relations between the the USSR and the GDR on a level commensurate with relations between the Soviet Union and West Germany. These two treaties marked acceptance by Soviet policy of two German states.

CONCLUSIONS

The East German uprising forced a change in Kremlin policy to economic support and consolidation of the Ulbricht government.   The Soviets needed to strengthen the GDR and, thereby, their own position in order to maintain their policy options in Germany.   The circumstances for reunification had changed.   The Kremlin could not advantageously enter into negotiations for the reunification of Germany from such as weakened position.   Nor would the GDR be a useful member of the East bloc unless conditions improved significantly. Under prevailing conditions, East Germany would become an economic drain and/or a political fuse threatening the security and stability of East Europe.   Renewed support for the Ulbricht faction of the SED appeared to be the major inconsistency in the political and

economic policy initiatives of the Kremlin following
the summer unrest, but Ulbricht's presence was apparently deemed more important as a symbol of continuity
and Soviet commitment to the GDR than as a symbol of
German Stalinism.

The shift in Soviet policy toward the GDR coincided with a new approach to solving the German problem. The Kremlin pursued a policy whereby the German
issue had to be solved within the context of a general
rapprochement between East and West anchored in a comprehensive European security agreement. This reflected
the inapplicability of the old formulae for German
reunification to the changed conditions which resulted
from the June events. During the long and unfruitful
process of bargaining and bickering over Germany, the
Kremlin did modify its position several times. In
addition, the agreement on the Austrian State Treaty
promoted the image of the Soviets as reliable, if
tough, negotiators as well as hopes for a similar
agreement on Germany. The Western Allies, on the other
hand, felt no need for compromise over Germany, being
fully confident of the inherent weakness of the GDR
regime. The West expected that a reunited Germany
would freely choose to become a part of the Western
alliance. The difference in position and perspective
of opposing sides is reflected in the approaches of
each to settlement of the German problem. The West
could stand fast on their original conditions for reunification, confident in the majority support of the
German people. The Soviets, on the other hand, modified their proposals and changed their total approach
to try to halt the momentum toward West German integration into the Western alliance.

The Two State Thesis was adopted by the Soviet
Union in the face of Western intractability to overcome
the disadvantages to their interest of continuing the
status quo in Germany. This policy provided the basis
from which the Kremlin could pursue a relationship with
the Federal Republic which could mitigate the threat of
West German membership in NATO by opening channels for
Soviet political influence as well as by creating valuable economic ties. The effect of this policy was not
only to provide the Soviets important access to West
Germany but also to strengthen the position of the East
German leadership and secure the GDR's future by com-
mitting the USSR to continuation of the status quo in
Germany.

NOTES

1.   *Dokumente der Sozialistischen Einheitspartei Deutschlands* (Berlin: Dietz Verlag, 1952-1954), 4:436-40; Victor Baras, "Beria's Fall and Ulbricht's Survival," *Soviet Studies* 27 (July 1975), p. 387.

2.   *Dokumente der SED*, 4:453.

3.   "Über die sozialdemokratische Ideologie der Gruppe Zaisser-Herrnstadt," *Neues Deutschland* (22 August 1953).

4.   Ibid.; *Dokumente der SED*, 4:470.

5.   *Neues Deutschland* (20 June 1953, 30 June 1953); *Tägliche Rundschau* (1 July 1953); Baras, "Beria and Ulbricht," p. 389.

6.   Walter Osten, "Die Deutschlandpolitik der Sowjetunion in den Jahren 1952-53," *Osteuropa* (January 1964), p. 7.

7.   Report by Charles Hulick, Jr., Acting Chief of Eastern Affairs Division, to the Secretary of State, 5 October 1953. National Archives documents.

8.   *Dokumente der SED*, 4:471; Heinz Brandt, *The Search for a Third Way* (Garden City, N.Y.: Doubleday & Co., 1970), p. 231; Melvin Croan and Carl J. Friedrich, "The East German Regime and Soviet Policy in Germany," *Journal of Politics* 20 (April 1958), p. 57; Fritz Schenk, *Im Vorzimmer der Diktatur* (Cologne: Kiepenheuer & Witsch, 1960), p. 213. Ackermann, Jendretzky and Schmidt were rehabilitated in March 1956.

9.   Klaus Erdmenger, *Das folgenschwere Missverständnis* (Freiburg i. Br.: Verlag Rombach, 1959), p. 142; Carola Stern, *Porträt einer bolschewistischen Partei* (Cologne: Verlag für Politik und Wirtschaft, 1957), p. 208.

10.   Brandt, *Search for a Third Way*, p. 188. Ambassador Bohlen wrote that in his judgment, the main cause of Beria's demise was his unwillingness to subordinate the secret police to the party. Charles E. Bohlen, *Witness to History, 1929-1969* (New York: W.W. Norton & Co., 1973), p. 356.

11.   Wolfgang Leonhard, The Kremlin since Stalin (New York: Frederick A. Praeger, 1962,) pp. 91-92.

12.   David O. Childs, The GDR: Moscow's German Ally (London: George Allen & Unwin Ltd., 1983), p. 38; Osten, "Deutschlandpolitik der Sowjetunion," p. 8.

13.   N.S. Khrushchev, Khrushchev Remembers (Boston: Little, Brown and Co., 1967), pp. 310-53.

14.   Arnulf Baring, Uprising in East Germany (Ithaca, N.Y.: Cornell University Press, 1972), p. 109; Brandt, Search for a Third Way, p. 218; Croan, "Reality and Illusion in Soviet-German Relations," Survey (October 1962), p. 19; Harold Laeuen, "Berijas Deutschlandpolitik," Osteuropa (April 1964), p. 259.

15.   Brandt, Search for a Third Way, pp. 222-23; Baras, "Beria and Ulbricht," pp. 394-95; Fritz Schenk and Richard Löwenthal, "Soft Goods vs Hard Goods," in New Leader (5 January 1959), p. 7; Harry Schwartz, Eastern Europe in the Soviet Shadow (New York: The John Day co., 1973),p. 39; Stern, Porträt, p. 169.

16.   Dokumente der SED, 4:442-44.

17.   Ibid., pp. 449-69; Brandt, Search for a Third Way, p. 231.

18.   Dokumente der SED, 4:449.

19.   Ibid., p. 467.

20.   The correctness of the Construction of Socialism Program was qualified by the admission of party failures in implementing that policy.   The party criticized its own performance in overlooking concrete domestic and foreign conditions whch led to too rapid development of the economy, especially heavy industry, and the premature attempt to liquidate the middle classes, among other things. Dokumente der SED, 4:467-68.

21.   Like the New Economic Policy, the New Course was presented as more than a short-term deviation in policy.   Grotewohl presented the policy as one which would be in effect for many years to come.   Stern, Porträt, p. 172.

22.   Ibid.; "Eastern Germany Since the Risings of June 1953," World Today (February 1954), p. 59.

184 Soviet Policy Toward East Germany Reconsidered

23.   Dokumente zur Aussenpolitik der Regierung
der Deutschen Demokratischen Republik (Berlin: Rütten &
Loening, 1954) band 1, p. 286; Deutsches Institut für
Zeitgeschichte, Dokumente zur Deutschlandpolitik der
Sowjetunion 3 vols., (Berlin: Deutscher Verlag der
Wissenschaften, 1957-1968), 1:347-48. The text in each
is somewhat different. The Soviet government had announced on 26 June the early release and return of
6,994 German prisoners of war to begin on 1 July in
accord with the 27 March amnesty proclamation of the
Praesidium of the Supreme Soviet. Beziehungen DDR-
UdSSR, 1949 bis 1955: Dokumentensammlung, 2 vols., (Berlin: Staatenverlag der Deutschen Demokratischen Republik, 1975),2:677.

24.   Dokumente zur Aussenpolitik der DDR, band 1,
p. 296. Semyonov was promoted to Deputy Foreign Minister for German Affairs in March 1955.

25.   Ibid., pp. 370, 422-23, 446, 457, 468.

26.   Dokumente zur Deutschlandpolitik der Sowjetunion, 1:501-2. This declaration occurred shortly
after the failure of the Berlin Conference of Foreign
Ministers, which will be discussed.

27.   Schenk, Im Vorzimmer der Diktatur, pp. 221-
23, 256.

28.   Werner Erfurt, Die sowjetrussische
Deutschland-Politik (Esslingen: Bechtel Verlag, 1959),
pp. 92-93.

29.   Beziehungen DDR-UdSSR, 2:667.

30.   Dokumente zur Deutschlandpolitik der Sowjetunion, 2:111-12. In this action the Soviet Union also
trailed the Western powers, who had ended the state of
war with Germany in July 1951.

31.   Beziehungen DDR-UdSSR, 2:827. Statement of
the Council of Ministers of the GDR on the Soviet
action.

32.   Dokumente zur Deutschlandpolitik der Sowjetunion, 2:137-42.

33.   Ibid., p. 143; Stern, Porträt, pp. 174-75;
Studiengesellschaft für Zeitprobleme, Die sowjetische
Deutschlandpolitik 4 parts (Duisdorf bei Bonn: Studien-

gesellschaft für Zeitprobleme, 1962-1963), 4:46.

34.   Studiengesellschaft, Deutschlandpolitik,
4:99-100; Peter Bender, East Europe in Search of Security (Baltimore: Johns Hopkins University Press, 1972),
p. 13.

35.   Dokumente zur Deutschlandpolitik der Sowjetunion, 2:209, text of the treaty, pp. 208-11.

36.   Ibid., pp. 190, 197.

37.   Ibid., p. 196.

38.   Ibid., pp. 209-10.

39.   West German remarks indicated that there
were many more than this involuntarily in the USSR.
Dokumente zur Deutschlandpolitik (Frankfurt am Main:
Allfred Metzner Verlag, 1961), III Reihe, band 1,
p. 339.

40.   Dokumente zur Deutschlandpolitik der Sowjetunion, 2:213-14.

41.   Ibid., 3:342-45. The treaty also promoted
economic integration through socialist division of
labor in conjunction with Khrushchev's campaign to
revitalize the CMEA.
    East Europe's reluctant acceptance of the GDR in
the bloc was reflected in the fact that no East European country concluded a Treaty of Friendship with the
GDR until 1967. Dokumente zur Aussenpolitik der DDR,
Vol. 15, no. 2. Bulgaria, September 1967, pp. 816-22;
Poland, 15 March, pp. 951-57; Czechoslovakia, 17 March,
pp. 1036-41; Hungary, 18 May, pp. 1053-58. Ulbricht
and Khrushchev pushed for this equalization probably in
response to West Germany's Ostpolitik. Bender, East
Europe in Search of Security, p. 14; Bender, "The
Special Case of East Germany," Studies in Comparative
Communism 2 (April 1969):17.

42.   This was not the first economic aid from the
Soviet Union. East Germany had received food aid in
the immediate postwar years. See Chapter 2. Prior to
the uprising, it will be recalled, the Kremlin had
refused Ulbricht's plea for aid.

43.   Baring, Uprising in East Germany, p. 98;
Schenk, Im Vorzimmer der Diktatur, p. 226.

44.   Dokumente zur Aussenpolitik der DDR, 1:273-74.

45.   Ibid., pp. 274-75.

46.   Schenk, Im Vorzimmer der Diktatur, p. 231. Schenk contends that the U.S. offer of food aid to ease the plight of the population spurred the Soviets to improve living conditions in the GDR. The Kremlin ordered East Germans to reject the U.S. offer, p. 230. Jonathan Steele, Socialism with a German Face (London: Jonathan Cape, 1977), p. 99.

47.   Dokumente zur Deutschlandpolitik der Sowjet-union, 1:345-48. In negotiating the reduction of East Germany's financial burden, which arose as a conse-quence of the war, it was taken into consideration that the GDR had "already fulfilled a considerable part of her financial and economic obligations" and that during the last years these obligations had been conscien-tiously fulfilled. This was stated to reflect the generosity of the Soviets.

48.   Ibid., p. 347.

49.   Ibid.; Heinz Köhler, Economic Integration in the Soviet Bloc with an East German Case Study (New York: Frederick A. Praeger, 1965), p. 310.

50.   Credit for 100 million rubles in 1949 and 149 million rubles in 1950 was extended by Moscow primarily to finance the importation of badly needed foods and raw materials. Köhler, Economic Integration, pp. 309-11. See Chapter 3.

51.   Ibid., p. 311; United Nations, Economic Commission for Europe, Economic Survey of Europe, 1957 (Geneva: Economic Commission for Europe, 1958), Ch. 6, p. 56. See Appendix E for a complete chart of Soviet credits to the GDR.

52.   Fritz Schenk, Magie der Planwirtschaft (Cologne: Kiepenheuer & Witsch, 1960), p. 87.

53.   Dokumente zur Deutschlandpolitik der Sowjet-union, 1:348-50.

54.   The SAGs returned earlier were to be paid for by the East Germans. The last SAGs were allegedly overvalued by the Soviets for propaganda purposes since

they were returned gratis as well as to compensate somewhat for the earlier transfers for which the GDR had to pay inflated prices. Franz Rupp, _Die Reparationen der sowjetischen Besatuzungszone in den Jahren 1945 bis Ende 1953_ (Bonn: Bonner Berichte aus Mittel- und Ostdeutschland, 1954), p. 5.

55.   Ibid., p. 19.   These figures should probably be lower because of the SAGs shift from priority status in the GDR economy and because of the cost of replacing equipment, and inventories taken by the Soviets prior to turning the plants over.

56.   _Sowjetische Auffassungen zur Deutschlandfrage, 1945-1953_ (Bonn: Deutscher Bundes-verlag, Bundesministerium für gesamtdeutsche Fragen), p. 17.

57.   Boris Meissner, "Sowjetrussland und der Ostblock: Hegemonie oder Imperium?" _Europa Archiv_ (10 May 1962), p. 297.

58.   David J. Dallin, _Soviet Foreign Policy after Stalin_ (New York: J.P. Lippincott Co., 1961), p. 197; Leonhard, _Kremlin since Stalin_, p. 107.

59.   _Dokumente zur Deutschlandpolitik der Sowjetunion_, 1:350.

60.   Ibid., 2:316-17.

61.   Ibid., 2:618.

62.   See Appendix D.

63.   Paul Marer, "Soviet Economic Policy in Eastern Europe," in _Reorientation and Commercial Relations of the Economies of Eastern Europe_ (Washington, D.C.: Government Printing Office, 1974), p. 145. This includes debts forgiven on returned SAGs and occupation costs up to 1954.

64.   _Khrushchev Remembers_, p. 456.

65.   Schenk, _Im Vorzimmer der Diktatur_, p. 128; Stern, _Porträt_, p. 188; Edwin M. Snell and Marilyn Harper, "Postwar Economic Growth in East Germany," in _Economic Developments in Countries of Eastern Europe_ (Washington, D.C.: Government Printing Office, 1970), p. 580.

66.   Köhler, "East Germany's Terms of Trade," _Kyklos_ 16 (1963):300; Konstantin Pritzel, _Die wirtschaftliche Integration der sowjetischen Besatzungszone Deutschlands in den Ostblock und ihre politischen Aspekte_ (Bonn: Deutscher Bundes-Verlag, 1962), p. 69; "Eastern German Since the Risings," p. 66. See also P.J.D. Wiles, "Settling the Terms of Trade," in _Communist International Economics_ ((New York: Frederick A. Praeger, 1969), pp. 210-53 for a discussion of the terms of trade issue.

67.   Hirschman's foreign trade theory described the impact of colonialism on later economic relations. Hirschman stated that an initial power disequilibrium between two countries is necessary for the implementation of economic policies designed to enhance the power of the stronger nation over the weaker. In a colonial relationship, the supremacy of the colonial power enables it to shape and direct the colony's trade; the ensuing trade further strengthens the hold of the imperial power. Conditions of bilateralism were further cited as a tool to maximize the power of the dominant economy. Hirschman, _National Power and the Structure of Foreign Trade_ (Berkeley: University of California Press, 1945), pp. 13-33. See also Francois Perroux, "Entwurf einer Theorie der dominierenden Wirtschaft," _Zeitschrift für Nationalökonomie_, band 13, 1952.

68.   _Dokumente zur Deutschlandpolitik der Sowjetunion_, 2:31. Mikoyan noted at the SED's Fourth Party Congress in 1954 that in united Germany, goods exchanged between the eastern and western parts were valued at more than 4 billion marks. During 1953 inter-German trade was a little over 500 million marks. From this, he concluded that a return to comprehensive goods exchange was necessary.

69.   _Dokumente zur Aussenpolitik der DDR_, 2:20-21; Baring, _Uprising in East Germany_, p. 97.

70.   _Dokumente der SED_, band 4, pp. 449-50.

71.   _Protokoll des IV Parteitages der sozialistischen Einheitspartei Deutschlands_, 2 vols., (Berlin: Dietz Verlag, 1954), 2:143.

72.   Pritzel, _Die wirtschaftliche Integration_, p. 65; Karl C. Thalheim, "Die sowjetische Besatzungszone Deutschlands," in _Sowjetisierung Ost-Mitteleuropa_, ed. by Ernst Birke (Frankfurt am Main: Alfred Metzner Ver-

lag, 1959), p. 354. Collectivization of agriculture
was not completed until 1960.

73.   Dokumente der SED, band 4, p. 450; Schenk,
Im Vorzimmer der Diktatur, p. 275.

74.   Horst Duhnke, Stalinismus in Deutschland
(Cologne: Verlag für Politik und Wissenschaft, 1955),
p. 102.

75.   In sharp contrast to the moderation in economic policy, the Fourth Party Congress pursued a policy to tighten political controls. The new party statutes adopted at the Fourth Party Congress confirmed the
SED's leading role in society and followed the organizational principles of the CPSU. The new statutes
provided for centralization of the decision-making
process to tighten control within the party. The Party
Congress, theoretically the highest party organ, was to
meet less often. The Central Committee was to meet at
least once every four months, and real decision-making
authority was transferred to the Politburo. Protokoll
des IV Parteitages der SED, 2:1128-29. The contrast in
economic and political policy, i.e. , economic reform
and political orthodoxy, reflected a continuation of
the tension between Ulbricht and the New Course. But
these apparent inconsistencies of countervailing policies are virtually standard patterns in Soviet-type
systems and are conceived as complementary changes,
each making the other possible.

76.   Ibid., 1:80.

77.   The same situation in 1952 and early 1953
had led to inflationary pressures on the economy which
had called forth the price increases, increased work
norms, and other measures which had sparked the June
uprising.

78.   Protokoll des IV Parteitages der SED, 1:140-
41.

79.   Schenk, Im Vorzimmer der Diktatur, pp. 227-
29.

80.   Köhler, Economic Integration, p. 204.
Köhler himself notes the unreliability of this investment data.

81.   Hermann Weber, Von der SBZ zur "DDR" 2
vols.,   (Hannover: Verlag für Literatur und Zeitgeschehen, 1966-1967), 2:30.

82.   Protokoll des IV Parteitages der SED, 1:145-
56; Schenk, Magie der Planwirtschaft, p. 95. Schenk
attributed the inability to lift rationing as promised
to the failure of the Soviet Union to meet Ulbricht's
request for special deliveries. p. 96.

83.   Protokoll des IV Parteitages der SED,
p. 146.

84.   Beziehungen DDR-UdSSR, 2:678.

85.   Paul Marer, Soviet and East European Foreign
Trade, 1946-1969: Statistical Compendium and Guide
(Bloomington: Indiana University Press, 1972), pp. 27,
37.

86.   Köhler, Economic Integration, p. 350.

87.   Pritzel, Die wirtschaftliche Integration,
p. 66; Schenk, Magie der Planwirtschaft, pp. 77-87.

88.   Schenk, Magie der Planwirtschaft, p. 87;
Pritzel, Die wirtschaftliche Integration, p. 160.

89.   Bohlen, Witness to History, pp. 368-69.

90.   Ibid., pp. 370-71.

91.   Schenk, Magie der Planwirtschaft, p. 75.

92.   Ibid.; Brandt, Search for a Third Way,
p. 241; Pritzel, Die wirtschaftliche Integration,
p. 53; Stern, Porträt, p. 173.

93.   This plan was aborted in 1957 but, nevertheless, illustrates the trend in policy after the New
Course.

94.   Protokoll des III Parteikonferenz der SED,
p. 1026; Karl C. Thalheim and Peter D. Propp, Die
Entwicklungsziele in der zweiten Fünfjahrplan (Bonn:
Bundesministerium   für   Gesamtdeutsche   Fragen,
1957), provides a detailed analysis of the plan.

95.   Economic Survey of Europe, 1956, p. A-35.

96.   Protokoll   des III Parteikonferenz der SED,
p. 1030.

97.   Ibid., pp. 63-67.

98.   Townsend Hoopes, "A Critique of the Prime
Mover, John Foster Dulles," in Major Problems in Ameri-
can Foreign Policy, 2nd ed. ed. by Thomas G. Paterson
(Lexington, Mass.: D.C. Heath & Co., 1984), pp. 483-94.

99.   Bohlen, Witness to History, p. 356.

100.   Dokumente zur Deutschlandpolitik der Sowjetunion, 1:320-21. Complete text of Western note in
Johannes Hohlfeld, ed., Dokumente der deutschen Politik
und Geschichte (Berlin: Dokumenten-Verlag, 1956),
8:205-6.

101.   Dokumente zur Deutschlandpolitik der Sowjetunion, 1:322-23, 354-57, 364-65, 461-66, 471-78; 2:56,
67-70, 84-85, 94-96, 151-54. Dokumente zur Deutschlandpolitik, pp. 166-72.

102.   Dokumente zur Deutschlandpolitik der Sowjetunion, 1:323-35.

103.   Ibid., p. 322.

104.   Erdmenger, Das folgenschwere Missverständnis, pp. 140-41.

105.   The Bonn Treaty granted West Germany circum-
scribed sovereignty, and the Paris Treaty provided for
West German membership in the EDC.

106.   Dokumente zur Deutschlandpolitik der Sowjetunion, 1:329-39.

107.   This section included reduction in cost for
maintenance of occupation troops and freeing Germany
from debts incurred as a result of those occupation
costs.

108.   Dokumente zur Deutschlandpolitik der Sowjetunion, 1:346.

109.   Notes were exchanged on 2 and 28 September,
18 October, 3, 16, and 26 November, and 8 December
1953. Complete texts of notes in Dokumente der
Deutschen Politik und Geschichte, 8:219-43.

110.   Ibid., pp. 332-33; Dokumente zur Deutsch-landpolitik der Sowjetunion, 1:494-95.

111.   Andrew H. Berding, Dulles on Diplomacy (Princeton, N.J.: D. Van Nostrand Co., 1965), pp. 37-39.

112.   A symbolic level of forces was to remain in place, reflecting the retained right of the occupying powers to intervene if the security of their respective parts of Germany were threatened.

113.   Dokumente zur Deutschlandpolitik der Sowjet-union, 1:388-499, provides text of Soviet positions. Note pp. 473-74, 481, 497-98; Frederick M. Hartmann, "Soviet Russia and the German Problem," The Yale Review (Summer 1954), pp. 513-14; Studiengesellschaft, Deutschlandpolitik, p. 90.

114.   Text on the exchanges at the conference in Dokumente der Deutschen Politik und Geschichte, 8:326-38. See also Dokumente zur Deutschlandpolitik der Sowjetunion, 1:487-98. For an informed discussion of the Conference, see Hartmann, "German Problem," pp. 513-18, 521-22. The participants did agree to a con-ference on Korea and Indochina including the People's Republic of China, and North and South Korea, which began on 26 April in Geneva.

115.   Protokoll des IV Parteitages der SED, pp. 407, 409.

116.   Ibid., pp. 21-26, 64-68, 186-87, 856-57, 864-65. Complete text of Ulbricht's speech appears on pp. 18-194 and concluding remarks on pp. 855-91.

117.   Studiengesellschaft, Deutschlandpolitik, 4:30.

118.   Dokumente zur Deutschlandpolitik der Sowjet-union, 1:501.

119.   Dokumente der Deutschen Politik und Ge-schichte, 8:211-43, 363-80.

120.   Ibid., p. 367.

121.   Ibid., pp. 468-70. Agreement was also reached on ending the occupation regime in West Germany.

122. *Dokumente zur Deutschlandpolitik der Sowjet-union*, 2:63. Complete text of note, pp. 55-64.

123. Ibid., pp. 60-61.

124. *Dokumente der Deutschen Politik und Ge-schichte*, 8:503-7.

125. Ibid., pp. 508-10.

126. *Dokumente zur Deutschlandpolitik der Sowjet-union*, 2:85-99.

127. Ibid., pp. 100-9.

128. Ibid., pp. 107, 109.

129. Final consideration of the Paris Treaty by the Bundestag was scheduled for February.

130. *Dokumente zur Deutschlandpolitik der Sowjet-union*, p. 106.

131. Ibid., p. 109.

132. Werner Weber and Richter W. Jahn, *Synopse zur Deutschlandpolitik, 1941 bis 1973* (Göttingen: Ver-lag Otto Schartz & Co., 1973), pp. 219, 222; *Dokumente zur Deutschlandpolitik der Sowjetunion*, 2:128; *Doku-mente zur Deutschlandpolitik*, pp. 9-10. In conjunction with the Paris Treaty ratification, the Allied High Commission was dissolved and the occupation statutes were lifted. The Federal Republic was declared a sov-ereign state.

133. Bohlen, *Witness to History*, p. 366.

134. *Dokumente zur Deutschlandpolitik der Sowjet-union*, 2:137-42. Text of treaty.

135. Ghita Ionescu, *The Break-up of the Soviet Empire in Eastern Europe* (London: Cox & Wyman, Ltd., 1965), p. 47.

136. The Austrian State Treaty and the Warsaw Treaty were signed just one day apart. The Austrian Treaty eliminated the legitimate need for Soviet troops in Rumania and Hungary to maintain lines of communica-tion with its occupied zone.

137.   Dokumente zur Deutschlandpolitik der Sowjetunion, 2:140-41.

138.   Ibid., p. 141.

139.   William Lloyd Stearman, The Soviet Union and
the Occupation of Austria (Bonn: Verlag für Zeitarchive, 1961), pp. 151-53. Bohlen, Witness to
History, p. 374.   The Soviets agreed that they would
drop their demand for the right to use troops in
Austria following signature of the peace treaty, should
Austrian independence be threatened.   Molotov first
informed Ambassador Bohlen of the concession.

140.   Stearman, Occupation of Austria, pp. 164,
167; Dokumente zur Aussenpolitik der DDR, 2:82-83. It
is important to note that neutrality is not mentioned
in the State Treaty.   It was a status adopted freely by
the Austrians.   Bohlen says the Austrian Treaty was not
intended by the Soviets to be a model for Germany but
rather to preclude integration of Western zones of
Austria into NATO.   Bohlen, Witness to History, p. 374.

141.   Stearman, Occupation of Austria, p. 165.

142.   Ibid.

143.   This thesis is developed by Wolfgang Höpker
in Europäisches Niemandsland (Düsseldorf: Eugen
Diederichs Verlag, 1956).   Also Ernst Richert,
"Zwischen Eigenständigkeit und Dependenz," Europa
Archiv (September 1974), p. 156.

144.   Stearman, Occupation of Austria, pp. 162-63.

145.   Domestically, Khrushchev rehabilitated some
prominent purge victims, encouraged a cultural thaw,
brought new faces into the party leadership, and generally eased police controls in preparations for the
dramatic Twentieth Party Congress in 1956.   Khrushchev
was methodically distancing himself from the abuses of
Stalin's rule without addressing the roots of those
abuses or his own role in them.

146.   Dokumente zur Deutschlandpolitik, summit
proceedings, pp. 148-219.   The GDR and the FRG sent
observer delegations to the conference.

147.   Churchill was replaced by Anthony Eden as
Prime Minister before the summit convened.

148.   Dwight D. Eisenhower, _Mandate for Change,_ _1953-1956_ (Garden City, N.Y.: Doubleday & Co., 1963), p. 508.

149.   Robert A. Divine, _Eisenhower and the Cold War_ (New York: Oxford University Press, 1981) p. 118.

150.   _Khrushchev Remembers,_ p. 395.

151.   Eisenhower, _Mandate for Change,_ pp. 512-13.

152.   Bohlen recalls that Adenauer was suspicious that Eisenhower might reach an agreement with the Soviets through Zhukov which would be at West German expense. _Witness to History,_ p. 386.

153.   _Dokumente zur Deutschlandpolitik,_ p. 150. Bulganin's agenda: discontinue the Cold War and strengthen trust between states; neutrality policy; the question of Asia and the Far East. Subsequently, he addressed the German question.

154.   Eisenhower, _Mandate for Change,_ p. 508.

155.   It was in the summer of 1955 that Khrushchev began the campaign to make the GDR the showcase of socialism.

156.   Erdmenger, _Das folgenschwere Missverständnis,_ p. 136.

157.   Ibid., pp. 141-42.

158.   _Dokumente zur Deutschlandpolitik der Sowjetunion,_ 2:156-58.

159.   _Dokumente zur Deutschlandpolitik,_ p. 188.

160.   Eisenhower, _Mandate for Change,_ p. 523.

161.   Berding, _Dulles on Diplomacy,_ pp. 35-37.

162.   _Khrushchev Remembers,_ p. 394.

163.   Eisenhower, _Mandate for Change,_ pp. 520-21.

164.   Bohlen, _Witness to History,_ p. 384.

165.   _Dokumente zur Deutschlandpolitik der Sowjetunion,_ 2:148-49.

166.   Ibid., p. 160. Entire statement, pp. 158-62.

167.   *Dokumente zur Deutschlandpolitik*, pp. 78-80.

168.   Ibid., pp. 123, 251, 262, 277.

169.   Ibid., p. 318. Text of proceedings, pp. 302-38.

170.   In fact, the Soviets were to pay through the release of imprisoned Germans. In a side agreement, the West Germans exacted the promised release of 9,626 Germans. Ibid., p. 339.

171.   Ibid., p. 337. West Germany did not recognize the GDR or the Oder-Neisse border. The Soviets responded through Tass that they considered the German border question resolved by the Potsdam Agreements. The Hallstein Doctrine was formulated in the fall to prevent the GDR from gaining international recognition.

172.   Bohlen, *Witness to History*, p. 387.

173.   *Dokumente zur Deutschlandpolitik*, pp. 3-4, 318, 322.

174.   Ibid., pp. 332-34.

175.   *Dokumente zur Deutschlandpolitik der Sowjetunion*, 2:190-208. The Soviets acted as if they agreed to the release of Germans in the USSR as a favor to the GDR government, when, in fact, they had already promised this to Adenauer.

6
The GDR:
A Special Case in East Europe

For too long, Soviet policy toward East Europe after
World War II was viewed as undifferentiated, just as
East European societies were considered uniformly grey
under Soviet domination. This was part of the "iron
curtain" image created by the Cold War, which for some
time remained unchallenged due in part to the lack of
reliable information. In time, greater access to information and a less politicized environment allowed
scholarly research to dispel the notion of East European homogeneity under Soviet influence without overlooking the changes wrought by socialization and Soviet
control. It is, nonetheless, useful to recognize that
there was an identifiable pattern of socialist transformation and integration into a bloc common to the
region.(1) In the most general terms, this pattern was
characterized by the establishment of coalition governments throughout East Europe with loyal communist party
members in critical positions, which allowed the respective communist parties to expand their influence
and then consolidate power. Other basic elements included the transformation of the economies according to
the Soviet model and integration of the countries into
a bloc bound by economic, political, and military ties.

Today the German Democratic Republic is numbered
among the countries of the "socialist commonwealth" and
regarded as one of the staunchest supporters of Soviet
orthodoxy within the bloc. In the decade following
World War II, however, East Germany deviated from the
pattern of Soviet policy toward the rest of East Europe
to a significant degree. There were, of course, elements of commonality with the rest of the bloc, which
must not be overlooked in consideration of East Ger-

many's position.   This chapter will examine first   the
parallel developments in East Germany and the East bloc
and then focus on the differentiation of Soviet political and economical policy which made the GDR a special
case in East Europe.

COMMON ELEMENTS

     The   development of   the party and   its role in
society in East Germany followed the pattern of change
directed from the Kremlin and imposed throughout East
Europe.   Immediately following World War II, the
Popular Front strategy was adopted throughout the territories where the Soviets had occupying forces.   Communist parties were to acquire power through influence
over broad-based, national coalitions.(2)   This strategy of evolving into socialism was reflected in the
fusion of the SPD and KPD in East Germany.   The SED was
to provide political leadership throughout Germany.
The coalition approach prevailed throughout East Europe
until the summer of 1948,   when the break with Tito and
growing hostile activity by the West precipitated the
transformation of all communist parties into parties of
the New Type.   The Soviet need to assert control over
the international communist movement took precedence
over advancing the communist position.   The SED was the
first to undertake the transformation.(3)

     During the Popular Front period, the Separate
Roads to Socialism theory provided the formulation in
East Europe for socialist transformation molded by
national conditions and characteristics.   The Separate
German Road to Socialism theory developed by Anton
Ackermann, exemplified this period of experimentation
and diversity.   Separate Roads to Socialism became
heresy when the Popular Front was abandoned.   The purge
of "Titoists" from all European communist parties followed.   The SED continued to follow the general fluctuations of Soviet strategy in Europe from confrontation to accommodation and negotiation, as presented in
the preceding chapters.

     The role of the SED in society also conformed to
the East European formula.   While maintaining a coalition government and formal multi-party system, the SED
took   over critical positions in the government.   The
other parties functioned in concert with, not in oppo-

sition to, the SED. Real authority was rapidly concentrated in the hands of the SED as the instrument of
Soviet power.(4)

     Economically, the focus on development of heavy
industry, coupled with reorientation of trade in East
Germany, paralleled changes in the East bloc.   The
shift from East-West to intrabloc trade was imposed by
the international political climate as well as by Soviet reconstruction requirements.   All East European
nations, including the Soviet Union, suffered economic
losses as a result.   Soviet exports had a natural
market in West Europe, and the needs of Soviet industrialization would have been filled most efficiently by
imports of capital goods and technical assistance from
the West.(5) The reorientation of trade was much more
costly to the East European nations, however, because
of their greater trade dependency.(6) The fact that
Stalin vetoed Soviet and East European participation in
the Marshall Plan underlined the importance of strategic and political considerations over purely economic
requirements.

     The already limited East-West trade deteriorated
with the outbreak of the Korean conflict and the imposition of strategic controls on exports from many Western countries orchestrated by the United States.(7)
Table 18 shows the shift in trade patterns for the East
bloc.   The most dramatic change occurred in East Germany, due to the division of the German economy and the
flow of reparations eastward.

Table 18
Proportion of Trade Turnover of CMEA Nations
with the East Bloc, in Percentages

	Bulgaria	Czech.	GDR	Hungary	Poland	Rumania	USSR
1938	30	22	4	23	13	25	13
1948	78	32	75	34	41	71	-
1950	85	53	72	61	59	84	81
1951	90	60	76	67	57	80	-
1952	89	71	75	73	66	85	-
1953	86	78	78	76	70	84	-
1954	87	74	76	71	70	80	-
1955	87	69	72	61	64	79	78
1956	80	65	73	61	62	78	74

Source: Frederic L. Pryor, The Communist Foreign Trade
System (Cambridge: MIT Press, 1963), p. 165.

Restructuring of economies throughout the Soviet controlled area went hand in hand with reorientation of trade. East European countries, which traditionally supplied raw materials and light industrial products to the West, became suppliers of heavy industrial products to meet Soviet needs. Until the end of 1953, these economies concentrated on development of heavy industry regardless of experience, factor endowments, or economies of scale. East Germany and Czechoslovakia, the two most industrialized economies, retarded their development by being tied to less advanced economies.

In sum, the common political elements represented the Kremlin's stake in consolidating control over the international communist movement and guaranteeing the presence of friendly governments along Soviet borders. The parallel elements of economic policy pursued in East Germany and East Europe reflected the need for reliable supplies of industrial equipment and products to rebuild and strengthen the Soviet economy. The political climate made such guarantees in trade with the West impossible. The need for a buffer of friendly governments and reliable supplies of industrial goods went to the heart of Soviet national security requirements. The achievement of the former, important in and of itself, provided a guarantee of the latter. Control over the communist movement touched the _raison d' être_ of the CPSU and secured Soviet influence in communist-governed states. The combination of these policies had an internal consistency which made them mutually supporting. All of them served priority goals of Moscow in East Europe.

DIFFERENCES IN ECONOMIC POLICY

The Potsdam Agreements awarded the Soviet Union German holdings and investments in East Europe. The Kremlin generally interpreted this very broadly to include even those assets recently confiscated during German occupation. The burden of this provision fell heavily on Poland and to a lesser extent on Czechoslovakia, against which the Soviets otherwise had no legitimate claims. Most of the industrial and transportation equipment and livestock from the new Polish territories were removed as German assets despite an agreement signed by the Soviets on 16 August 1945 in which they renounced all claims to German property in

Poland.(8)   Among the properties confiscated were some
of the largest industrial plants of Germany's wartime
economy.   It has been conservatively estimated that $.5
billion in equipment was removed from   western   Poland
before   the   Potsdam   Conference met in   July   1945.(9)
Czechoslovakia's loss of assets to the Soviet Union   in
industrial equipment, cash, and commodities confiscated
as   German property has been valued at $387 million   in
prewar dollars.   An end to the seizures was negotiated
in   Moscow in July 1946.(10)   Of all the East   European
countries,   only Czechoslovakia, Poland, and Yugoslavia
managed   to   retain or recover assets that the   Germans
had   taken.(11)   The Polish economy was   further   exploited by an agreement with the Soviets to sell   coal
at   much below market price ostensibly in exchange   for
being   allowed   to retain German assets and for   Soviet
transfer of the Polish portion of reparations extracted
from East Germany.   The Poles were to receive 15   percent   of   reparations according to the   Potsdam   Agreements,   but   it   is generally recognized they   received
only   a   small   fraction of the   amount   due.(12)   The
delivery of coal at unconscionably low prices apparently continued until the mid 1950s,   long after the Soviets   had ceased any reparations deliveries from   Germany.   Some measure of restitution for this policy was
made in November 1956, after the Polish October and the
Hungarian revolt.(13)

The Soviet Union demanded reparations from Rumania
and Hungary,   former Axis countries.   Rumania was   required to pay $300 million in 1938 dollars primarily in
crude   oil and oil by-products,   while $200 million   in
1938   dollars in deliveries from current production was
demanded   from Hungary in addition to an   estimated $1
billion   worth   of goods and equipment   dismantled   and
confiscated   in   the immediate postwar   period.   These
amounts   were subsequently reduced to $266 million   and
$134   million   respectively.(14)   The   Soviets   also
claimed   restitution for equipment and goods taken   and
supplies   used by Rumanian and Hungarian troops   during
their   occupation   of   Soviet   territories   during   the
war.(15)   The value of debts to Germany incurred during
the   war   was to be paid to the USSR,   while   each   was
forced   to   renounce any   claims   against Germany.(16)
Occupation costs were an additional common burden.   The
Rumanian economy had the added burden of selling oil to
the   Soviets   at below market prices,   similar   to   the
Polish coal situation.(17)

Bulgaria was spared payment of direct reparations and removal of industrial equipment.(18) Transfer of wealth to the USSR did, however, take place through forced exports of foodstuffs and the establishment of joint stock companies.(19)

Joint stock companies, similar to the SAGs in East Germany, were formed in Hungary, Rumania, Bulgaria, Yugoslavia, and Czechoslovakia. They were unevenly distributed: in Czechoslovakia only the uranium indus- try was operated as a joint company, whereas in Rumania sixteen joint companies dominated raw material and energy production.(20) One calculation of joint compa- nies values the properties thus transformed at $200 million in the GDR, $250 million in Hungary, and $900 million in Rumania, a surprising indication of the extent to which Rumania suffered under this policy, particularly when compared with East Germany.(21) By contrast, joint companies played almost no role in Czechoslovakia, Poland, and Yugoslavia.(22) Between 1954 and 1956 almost all joint stock companies were turned over or sold to the respective governments in concert with the shift in Soviet-East European rela- tions precipitated by the death of Stalin and the East German rising in the summer of 1953.(23) The debts resulting from those transactions were cancelled after the Hungarian and Polish revolts of 1956. The uranium- producing mixed companies were the last to be dis- solved, in late 1956. Only the German Wismut, A.G., remained a joint company after that.

In sum, there was a tremendous transfer of wealth from East Europe to the Soviet Union in the first postwar decade. It is, nevertheless, generally accept- ed that the total transfer of wealth from all of East Europe, excluding the GDR, was much less than that transferred from East Germany. The East European share is estimated to range from one-half to one-eighth of the total.(24) A calculation of the "cumulative grant equivalent" estimates East Europe's sacrifice between 1945 and 1960 at $23.2 billion. Of this, the GDR contributed $19.5 billion, or seven-eighths of the total.(25) A further calculation which balances Soviet aid against economic losses to the USSR by country shows that the GDR accounted for an even greater share of the wealth transferred from East Europe--approxi- mately nine-tenths of the total.(26) Thus, although former enemy and ally alike had to contribute to the economic reconstruction of the Soviet Union, the GDR's share overwhelmed that from all other East European countries combined. This was perhaps a justifiable apportionment of the burden, commensurate with Germany's wartime role. Nevertheless, the magnitude of difference in economic burden demonstrated that satisfying Soviet economic requirements was a primary objective of Soviet policy toward East Germany but not toward East Europe. This had political and economic ramifications which constituted a qualitatively distinct policy.

Trade relations between the USSR and GDR were dominated by reparations transfers until January 1954. East Germany and Czechoslovakia rapidly became the Soviet Union's most important trading partners because of their advanced level of industrial development, skilled labor, and technological know-how. The other East European countries were to varying degrees behind the Soviets in level of economic development and, therefore, were not in a position to contribute to Soviet development. Western restrictions on exports of technology and other products made East Germany that much more important to the USSR.

The reparations burden imposed on the East German economy, particularly the extensive dismantling, contributed significantly to the lag in the GDR's economic recovery compared with the rest of East Europe. Table 19 shows that only East Germany and Hungary failed to reach prewar levels of GNP by 1950.

Table 19
Growth of GNP
(1955=100%)

	Prewar	1950	1955	1960
Bulgaria	68	75	100	142
Czechoslovakia	79	84	100	137
GDR	84	71	100	127
Hungary	80	76	100	123
Poland*	72	79	100	127
Rumania	66	66	100	119

Source: Maurice Ernst, "Postwar Economic Growth in Eastern Europe," in New Direction in the Soviet Economy (Washington, D.C.: Government Printing Office, 1966), p. 880.
*Poland's recovery by 1950 was due to the acquisition of former German territories. Within her old boundaries, she would not surpass prewar GNP.

Other factors such as a low rate of investment hampered
East Germany's recovery. It should also be noted that
the rest of East Europe, with the exception of Czechoslovakia, was not as industrialized as the GDR: Bulgaria and Rumania were the least developed, while
Poland and Hungary occupied a middle ground. The lower
the level of industrialization, the more rapid the rate
of recovery. This was particularly true in East
Europe, where the push for industrialization and development of a full complement of industries began in
1948.

     A comparison of the size and distribution of gross
fixed investment, seen in Table 20, illustrates the
very low rate of investment in the GDR compared with
other East European countries.

Table 20
Gross Fixed Investment

	Years	Total	Ind.	Agr.	Services
			% of GNP		
Bulgaria	1950-54	23.7	10.6	4.1	9.0
	1955-59	27.7	12.1	7.6	8.0
	1960-63	41.5	19.3	11.2	11.2
Czech.	1950-54	23.5	10.6	2.3	10.6
	1955-59	27.3	11.4	4.3	11.6
	1960-63	27.7	12.9	4.4	10.4
GDR	1950-54	14.5	5.8	1.8	6.9
	1955-59	19.4	8.3	2.2	8.9
	1960-63	23.6	11.4	2.9	9.3
Hungary	1950-54	25.9	12.2	3.6	10.1
	1955-59	24.2	11.0	3.9	9.3
	1960-63	27.2	12.0	5.3	9.9
Poland	1950-54	21.2	9.9	2.0	9.2
	1955-59	25.1	11.0	3.2	10.9
	1960-63	28.1	12.5	3.4	12.2

Source: Ernst, "Economic Growth in Eastern Europe,"
p. 890.

The differential reflected not only East Germany's
heavy reparations burden but also the policy emphasizing consumption over investment. The GDR was also
at odds with the others in trends in investment distri-

bution.   Industry's share of investment increased significantly   in   East   Germany,   while in   Bulgaria   and
Czechoslovakia industry's share increased slightly   and
in   Hungary   and Poland it actually declined.(27)   Despite   the increase in industrial investment,   the   GDR
remained   considerably behind the rest of the   bloc   in
industrial   investment   as   a percentage of   GNP   until
1960.

As with investment,   the GDR was a mirror image of
the   rest of the East bloc in the emphasis on   consumption.   East Germany was the only country in East Europe
in which consumption was higher than investment in   the
early 1950s.(28)   It was also the only country in which
consumption grew much faster than GNP at that same time
as seen in Table 21.

Table 21
Growth of Personal Consumption in Relation to GNP

	Ratio of growth rates in percent	
	1951-55	1956-60
Czechoslovakia	31	55
GDR	160	90
Hungary	36	100
Poland	85	84

Source: Ernst, "Economic   Growth in   Eastern   Europe,
p. 886.

The   special   conditions prevailing   in   East   Germany,
i.e.,   the   open border with West Germany and the unresolved   German question,   prescribed this unique   policy.(29)   The emphasis on increasing   consumption,   however, did not translate into a higher level of personal
consumption   for   East Germans compared to   other   East
Europeans.   War   damage   plus reparations brought   the
level of personal consumption per capita in the GDR   in
1950   below   levels   in   Czechoslovakia,   Hungary,   and
Poland.   Not until 1955 were East German levels roughly
equivalent to Czech levels.   By 1960,   the GDR resumed
its   prewar position,   enjoying a higher level of   consumption   than   the other East European   countries.(30)
In   accordance with the emphasis on   consumption,   real
wages   in   the GDR for the same period rose   an   annual
rate of 18 percent, much higher than in the rest of the
bloc.(31)

Socialization of the East German economy, by contrast, proceeded at a markedly slower rate than in the rest of East Europe. Nationalization of the means of production in East Europe took place in essentially two waves. In the former allied countries--Czechoslovakia, Poland, and Yugoslavia--the process began with German and/or Italian assets. In former enemy states, nationalization began in full force after Stalin's split with Tito in a move toward consolidation of the bloc. It is ironic that nationalization of basic industries was imposed most rapidly in Poland and Czechoslovakia because of the German predominance in their economies during the war.(32) Real resistance to nationalization was found only in Czechoslovakia because that was the only country with a significant entrepreneurial class.(33) In East Germany, foreign trade, finance, and businesses owned by Nazis were immediately nationalized. The establishment of SAGs further expanded that sector. But private enterprise was also tolerated for economic as well as political reasons. The evidence of that policy was seen in the relatively high contribution of private business to the total production as late as 1955.(34) It will be recalled that the GDR did not adopt a program for the socialist transformation of the society until the Second Party Conference in 1952, a plan which was officially aborted when the Soviets imposed the adoption of the New Course. Table 22 illustrates the East German lag behind the rest of East Europe in all areas of socialization except transport.

Table 22
Degree of Socialization in East Europe in 1952
(State and Cooperative, in percentages)

	Poland	Czech.	GDR	Hungary	Rumania	Bulgaria
Industry: gross output	99	98	77	97	97	100
Retail trade	93	97	54	82	76	98
Transport	100	96	100	100	85	-
Agriculture	15	43	7	27	16	53
National income	73	88	-	76	-	77

Source: Economic Survey of Europe, 1952, p. 37.

In agriculture, major collectivization drives were begun at various times, but nowhere were they begun as

late as in East Germany.   Collectivization in the   GDR
was not completed until 1960.(35)

   In   economic planning,   the distinction is not   so
clear.   Reconstruction plans were introduced in Czechoslovakia,   Poland,   Hungary,   and   Bulgaria in 1947 for
varying durations.   There was no real planned   economy
in   East   Germany until the second half of 1948 and   no
reconstruction   plan until 1949.(36)   Only Rumania   was
as late in instituting planning.

POLITICAL LAG BEHIND EAST EUROPE

   Because   Germany was carved into zones of   occupation   by   the World War II Allies while expressing   the
intention of restoring a reunited state,   the status of
the   Eastern   Zone was very different   from   the   other
countries   in   East Europe which fell under the   Soviet
sphere,   former enemy and ally alike.   The very nature
of joint occupation and ongoing negotiations for German
reunification, despite obvious difficulties between the
Soviet Union and the Western Allies, made the future of
East Germany and SED leadership uncertain indeed.   The
issue of continuation as a recognized political   entity
did not touch the rest of East Europe in a serious way,
whereas   it   formed   the   core   preoccupation   of   the
Ulbricht wing of the SED.(37) This fundamental difference underlies all the manifestations of East Germany's
political lag behind East Europe in relations with   the
Soviet   Union   and   integration   into   the   East   bloc.

   The   Soviet occupation zone did not become a state
until   October   1949.   This move was followed   by   the
exchange   of diplomatic missions with the Soviet   Union
and other East bloc countries.   By contrast,   the   Soviets had re-established full diplomatic relations with
former   enemy   states of Bulgaria and Hungary in   1945.
No   further   significant change in the GDR's   political
status   appears   to have been   contemplated until   the
summer   events of 1953 dramatized the vulnerability   of
the   regime.   The Soviet Union then undertook a series
of steps designed to enhance the GDR's prestige. In the
fall,   diplomatic missions were upgraded to   embassies;
the   East Europeans rapidly followed suit.   Not   until
March 1954,   however, did Moscow recognize the GDR as a
sovereign state, signifying that the GDR since 1949 had
retained   the character of an occupied zone.   Even the

1954 declaration did not elevate the GDR to a status commensurate with the rest of the bloc. The state of war with Germany was not terminated by the Soviets until January 1955, whereas peace treaties had been signed with Hungary, Rumania, and Bulgaria in 1947.

The most significant boost to East German prestige occurred in September 1955, when a state treaty was signed between Berlin and Moscow officially ending the occupation regime. Relations henceforth were to be based on mutual respect, equality, and noninterference. The treaty reaffirmed the earlier unilateral Soviet recognition of East German sovereignty. A Treaty of Friendship, Mutual Assistance, and Cooperation between the GDR and the USSR was not concluded until June 1964, however, marking the first time that the territorial integrity of the GDR had been guaranteed. Only from that time were East German-Soviet relations on a par with Soviet-East European relations. Parity had been a long time coming. By February 1948, Stalin had concluded Treaties of Friendship with all the East European countries except Albania. Treaties had been signed with Czechoslovakia, Yugoslavia, and Poland during the war and with the ex-enemy states in early 1948. During 1946 and 1947, a series of similar treaties was concluded among the East European states. Thus, at an early date an interlocking network of treaties bound the bloc countries to the Soviet Union and each other.(38) The GDR, on the other hand, was not favored by a Treaty of Friendship with any other East European state until 1967, three years after the treaty with the USSR and two decades after the pattern of treaties was established in East Europe. The delay by the East European states no doubt stems from the deep-seated animosity toward Germany, which SED comrades had not been able to overcome.

Concomitantly, East Germany's integration into the Soviet bloc was delayed. The SED was excluded from the September 1947 meeting in Warsaw at which the Cominform was established by the communist parties of Bulgaria, Czechoslovakia, Hungary, Poland, Rumania, the Soviet Union, Yugoslavia, France, and Italy.(39) The SED's exclusion was particularly significant because the nonruling parties of France and Italy were among the founding members. East Germany was also not included in the Warsaw conference which met in June 1948 to formally oppose the impending fusion of the three West German zones. Nor was the SED a participant in the November 1949 conference of communist parties in Hungary, convened to broaden the base of support for Moscow's Peace Movement and National Front initiatives. Only the founding members of the Cominform, with the exception of Yugoslavia, were in attendance. Further- more, East Germany was not included as a full and equal member of the Council for Mutual Economic Assistance until almost two years after its founding. The Prague Conference of Foreign Ministers in October 1950 marked the beginning of the GDR's regular participation in bloc affairs. The formal integration of the GDR into the Soviet bloc did not begin until after the formation of the two German states.

Even after the GDR's official initiation into the bloc in 1950, East Germany did not enjoy equal status with other East European countries. When the Warsaw Treaty Organization was established in 1955, the GDR, although a founding member, was not integrated militar- ily with the other Pact forces until 1956. And, as previously mentioned, East Germany did not enjoy the full protection of Treaties of Friendship and Mutual Assistance with the entire bloc until 1967.

CONCLUSIONS

In sum, the Kremlin pursued a combination of po- litical and economic policies unique to East Germany in response to the unsettled German question and the open border with the West. These policies expressed a po- litical decision to modify the socialist transformation of the economy and delay political integration of East Germany into the Soviet bloc in order to promote reuni- fication on acceptable terms or use the reunification issue to prevent incorporation of West Germany into the Western camp.

The exception to the restrained quality of the policies which set the GDR apart from the bloc was the reparations policy. This policy underscored a primary interest in Germany as a source of resources needed to rebuild the devastated Soviet economy. The same prior- ity did not hold for East Europe, as was reflected in the difference in economic burdens imposed as well as the early political consolidation of the bloc. This policy, nevertheless, went hand in hand with the poli- cies common to all which served to guarantee availabil- ity of badly needed industrial supplies. Political

control and the reparations policy ensured the supply,
while restructuring the economies provided the assort-
ment of industrial products the Soviet economy required
in some cases and established the economic basis for
socialism in others.   Thus, in this area the GDR and
East Europe received common treatment despite the difference in priority.

     The early exclusion of East Germany from bloc
affairs appears to have been a deliberate policy which
logically accompanied and complemented Soviet efforts
to bring about German reunification on favorable terms
or at least keep open the opportunity for Soviet influence in West Germany.   The partial integration beginning in 1950 really represented a continuation of
the same Soviet interests, modified to respond to
changed conditions.   The Soviets increased emphasis on
securing their position in the GDR in light of Western
movement toward integrating the FRG into its own alliance in order to preclude the threat of a reunited,
anti-Soviet Germany.

     The policies which distinguished East Germany from
the bloc corresponded to its unique status and uncertain future.   Soviet pursuit of varied and often contradictory options in Germany served to keep the GDR
outside the process of transformation in the bloc for
almost a decade.

NOTES

1.   Hugh Seton-Watson, The East European Revolution (New York: Frederick A. Praeger, 1951).

2.   Henry Krisch, German Politics under Soviet Occupation (New York: Columbia University Press, 1974), p. 19.   This was the same period during which Varga's analysis of capitalism's future was being debated, indicating the uncertain propects for socialism in the West and the doubt regarding optimal strategy for dealing with the West.

3.   The SED, however, was not one-dimensional. It was the product of two separate and very different parties.   Sovietization of the party did eliminate former SPD members from critical positions, although parity between former KPD and SPD members was not officially dropped until January 1949.   Some who were considered completely reliable, such as Grotewohl, were maintained in high positions. Even after the transformation of the party and the purge of "Titoists," unanimity did not prevail, as demonstrated in the 1953 challenge to Ulbricht's leadership.

4.   The October 1946 election was a turning point in this development.

5.   Franklyn D. Holzman, International Trade under Communism: Politics and Economics (New York: Basic Books, 1976), pp. 66-67; Alexander Gerschenkron, "Russia's Trade in the Postwar Years," American Academy of Political and Social Science Annals (May 1949), p. 93.

6.   Holzman, International Trade under Communism, p. 74.

7.   United Nations, Economic Commission for Europe, Economic Survey of Europe, 1957 (Geneva: Economic Commission for Europe, 1958), ch. 6, p. 3.

8.   Paul Marer, "Soviet Economic Policy in Eastern Europe," in Reorientation and Commercial Relations of the Economies of Eastern Europe (Washington, D.C.: Government Printing Office, 1974), p. 139; Jan Wszelaki, Communist Economic Strategy: The Role of East-Central Europe (Washington, D.C.: National Planning Association, 1959), p. 69.

9.   Wszelaki, _Communist Economic Strategy_, pp. 69-70.

10.   Ibid., p. 70.

11.   Marshall I. Goldman, _Soviet Foreign Aid_ (New York: Frederick A. Praeger, 1967), p. 6

12.   Ibid., p. 7; Marer, "Soviet Economic Policy in Eastern Europe," p. 140; Nicolas Spulber, _The Economies of Eastern Europe_ (New York: John Wiley & Sons, 1957), pp. 176-78.

13.   Spulber, _Economies of Eastern Europe_, pp. 177-78; Wszelaki, _Communist Economic Strategy_, p. 61.

14.   Marer, "Soviet Economic Policy in Eastern Europe," p. 140.   Deliveries from both countries were worth more than the mentioned dollar values because of the low accounting prices given to deliveries and to the use of 1938 dollars.   Janos Horvath, "Grant Elements in Intra-Bloc Aid Programs," _ASTE Bulletin_ (Fall 1971), p. 8.

15.   Spulber, _Economies of Eastern Europe_, pp. 39-40.   Rumania is estimated to have paid one-third of the $500 million demanded. p. 175.

16.   Marer, "Soviet Economic Policy in Eastern Europe," p. 140; Goldman, _Soviet Foreign Aid_, p. 6. For a detailed discussion of Hungarian and Rumanian deliveries, see Spulber, _Economies of Eastern Europe_, pp. 167-76.

17.   Horvath, "Grant Elements," p. 8.

18.   Marer, "Soviet Economic Policy in Eastern Europe," p. 141; Wszelaki, _Communist Economic Strategy_, p. 71.

19.   Wszelaki, _Communist Economic Strategy_, p. 71.

20.   Ibid., p. 69.

21.   Horvath, "Grant Elements," p. 9.

22.   Erich Klinkmüller and Maria Elisabeth Ruban, _Die wirtschaftliche Zusammenarbeit der Ostblockstaaten_ (Berlin: Duncker & Humbloc, 1959), p. 247.

23.   Ibid.; Goldman, Soviet Foreign Aid, pp. 17-19; Marer, "Soviet Economic Policy in Eastern Europe," p. 142.

24.   Marer, "Soviet Economic Policy in Eastern Europe," p. 142; Wszelaki, Communist Economic Strategy, pp. 68-69; Horvath, "Grant Elements," pp. 14-15.

25.   Marer, "Soviet Economic Policy in Eastern Europe," pp. 143-45, 161. Grant equivalent is defined as the measure of unilateral transfer component of each transaction. p. 143.   These figures do not include uranium shipped by Czechoslovakia and Hungary or Rumanian and Hungarian occupations costs.   They also do not calculate the cost to East European countries of supplying the USSR with products at unfavorable prices with the exception of Polish coal. Figures on East Germany's sacrifices are most complete, which exaggerates its burden slightly. p. 144.

26.   Ibid., pp. 144-45

27.   Maurice Ernst, "Postwar Economic Growth in Eastern Europe," in New Directions in the Soviet Economy (Washington, D.C.: Government Printing Office, 1966), p. 890.

28.   Edwin M. Snell and Marilyn Harper, "Postwar Economic Growth in East Germany: A Comparison with West Germany," in Economic Developments in Countries of Eastern Europe (Washington, D.C.: Government Printing Office, 1970), p. 576.

29.   There was a sharp drop in growth of personal consumption after the Wall was built.

30.   Ernst, "Economic Growth in Eastern Europe," p. 887.

31.   Economic Survey of Europe, 1965, ch. 7, pp. 44-45. Bulgaria's average annual real wage increase for 1953-1956 was 13.3 percent; the USSR's for 1951-1955, 6.8 percent; Rumania's, 4.6 percent; Czechoslovakia's and Poland's were both 1.9 percent and Hungary's was 0.9 percent.

32.   Ibid., 1952, pp. 22, 27; Spulber, Economies of Eastern Europe, pp. 45-87.

33.   Spulber, Economies of Eastern Europe, p. 83. This excludes East Germany.

34.   See Table 7, p. 83.

35.   Poland, of course, remains the exception, which restored agriculture largely to private production.

36.   Economic Survey of Europe, 1952, p. 23; Horst Duhnke, Stalinismus in Deutschland (Cologne: Verlag für Politik und Wirtschaft, 1955), pp. 88-89.

37.   In the early postwar period there were discussions of creating a South Slav Confederation including Yugoslavia, Albania, and Bulgaria and integrating all East European states into the USSR much as Estonia, Latvia, and Lithuania had been absorbed, but the Soviets terminated such proposals at an early date.   The first suggestion had advanced to the stage of negotiation.

38.   Keesing's Contemporary Archives (Bristol: Keesing's Publications Limited) 21, 8 February 1948, p. 9118.

39.   Royal Institute of International Affairs, Documents on International Affairs, 1947-1948 (London: Oxford Univeristy Press, 1952), pp. 122-25.

7
Conclusions

The study of Soviet policy toward the GDR has shown a policy of complexity and ambivalence evolving as Allied relations in Germany and throughout the world changed. Soviet policy was developed to meet the intertwining national security and economic needs of the USSR first and foremost, within the constraints imposed by deteriorating relations with the United States on a considerably weaker Soviet Union. The international environment, the German situation, and Soviet policy toward East Germany interacted dynamically to provide both opportunities for and restraints on the Kremlin.

Any attempt to divine the true intentions of Soviet policy toward Germany must begin with the interdependent goals of the Soviet Union in the postwar period: enhancement of national security and reconstruction of a devastated economy. Stalin went to considerable lengths to conceal the extent of ruin from his Western Allies. The Soviet Union was in no positon to confront the West in a military contest but camouflaged weakness with aggressive posturing. Soviet reparations policy, the rejection of Marshall aid, and the Berlin blockade were all expressions of weakness. With regard to the division of Germany, as has been shown, Soviet policy was generally one of reaction to the progressive steps by the West to integrate West Germany into their alliance. The Soviets had no reason to expect Western aid or cooperation in reaching their goals, given their wartime experiences, particularly the delay of the Second Front, and the duplicitous behavior perceived in the American position toward the USSR between Yalta and Potsdam. The historical basis for mutual fear and distrust was not overcome by war-

time alliance and was only fueled by competing interests in the postwar world.   What the Soviets perceived
as their legitimate security interests, the United
States perceived as communist aggression.

In the extensive Western literature on culpability
for the division of Europe and Germany in the postwar
period, a great deal of attention is devoted to Soviet
violations of the Yalta and Potsdam agreements.   Little, if any, is given Western violations as seen from
the Soviet perspective.   The West essentially abandoned
policies of denazification, demilitarization, and restrictions on war-related industry agreed to by the
World War II Allies.   The West failed to live up to
these agreements in large part because they shifted
their attention and energies from the defeated enemy to
the new adversary, the USSR.   And the two sides had
different notions of what compliance entailed.   That
the West acted out of fear no doubt seemed inconceiv-
able to the Kremlin, given the tremendous imbalance of
power between the two major rivals.   Even granting that
motivation, the actions would appear no less ominous to
the Soviets.

The ambivalence in Soviet policy toward East Germany, heightened by uncertain but deteriorating relations between East and West, was a function of Soviet
pursuit of the greatest possible influence throughout
Germany, which they needed to attain their primary
policy goals.   Factions within the Soviet leadership
disagreed over the critical issue of enhancing Moscow's
influence until the issue was resolved, more by a
combination of circumstances than by decision, in 1955.
Experimentation in Soviet policy was reflected in the
shift from a militant, confrontational strategy to one
of negotiaton and peaceful coexistence after 1948,
marked by the failure of the Berlin blockade and the
demise of Zhdanov.   But the complexity of Soviet policy
is not in a shift from one strategy to another.   It is,
rather, in the internal contradictions of the political
and economic aspects of that policy which were present
until 1955.   Competing interpretations of how best to
extend Soviet influence in Germany permeated Soviet
policy throughout the postwar decade despite the temporary ascendance of one group or another.

The contradictions in Soviet economic policy
toward the GDR have been shown in the juxtaposition of
a harsh reparations policy with policies of moderation
which included emphasis on improved consumption, direct

economic aid, and toleration of private trade and production.   Contradictions in the political sphere were
also present.   Soviet-East German political   relations
and East German integration into the bloc lagged behind
Western policy toward the Federal Republic and Soviet
policy toward the other East European states.   At the
same time, the SED was in the forefront of transformation into a party of the New Type when that change was
dictated by Stalin in 1948.   The role the SED assumed
in East German society was orthodox, yet the Soviets
continually mortgaged the future of the GDR by ongoing
initiatives for German reunification.

     How can these contradictions be understood?   So-
viet policy toward East Germany was dictated by geopolitical facts.   In the immediate postwar period,
Stalin's top priority was to reconstruct the Soviet
economy as a key element of national security.   The
USSR needed to draw on all resources at its disposal in
order to strengthen itself before it could project its
power, even to secure the buffer zone in East Europe.
Thus, Soviet emphasis on reparations in its overall
policy toward East Germany was a pragmatic response to
the situation.   The importance of reparations to the
Kremlin was attested to by the detailed proposal sub-
mitted by the Soviets at the Yalta Conference (the USSR
was the only nation to have prepared one) and the
willingness of the Soviets to compromise in order to
achieve Allied agreement on the issue.   The reparations
policy served to bolster the economic base of the USSR
while cutting potential losses in case East Germany was
"lost."   Orthodoxy of SED organization and societal
role was necessary to provide the instrument for administering Soviet policy in East Germany and guaranteeing
reparations deliveries. At the same time, the moderate
elements of Soviet policy served practical economic
needs by encouraging better economic performance as
well as appealing to East German workers to remain.   In
addition, Soviet moderation in East Germany was appropriate to the unsettled nature of conditions in Germany
as a whole and served to enhance the potential for
favorably influencing West German public opinion.

     The picture of moderation in the GDR was shown
most clearly in the comparison of Soviet policy toward
East Germany with its policy toward the rest of East
Europe.   The combination of less orthodox policies and
the emphasis on reparations which set the GDR apart
indicated that East Germany's future as a member of the
bloc was not secure until all prospects for advanta-

geous reunification were removed in 1955.

Ideologically, the Soviets were undoubtedly always committed to the conversion of East Germany and prefer- ably all of Germany, but realized that they were inca- pable of forcing the issue without jeopardizing their own security. Not only would early sovietization of the Soviet Zone have precluded the extension of Soviet influence throughout Germany and risked Western mili- tary confrontation, it also would have undermined the Soviet claim to extensive reparations. It will be recalled that following the Russian revolution, Lenin denounced the capitalist war and renounced all respon- sibility of the new government for Tsarist debts. A new people's republic in East Germany could conceivably make the same case regarding its responsibility for the acts of the Nazi regime. This ambivalence in Soviet policy toward the GDR exemplified concretely the dilem- ma inherent in the Soviet Union's position after World War II as the head of the international communist movement and as a leading world power. The interests of these two roles were often contradictory and incom- patible.

A reunified, communist Germany appeared beyond realistic calculation following the Berlin blockade. The United States had been moving consistently and determinedly to unite the Western Zones and integrate West Germany into an allinace since 1946, largely in response to a perceived inability to reach any legiti- mate compromise with Soviet interests. Revival of the Rapallo policy by the Kremlin as an acceptable alterna- tive evoked Western intransigence toward the possibili- ty of a reunified, neutral Germany. Although revival of Rapallo may not have been the Soviets' first choice, it was far preferable to any of the other options. It offered the prospect of political and economic access to all of Germany, which the United States found unten- able and refused to seriously consider.

The interplay of political and economic policies over the postwar decade illustrates the inseparability of the two spheres. Power and wealth combine to ensure national security. The contradiction in Soviet goals and policies in East Germany did not divide neatly between politics and economics but rather crossed po- litical-economic lines. For example, national security was sought through the political safeguard of an Allied agreement prohibiting Germany from entering into an alliance directed against any former enemy and by establishing a regime friendly to the Soviet Union in their occupation zone. Elimination of Germany's war-making capability through dismantling of military and related industries as well as general reduction in industrial capacity constituted an economic component of Soviet national security policy. Soviet reparations policy also served the political need of national re-venge for the damage and suffering inflicted by the Nazis.

Simultaneously, the Kremlin pursued a countervail-ing goal of extending their influence throughout Ger-many after the breakdown of the Allied agreement on reparations in the spring of 1946. This goal promoted policies of moderation and restraint in the transforma-tion of East Germany according to the Soviet model compared with Soviet policy in East Europe. Thus, a policy of improving economic conditions in East Germany paralleled a policy of extraction.

The Soviet leadership likewise pursued an economic goal which, while not independent of the other goals, was significant in its own right: reconstruction and development of the Soviet economy through the use of German resources. The requirements of Soviet economic recovery and growth supported both a harsh reparations policy and a policy of moderation in the interest of rejuvenating the East German economy and regaining access to West German resources, industry, and technol-ogy.

In sum, one Soviet goal called forth policies to reduce German economic and political power as much as possible, while competing Soviet interests promoted policies of moderation in order to enhance Soviet in-fluence throughout Germany. These policies were played out in East Germany because of the occupation formula reached at Potsdam and the subsequent falling out among the Allies. The distinction between political and economic goals becomes blurred because economic poli-cies serve political goals and vice versa.

The development and illustration of the tension between competing goals in Soviet policy toward East Germany has provided the evidence for the ambivlent and undecided nature of that policy until the transition to support in the 1953-1955 period.

At first glance, it appears that Soviet policy in Germany was something of a failure. The harsh repara-

tions policy, the fear of Soviet aggression which hastened West German integration into the NATO alliance,
and the adoption of a Soviet style system in the GDR
not only excluded Soviet influence from West Germany
but also limited the economic contribution of the GDR
to the bloc. Or did it? The division of Germany
provided the Soviet Union for many years with one of
its staunchest supporters in the bloc as well as an
economic powerhouse by East European and world standards. The GDR has also served as a valuable conduit
of Western technology to the East bloc by virtue of its
special relationship with West Germany and the European
Economic Community (EEC). In addition, East German
membership in the Soviet bloc eliminated the fear of a
reunited, anti-Soviet Germany and provided the Kremlin
leverage over West Germany because of the Federal Republic's interest in improving ties with the GDR.

At the same time, once the Soviet Union accepted
the status quo in Germany, represented by the Two State
Thesis, Moscow pursued the establishment of diplomatic
relations with West Germany, concluded in September
1955, in order to create economic ties as well as to
open political channels for Soviet influence. Over the
years, Soviet-West German trade had grown immensely,
particularly during the 1970s in the wake of West
German Chancellor Willy Brandt's _Ostpolitik_. In purely
economic terms, West Germany is probably more valuable
to the USSR as a member of the EEC with a highly effi-
cient, progressive, capitalist economy than it might be
as a part of the East bloc. The West German _Ostpolitik_
has created an important network of political and economic ties between East and West Germany and the Soviet
Union in a triad of entangling interests. The GDR
might then be seen at least during the initial stages
of the _Ostpolitik_ as a bargaining chip used by the
Soviets to enhance their influence in West Germany.

Although both Germanies have been a cause of considerable concern to their respective superpower allies
in recent years, the overall situation in Germany would
seem to be acceptable from the Soviet perspective.
West German policies under the Social Democrats had not
assumed a neutral stance, but they were not anti-
Soviet. The West German stake in detente is particularly high, and a political consensus seems to have
been forged among virtually all segments of the population in support of the _Ostpolitik_. Even the new,
conservative West German government under Chancellor
Helmut Kohl has accepted its basic tenets while align-

ing the FRG more closely with the United States.   Relations between the USSR and the FRG have deteriorated in
recent years due to numerous intervening circumstance,
but contrary to the fears of some and hopes of others,
the Kohl government generally has not adopted the anticipated hard-line policies so popular in Washington
toward either the GDR or the USSR, but rather has tried
to promote a relaxation of tensions and restore dia-
logue between East and West.   The fact that Franz Josef
Strauss arranged the largest loan to the GDR ever made
in the period of East German-West German relations
illustrates the extent to which the <u>Ostpolitik</u> had
become a fundamental principle of West German policy.
As a result, West Germany may well remain an important
moderating force in Europe and in the development of
Allied policy toward the Soviet Union which serves to
dilute the resurgent anti-Soviet sentiment in the
United States that began in the last year of the Carter
presidency and has come to full flower in the Reagan
administration.

Appendix A
Protocol of Proceedings of the Crimea Conference

PROTOCOL ON GERMAN REPARATIONS

1. Germany must pay in kind for the losses caused by her to the Allied nations in the course of the war. Reparations are to be received in the first instance by those countries which have borne the main burden of the war, have suffered the heaviest losses and have organized victory over the enemy.

2. Reparations in kind are to be exacted from Germany in three following forms:

a. Removals within 2 years from the surrender of Germany or the cessation of organized resistance from the national wealth of Germany located on the territory of Germany herself as well as outside her territory (equipment, machine-tools, ships, rolling stock, German investments abroad, shares of industrial, transport and other enterprises in Germany, etc.), these removals to be carried out chiefly for purpose of destroying the war potential of Germany

b. Annual deliveries of goods from current production for a period to be fixed

c. Use of German labour

3. For the working out on the above principles of a detailed plan for exaction of reparations from Germany and Allied Reparation Commission will be set up in Moscow. It will consist of three representatives-- one from the USSR, the United Kingdom and the United States.

4.   With regard to the fixing of the total sum of
the reparations as well as the distribution of it among
the countries which suffered from the German aggression
the Soviet and American delegations agreed as follows:

The   Moscow Reparation Commission should   take   in
its   initial studies a a basis for discussion the   suggestion   of the Soviet Government that the total sum of
the   reparation in accordance with the points   (a)   and
(b) of the paragraph 2 should be 20 billion dollars and
that 50% of it should go to the Union of Soviet Socialist Republics.

The   British   delegation was of the   opinion   that
pending consideration of the reparation question by the
.   .   .   Commission no figures of reparation should   be
mentioned.

Source: U.S. Department of State, Foreign Relations of
the United States, Diplomatic Papers: The Conferences
at Malta and Yalta, 1945 (Washington, D.C.: Government
Printing Office, 1955), pp. 978-79.

Appendix B
Protocol of Proceedings
of the Potsdam Conference

WESTERN FRONTIER OF POLAND

Article VIII

The three Heads of Government reaffirm their opinion that the final delimitation of the western frontier
of Poland should await the peace settlement.

The three Heads of Government agree that, pending
the final determination of Poland's western frontier,
the former German territories east of a line running
from the Baltic Sea immediately west of Swinemunde, and
thence along the Oder River to the confluence of the
western Neisse River and along the western Neisse to
the Czechoslovak frontier, including that portion of
East Prussia not placed under the administration of the
Union of Soviet Socialist Republics in accordance with
the understanding reached at this conference and including the area of the former free city of Danzig,
shall be under the administration of the Polish State
and for such purposes should not be considered as part
of the Soviet zone of occupation in Germany.

Source: U.S. Department of State, Foreign Relations of
the United States, Diplomatic Papers: Conference of
Berlin (Potsdam) (Washington, D.C.: Government Printing
Office, 1960), pp.1491-92.

Appendix C
Reparations

The following table details all types of reparations paid by the GDR to the USSR from 1945 until 1960, including dismantling, reparations from current production, and German labor in the GDR. Total reparations in dollars at 1938 prices are estimated at $19.3 billion. (Köhler, Economic Integration, p. 29.)

Reparations Delivered to the Soviet Union
(in RM/DM-O* at current

Year	Capital stock official dismantling	Current Production			
		Direct to USSR	Direct to Red Army	Indirect to Red Army	SAG inventory
1945	2,300.00	2,294.66	746.96	-	-
1946	2,300.00	2,995.21	871.71	-	-
1947	200.00	3,692.10	979.68	-	-
1948	200.00	3,657.81	948.17	-	-
1949	-	3,481.59	925.57	211.40	-
1950	-	3,012.25	911.39	211.40	-
1951	-	2,570.38	1,069.45	211.40	-
1952	-	2,385.59	1,153.31	211.40	500.00
1953	-	2,028.75	997.16	211.40	500.00
1954	-	-	1,440.00		-
1955	-	-	1,440.00		-
1956	-	-	1,440.00		-
1957	-	-	720.00		-
1958	-	-	540.00		-
1959	-	-	-		-
1960	-	-	-		-
Total	5,000.00	26,118.34	15,240.40		1,000.00

Source: Heinz Köhler, Economic Integration in the Soviet Block with an East German Case Study (New York: Frederick H. Praeger, 1965), pp. 25-28.
*DM-O=East German Mark

from East Germany
prices)

Uranium	Subtotal current production	Labor services in GDR	TOTAL
-	3,041.62	290.16	5,631.78
96.00	3,962.92	378.04	6,640,96
413.00	5,084.78	485.06	5,760.84
647.00	5,252.98	501.11	5,954.09
763.00	5,381.56	493.21	5,874.77
1,081.00	5,216.04	477.42	5,693.46
1,594.00	5,445.23	497.14	5,942.37
1,434.00	5,684.30	519.86	6,204.16
1,275.00	5,012.31	456.00	5,468.31
876.00	2,316.00	160.00	2,476.00
750.00	2,190.00	160.00	2,350.00
706.00	2,149.00	160.00	2,309.00
406.00	1,126.00	80.00	1,206.00
350.00	890.00	60.00	950.00
292.00	292.00	-	292.00
250.00	250.00	-	250.00
10,936.00	53,294.71	4,718.00	63,012.74

Appendix D
Summation of Soviet Credits to the GDR, 1945-1960

1949 100 million ruble credit for purchase of fat, grain, agricultural machines and trucks from the Soviet Union at an interest rate of 2 percent per annum

1950 149 million ruble credit for import of meat, butter, vegetable oils, fish, cotton, wool, grain from the USSR at an interest rate of 2 percent per annum

1950- 30 million ruble credit for East German
1951 expenditures on diplomatic missions

1953 485 million ruble credit of which 350 million was to be used for commodity imports from the USSR and Poland. Of this, 231 million was to finance the import of foodstuffs and raw materials agreed to in the special trade agreement of July 1953. 135 million of the total was given in convertible currencies. Entire credit to be paid in 1955 and 1956 at an interest rate of 2 percent per annum

1956 80 million ruble credit in convertible currencies at 2 percent per annum

1957 340 million ruble credit in convertible currencies, repaid in 1959-1960 at 2 percent per annum. An additional 700 million ruble credit issued in September and used in 1958 of which 300 million was in convertible currencies. Repayable in goods from 1961-1965 at 2 percent interest.

1958   Credit   for development of chemical industry;
            amount   not certain but an estimated   minimum
            is 110 million rubles

1959   112   million ruble credit to finance   a
            potassium salt minimg investment

All of these credits were short-term; some of the debts
were later forgiven.

Sources: Heinz Köhler, Economic Integration in the
Soviet Bloc with an East German Case Study (New   York:
Frederick A.   Praeger,   1965), pp. 309-11; United
Nations, Economic Commission for Europe, Economic Sur-
vey of Europe, 1957 (Geneva: Economic Commission for
Europe, 1958), ch. 6, p. 56.

Selected Bibliography

DOCUMENTS

Die Beschlüsse des Westfriedensrates auf seiner Ausserordentlichen Tagung in Berlin vom 1-6 Juli 1952. Berlin: Union Verlag, 1952.

Beziehungen DDR-UdSSR. 1949 bis 1955: Dokumentensammlung. 2 vols. Berlin: Staatenverlag der Deutschen Demokratischen Republik, 1975.

A Decade of American Foreign Policy: Basic Documents. 1941-49. New York: Greenwood Press, 1968.

Deutsches Institut für Zeitgeschichte. Dokumente zur Deutschlandpolitik der Sowjetunion. 3 vols. Berlin: VEB Deutscher Verlag der Wissenschaften, 1957-1968.

Dokumente der Sozialistischen Einheitspartei Deutschlands. vols. 3,4,5. Berlin: Dietz Verlag, 1952-1954.

Dokumente zur Aussenpolitik der Regierung der Deutschen Demokratischen Republik. vols. 1-3. Berlin: Rütter & Loening, 1955-1956.

Dokumente zur Deutschlandpolitik. III Reihe/Band 1. Frankfurt am Main: Alfred Metzner Verlag, 1961.

Elias, Rolf, ed. Die Deutsch-sowietischen Beziehungen. Berlin: Dietz Verlag, 1965.

Hohlfeld, Johannes, ed. Dokumente der deutschen Politik und Geschichte von 1848 bis zur Gegenwart. vols. 6,7,8. Berlin: Dokumenten-Verlag, 1951-1956.

Oppen, Beate Ruhm von, ed. Documents on Germany under Occupation, 1945-1954. London: Oxford University Press, 1955.

National Archives documents. Soviet-German Relations series, Germany: East and West series.

Protokoll der II Parteikonferenz der sozialistischen Einheitspartei Deutschlands. Berlin: Dietz Verlag, 1952.

Protokoll der Verhandlungen des II Parteitages der sozialistischen Einheitspartei Deutschlands. Berlin: Dietz Verlag, 1947.

Protokoll der Verhandlungen des III Parteitages der sozialistischen Einheitspartei Deutschlands. Berlin: Dietz Verlag, 1951.

Protokoll der Verhandlungen des IV Parteitages der sozialistischen Einheitspartei Deutschlands. Berlin: Dietz Verlag, 1954.

Protokoll der III Parteikonferenz der sozialistischen Einheitspartei Deutschlands. Berlin: Dietz Verlag, 1956.

Stulz, Percy, and Thomas, Siegfried, eds. Die Deutsche Demokratische Republik auf dem Wege zum Sozialismus: Dokumente und Materialien. 2 vols. Berlin: Volk und Wissen Volkseigener Verlag, 1959-1961.

U.S. Department of State. Foreign Relations of the United States, Diplomatic Papers: The Conferences at Malta and Yalta, 1945. Washington, D.C.: Government Printing Office, 1955.

_____. Foreign Relations of the United States, Diplomatic Papers: Conference of Berlin (Potsdam). Washington, D.C.: Government Printing Office, 1960.

_____. Treaty of Peace with Japan, 1952.

STATISTICAL SOURCES

Marer, Paul. Soviet and East European Foreign Trade, 1946-1969: Statistical Compendium and Guide. Bloomington: Indiana University Press, 1972.

Statistische Jahrbucher der Deutschen Demokratischen Republik, 1955-1959. Berlin: VEB Deutscher Zentralverlag, 1956-1960.

United Nations, Economic Commission for Europe. Economic Survey of Europe, 1952-1958. Geneva: Economic Commission for Europe, 1953-1959.

UNPUBLISHED WORKS

Baras, Victor. "East Germany in Soviet Foreign Policy: The Objectives of the New Course and the Impact of the Uprising of June 17, 1953." Ph.D. diss., Cornell University, 1973.

Hughes, Richard D. "Soviet Foreign Policy and Germany, 1945-1948." Ph.D. diss., Claremont College, 1964.

Willging, Paul R. "Soviet Foreign Policy in the German Question: 1950-1955." Ph.D. diss., Columbia University, 1973.

BOOKS

Achminow, Hermann. Warum ändern die Sowjets ihren Kurs? Cologne: Rote Weissbächer, 1953.

Der Aussenhandel der sowjetischen Besatzungszone Deutschlands in 1. Halbjahr 1952. Bonn: Bundesministerium für Gesamtdeutsche Fragen, 1953.

Axen, Hermann. Fragen der internationalen Lage und der internationalen Beziehungen der SED. Berlin: Dietz Verlag, 1974.

Backer, John H. The Decision to Divide Germany. Durham, N.C.: Duke University Press, 1978.

Baring, Arnulf, _Uprising in East Germany: June 17, 1953_. Ithaca, N.Y.: Cornell University Press, 1972.

Beletskii, Victor N. _Die Politik der Sowjetunion in den deutschen Angelegenheiten in der Nachkriegszeit, 1945-1976_. Berlin: Staatsverlag der Deutschen Demokratischen Republik, 1977.

Bender, Peter. _East Europe in Search of Security_. Baltimore: Johns Hopkins University Press, 1972.

Berding, Andrew H. _Dulles on Diplomacy_. Princeton: N.J.: D. Van Nostrand Co., 1965.

Bohlen, Charles E. _Witness to History, 1929-1969_. New York: W.W. Norton & Co., 1973.

Böttcher, Bodo. _Industrielle Strukturwandlungen im sowjetisch besetzten Gebiet Deutschlands_. Berlin: Dunker & Humblot, 1956.

Brandt, Heinz. _The Search for a Third Way_. Garden City, N.Y.: Doubleday & Co., 1970.

Brant, Stefan. _The East German Rising_. New York: Frederick A. Praeger, 1957.

Bröll, Werner. _Die Wirtschaft der DDR: Lage und Aussichten_. Munich: Günter Olzog Verlag, 1974.

Brown, Alan A., and Marer, Paul. _Foreign Trade in the East European Reforms_. Bloomington: International Development Research Center, Indiana University, 1972.

Brown, J.F. _Relations between the Soviet Union and Its Eastern European Allies: A Survey_. Santa Monica, Calif.: Rand Corporation, 1975.

Brzezinski, Zbigniew K. _The Soviet Bloc: Unity and Conflict_. Cambridge: Harvard University Press, 1967.

Bundesministerium für Gesamtdeutsche Fragen. _Sowjetische Auffassungen zur Deutschlandfrage, 1945-1953_. Bonn: Deutscher Bundes-verlag, 1953.

Byrnes, James F. _Speaking Frankly_. Westport, Conn.: Greenwood Press, 1974.

Childs, David O. *East Germany*. New York: Frederick A. Praeger, 1971.

_____. *The GDR: Moscow's German Ally*. London: George Allen & Unwin Ltd., 1983.

Churchill, Sir Winston S. *Triumph and Tragedy*. Boston: Houghton Mifflin Co., 1953.

Clay, Lucius D. *Decision in Germany*. Garden City, N.Y.: Doubleday and Co., 1950.

Clemens, Diane Shaver, *Yalta*. New York: Oxford University Press, 1970.

Conquest, Robert. *Power and Policy in the USSR*. New York: Harper & Row, 1961.

Croan, Melvin. *East Germany: The Soviet Connection*. Beverly Hills, Calif.: Sage Publications, 1976.

Dallin, David J. *Soviet Foreign Policy after Stalin*. New York: J.B. Lippincott Co., 1961.

Dauerlein, Ernst, *Deutschland: Wie Chruschtschow es Will: Eine kommentierte Dokumentation*. Bonn: Berto Verlag, 1961.

DDR: Werden und Wachsen Berlin: Dietz Verlag, 1975.

DeSantis, Hugh. *The Diplomacy of Silence: The American Foreign Service, the Soviet Union and the Cold War, 1933- 1947*. Chicago: University of Chicago Press, 1980.

Diepenthal, Wolfgang. *Drei Volksdemokratien: Ein Konzept kommunistischer Machtstabilisierung und seine Verwirklichung in Polen, der Tschechoslowakei und der sowjetschen Besatzungszone Deutschlands*. Cologne: Verlag Wissenschaft und Politik, 1974.

Dietsch, Ulrich. *Aussenwirtschaftliche Aktivitäten der DDR*. Hamburg: Verlag Weltarchiv, 1976.

Divine, Robert A. *Eisenhower and the Cold War*. New York: Oxford University Press, 1981.

Djilas, Milovan. *Conversations with Stalin*. New York: Harcourt, Brace & World, 1962.

Doernberg, Stefan. Kurze Geschichte der DDR. Berlin:
    Dietz Verlag, 1968.

Dornberg, John. The Other Germany. Garden City, N.Y.:
    Doubleday & Co., 1968.

Duhnke, Horst. Stalinismus in Deutschland. Cologne:
    Verlag für Politik und Wirtschaft, 1955.

Edinger, Lewis J. Kurt Schumacher: A Study in Personal-
    ity and Political Behavior. Stanford: Stanford
    University Press, 1965.

Eisenhower, Dwight D. Mandate for Change, 1953-1956.
    Garden City, N.Y.: Doubleday & Co., Inc., 1963.

Die Entwicklung der Freundschaftliche Beziehung zwi-
    schen der DDR und der UdSSR. Berlin: Akademie
    Verlag, 1977.

Erdmenger, Klaus. Das folgenschwere Missverständnis:
    Bonn und die sowjetische Deutschlandpolitik, 1949-
    1955. Freiburg i. Br.: Verlag Rombach, 1967.

Erfurt, Werner. Die sowjetrussische Deutschland-
    Politik. Esslingen: Bechtel Verlag, 1959.

Feis, Herbert. Between War and Peace: The Potsdam Con-
    ference. Princeton, N.J.: Princeton Univeristy
    Press, 1960.

_____. Churchill Roosevelt Stalin. Princeton, N.J.:
    Princeton University Press, 1957.

Fischer, Ruth. Stalin and German Communism: A Study in
    the Origins of the State Party. Cambridge: Harvard
    University Press, 1948.

Förster, Wolfgang. Das Aussenhandelssystem der sowjet-
    ischen Besatzungszone Deutschlands. Bonn:
    Deutscher Bundes Verlag, 1957.

Freier, Udo, and Lieber, Paul. Politische Ökonomie des
    Sozialismus in der DDR. Frankfurt am Main: Makol,
    1972.

Gaddis, John Lewis. The United States and the Origins
    of the Cold War. New York: Columbia University
    Press, 1972.

Gajzago, Oliver von. *Der sowjetische Aussenhandel mit den kommunistischen Ländern*. Berlin: Duncker & Humblot, 1962.

Galkin, I.S. *DDR-UdSSR: Aus zwei Jahrzehnten wissenschaftlicher Zusammenarbeit*. Berlin: Deutscher Verlag der Wissenschaften, 1971.

Garthoff, Raymond L. *Soviet Strategy in the Nuclear Age*. New York: Frederick A. Praeger, 1958.

Gleitze, Bruno. *Ostdeutsche Wirtschaft*. Berlin: Duncker & Humblot, 1956.

Gniffke, Erich W. *Jahre mit Ulbricht*. Cologne: Verlag Wissenschaft und Politik, 1966.

Goldman, Marshall I. *Soviet Foreign Aid*. New York: Frederick A. Praeger, 1967.

Gottlieb, Manuel. *The German Peace Settlement and the Berlin Crisis*. New York: Paine-Whitman, 1960.

Gromyko, A.A., and Ponomarev, B.N. *Soviet Foreign Policy*. Vol II, 945-1980. 4th edition. Moscow: Progress Publishers, 1981.

Grotewohl, Otto. *Die Politik der Partei und die Entwicklung der SED zu einer Partei neuen Typus*. Berlin: Dietz Verlag, 1949.

Hangen, Welles. *The Muted Revolution: East Germany's Challenge to Russia and the West*. London: Victor Gollancz Ltd., 1967.

Harriman, W. Averell. *Peace with Russia*. New York: Simon & Schuster, 1959.

Hartl, Hans, and Marx, Werner. *Fünfzig Jahre sowjetische Deutschlandpolitik*. Boppard am Rhein: Harald Bolot Verlag, 1967.

Hirschman, Albert O. *National Power and the Structure of Foreign Trade*. Berkeley: University of California Press, 1945.

Hofmann, Otto, and Scharschmidt, Gerhard. *DDR: Aussenhandel Gestern und Heute*. Berlin: Verlag die Wirtschaft, 1975.

Höhmann, Hans-Hermann. Zur Wirtschaftsentwicklung in Ostmittel-und Sudosteuropa seit dem II Weltkrieg. Cologne: Bundesinstitut für Ostwissenschaftliche und Internationale Studien, 1967.

Holzman, Franklyn D. International Trade under Communism: Politics and Economics. New York: Basic Books, 1976.

Hull, Cordell. THe Memoirs of Cordell Hull. 2 vols. New York: The Macmillan Co., 1948.

Ionescu, Ghita. The Break-up of the Soviet Empire in Eastern Europe. London: Cox & Wyman Ltd., 1965.

Jahn, Wolfgang. Gemeinsamer Kurs: Sozialistische Ökonomische Integration. Berlin: Staatsverlag der Deutschen Demokratischen Republik, 1972.

Kampfgefährten--Weggenossen: Erinnerungen deutscher und sowjetischer Genossen an die ersten Jahre der antifaschistisch-demokratischen Umwälzung in Dresden. Berlin: Dietz Verlag, 1975.

Kennan, George F. Memoirs: 1925-1950. Boston: Little, Brown and Co., 1967.

Khrushchev, N.S. Khrushchev Remembers. Boston: Little, Brown and Co., 1970.

Kiesewetter, Bruno. Der Ostblock: Aussenhandel des östlichen Wirtschaftsblockes einschliesslich China. Berlin: Safari Verlag, 1960.

_____. Statistiken zur Wirtschaft Ost-und Südosteuropas. Deutsches Institut für Wirtschaftsfor-schung. Berlin: Duncker & Humblot, 1955.

Klein, J. Kurt. Die Bedeutung der DDR für die Sowjetunion. Hildesheim: Gebräder Gerstenberg, 1969.

Klimov, Gregorii Petrovich. Berliner Kreml. Cologne: Kiepenheuer und Witsch, 1951.

Klinkmüller, Erich. Die gegenwärtige Aussenhandelsver-flechtung der sowjetischen Besatzungszone Deutschlands. Berlin: Duncker & Humblot, 1959.

Klinkmüller, Erich, and Ruban, Maria Elisabeth. Die wirtschaftliche Zusammenarbeit der Ostblockstaaten. Berlin: Duncker & Humblot, 1960.

Köhler, Heinz. Economic Integration in the Soviet Bloc with an East German Case Study. New York: Frederick A. Praeger, 1965.

Krause, Heinz. Economic Structure of East Germany and Its Position within the Soviet Bloc. 2 parts. Washington, D.C.: Council for Economic and Industry Research, 1955.

Krisch, Henry. German Politics under Soviet Occupation. New York: Columbia University Press, 1974.

LaFeber, Walter. America, Russia and the Cold War, 1945-1966. New York: John Wiley and Sons, 1967.

Laqueur, Walter. Russia and Germany: A Century of Conflict. Boston: Little, Brown and Co., 1965.

Lemmer, Ernst. Manches war doch anders: Erinnerungen eines deutschen Demokraten. Frankfurt am Main: H. Scheffler Verlag, 1968.

Leonhard, Wolfgang. Child of the Revolution. Clinton, Mass.: Colonial Press Inc., 1958.

_____. The Kremlin since Stalin. New York: Frederick A. Praeger, 1962.

Leptin, Gert. Die deutsche Wirtschaft nach 1945: ein Ost-West Vergleich. Opladen: Leske Verlag, 1971.

Löwenthal, Fritz. News from Soviet Germany. London: Gollanz, 1950.

Ludz, Peter Christian. Deutschlands doppelte Zukunft. Munich: Carl Hanser Verlag, 1974.

_____. Die DDR zwischen Ost und West. Munich: Carl Hanser Verlag, 1977.

Lukas, Richard. Zehn Jahre sowjetische Besatzungsaone. Mainz-Gonsenheim: Deutscher Fachschriften Verlag, 1955.

McCauley, Martin. Marxism-Leninism in the German Democratic Republic. New York: Barnes & Noble, 1979.

McNeal, Robert H. _International Relations among Commu-
    nists_. Englewood Cliffs, N.J.: Prentice-Hall,
    1967.

Marer, Paul, _Postwar Pricing and Price Patterns in
    Socialist Foreign Trade, 1946-1971_. Bloomington:
    International Development Research Center, Indiana
    University, 1972.

Mastny, Vojtech. _Russia's Road to the Cold War_. New
    York: Columbia University Press, 1979.

Medvedev, Roy. _Khrushchev_. Garden City, N.Y.: Anchor
    Press, 1983.

Meier, Christian. _Trauma deutscher Aussenpolitik: Die
    sowjetischen Bemühungen um die internationale
    Annerkennung der DDR_. Stuttgart: Seewald Verlag,
    1968.

Meimberg, Rudolf. _Die wirtschaftliche Entwicklung in
    Westberlin und in der sowjetischen Zone_. Berlin:
    Duncker & Humblot, 1952.

Meissner, Boris. _Russland, die Westmächte und Deutsch-
    land: Die sowjetische Deutschlandpolitik, 1943-
    1953_. Hamburg: H.H. Nölke Verlag, 1953.

Merkl, Peter H. _German Foreign Policies: West and East_.
    Santa Barbara, Calif.: Clio Press, 1974.

Mitzscherling, Peter; Lambrecht, H.; Melzer, M.; et al.
    System und Entwicklung der DDR-Wirtschaft. Berlin:
    Duncker & Humblot, 1974.

Molotov, Viacheslav Mikhailovich. _Problems of Foreign
    Policy: Speeches and Statements, April 1945-Novem-
    ber 1948_. Moscow: Foreign Languages Publishing
    House, 1949.

Moseley, Leonard. _Dulles: A Biography of Eleanor, Allen
    and John Foster Dulles and Their Family Network_.
    York: The Dial Press, 1978.

Mosely, Philip E. _The Kremlin and World Politics_. New
    York: Vintage Books, 1960.

Müller, H., and Reissig, K. _Wirtschaftswunder DDR: Ein
    Beitrag zur Geschichte der Ökonomische Politik der
    SED_. Berlin: Institute für Gesellschaftswissen-

schaften beim Zentralkommittee der SED, 1968.

Nettl, J.P. <u>The Eastern Zone and Soviet Policy in Germany, 1945-1950</u>. London: Oxford University Press, 1951.

Nikolaev, Pavel Alekseevich. <u>Politika Sovetskogo Sojuza v Germanskom Voprose, 1945-1964</u>. Moscow: Izdatel-stvo Nayka, 1966.

Nikolaeva, Alla Valentinova. <u>Ekonomicheskoe Sotrud-nichestvo GDR s SSSR</u>. Moscow: Izdatelstvo Nayka, 1968.

Nolte, Ernst. <u>Der Weltkonflikt in Deutschland: Die Bundesrepublik und die DDR im Brennpunkt des Kalten Krieges 1949-1961</u> Munich: R. Piper & Co. Verlag, 1981.

Obst, Werner. <u>DDR Wirtschaft: Modell und Wirklichkeit</u>. Hamburg: Hoffmann und Campe Verlag, 1973.

Oelssner, Fred. <u>Zwanzig Jahre Wirtschaftspolitik der SED</u>. Berlin: Akademie Verlag, 1966.

Oschlies, Wolf, <u>Aktionen der DDR--Reaktionen in Ost-europa</u>. Cologne: Berichte des Bundesinstituts für Ostwissenschaftliche und Internationale Studien, 1973.

<u>Politische Ökonomie des Sozialismus und ihre Anwendung in der DDR</u>. Berlin: Dietz Verlag, 1969.

Pritzel, Konstantin. <u>Die wirtschaftliche Integration der sowjetischen Besatzungszone Deutschlands in den Ostblock und ihre politischen Aspekte</u>. Bonn: Deutscher Bundes-Verlag, 1962.

_____. <u>Die Wirtschaftsintegration Mitteldeutschlands</u>. Cologne: Verlag Wissenschaft und Politik, 1969.

Pryor, Frederic L. <u>The Communist Foreign Trade System</u>. Cambridge: MIT Press, 1963.

Rausch, Heinz Volker. <u>DDR: Das politische, wirtschaft-liche und soziale System</u>. Munich: Bayerische Landeszentrale für politische Bildungsarbeit, 1973.

Rubinstein, Alvin Z., ed. The Foreign Policy of the
    Soviet Union. New York: Random House, 1972.

Rupp, Franz. Die Reparationen der sowjetischen Be-
    satzungszone in den Jahren 1945 bis Ende 1953.
    Bonn: Bonner Berichte aus Mittel-und Ostdeutsch-
    land, 1954.

Salter, Ernest J. Deutschland und der Sowjetkommunis-
    mus: die Bewährung der Freiheit. Munich: R. Piper,
    1961.

Sandford, Gregory W. From Hitler to Ulbricht: The Com-
    munist Reconstruction of East Germany, 1945-46.
    Princeton, N.J.: Princeton University Press, 1983.

Schenk, Fritz. Im Vorzimmer der Diktatur. Cologne:
    Kiepenheuer & Witsch, 1962.

_____. Magie der Planwirtschaft. Cologne: Kiepenheuer
    & Witsch, 1960.

Schulz, Eberhard, and Schulz, Hans Dieter. Braucht der
    Osten die DDR? Opladen: C.W. Leske Verlag, 1968.

Schumacher, Kurt. Reden und Schriften. Berlin: Grune-
    wald Arami-Verlag GMBH, 1962.

Schwartz, Harry, Eastern Europe in the Soviet Shadow.
    New York: The John Day Co., 1973.

Seton-Watson, Hugh. The East European Revolution. New
    York: Frederick A. Praeger, 1951.

Shulman, Marshall D. Stalin's Foreign Policy Reap-
    praised. Cambridge: Harvard University Press,
    1963.

Smith, Jean Edward. Germany Beyond the Wall. Boston:
    Little, Brown and Co., 1969.

Sokolov, V.L. Soviet Use of German Science and Technol-
    ogy. New York: Research Program on the USSR, 1955.

Sontheimer, Kurt, and Bleek, Wilhelm. The Government
    and Politics of East Germany. New York: St.
    Martin's Press, 1975.

Soviet Views on the Post-War Economy: An Official Cri-
    tique of Eugene Varga's Changes in the Economy of

Capitalism _Resulting_ _from_ _the_ _Second_ _World_ _War_.
Translated by Leo Gruliow. Washington, D.C.:
Washington Public Affairs Press, 1948.

Die _sowjetische_ _Besatzungszone_ _Deutschlands_ _in_ _den_
Jahren _1945_ _bis_ _1954:_ _Eine_ _chronologische_ _Über-_
sicht. Bonn: Bundesministerium für Gesamtdeutsche
Fragen, 1956.

Die _sowjetische_ _Hand_ _in_ _der_ _deutschen_ _Wirtschaft_. Bonn:
Bonner Berichte aus Mittel-und Ostdeutschland,
1952.

Spulber, Nicolas. _The_ _Economies_ _of_ _Communist_ _Eastern_
Europe. New York: John Wiley & Sons, 1957.

Stalin, Iosif. _Economicheskie_ _Problemy_ _Sotsializma_ _v_
SSSR. Moscow: Gosydarstvenoe Izdatelstvo Politicheskoy Literatyri, 1952.

_____. _Über_ _den_ _grossen_ _vaterländischen_ _Krieg_ _der_
Sowjetunion. Berlin: Dietz Verlag, 1951.

Staritz, Dietrich. _Sozialismus_ _in_ _einem_ _halben_ _Land_.
Berlin: Verlag Klaus Wagenbach, 1976.

Stearman, William Lloyd. _THe_ _Soviet_ _Union_ _and_ _the_ _Occu-_
pation _of_ _Austria_. Bonn: Verlag für Zeitarchive,
1961.

Steele, Jonathan. _Socialism_ _with_ _a_ _German_ _Face_. London:
Jonathan Cape, 1977.

Stern, Carola. _Porträt_ _einer_ _bolschewistischen_ _Partei_.
Cologne: Verlag für Politik und Wirtschaft, 1957.

_____. _Ulbricht:_ _Eine_ _politische_ _Biographie_. Cologne:
Kiepenheuer & Witsch, 1963.

Stolper, Wolfgang F. _The_ _Structure_ _of_ _the_ _East_ _German_
Economy. Cambridge: Harvard University Press,
1960.

Studiengesellschaft für Zeitprobleme. _Die_ _sowjetische_
Deutschlandpolitik. 4 parts. Duisdorf bei Bonn:
Studiengesellschaft für Zeitprobleme, 1962-1963.

Thalheim, Karl C., and Propp, Peter D. _Die_ _Entwick-_
lungsziele _für_ _die_ _gewerbliche_ _Wirtschaft_ _der_
sowjetischen _Besatzungszone_ _in_ _der_ _zweiten_ _Fünf-_

jahrplan-Periode. Bonn: Bundesministerium für Gesamtdeutsche Fragen, 1957.

Thomas, Rüdiger. Modell DDR: Kie kalkulierte Emanzipation. Munich: Carl Hanser Verlag, 1972.

Timmermann, Heinz. Konflikt und Krise im Weltcommunismus. Cologne: Berichte des Bundesinstituts für Ostwissenschaftliche und Internationale Studien, 1971.

Toma, Peter, ed. Changing Faces of Communism in Eastern Europe. Tucson: University of Arizona Press, 1970.

Twenty Years External Economic Relations of the GDR. Berlin: Verlag die Wirtschaft, 1969.

Ulam, Adam B. Expansion and Coexistence: The History of Soviet Foreign Policy, 1917-1967. New York: Praeger, 1968.

_____. The Rivals: American and Russia since World War II. New York: Viking Press, 1971.

Ulbricht, Walter. Zur Geschichte der deutschen Arbeiterbewegung. Band V, 1954-1956. Berlin: Dietz Verlag, 1964.

The United States Strategic Bombing Survey. The Effects of Strategic Bombing on German Transportation. Transportation Division. November 20, 1945.

_____. The Effects of Strategic Bombing on the German War Economy. Overall Economic Effects Division, October 31, 1945.

_____. Over-all Report: European War. September 30, 1945.

Weber, Hermann. Von der SBZ zur "DDR". 2 vols. Hannover: Verlag für Literatur und Zeitgeschehen, 1966-1967.

Weber, Werner, and Jahn, Richter W. Synopse zur Deutschlandpolitik, 1941 bis 1973. Göttingen: Verlag Otto Schartz & Co., 1973.

Wettig, Gerhard. Community and Conflict in the Socialist Camp. New York: St. Martin's Press, 1975.

_____. Dilemmas der SED-Abgrenzungspolitik. Cologne:
Berichte des Bundesinstituts für Ostwissenschaftliche und Internationale Studien, 1975.

_____. Die Parole der nationalen Einheit in der so-
wjetischen Deutschlandpolitik, 1942-1967. Cologne:
Berichte des Bundesinstituts für Ostwissenschaftliche und Internationale Studien, 1967.

_____. Das Verhältnis zwischen Sowjetunion und DDR in
der Deutschland-Politik. Cologne: Berichte des
Bundesinstituts für Ostwissenschaftliche und
Internationale Studien, 1974.

Whetten, Lawrence L. Germany, East and West. New York:
New York University Press, 1980.

Wiles, P.J.D. Communist International Economics. New
York: Frederick A. Praeger, 1969.

Wszelaki, Jan. Communist Economic Strategy: The Role of
East-Central Europe. Washington, D.C.: National
Planning Association, 1959.

Zauberman, Alfred. Economic Imperialism: The Lesson of
Eastern Europe. London: Ampersand Ltd., 1955.

_____. Industrial Progress in Poland, Czechoslovakia
and East Germany, 1937-1962. London: Oxford University Press, 1964.

ARTICLES

Ackermann, Anton. "Uber den einzig möglichen Weg zum
Sozialismus." Neues Deutschland (24 September
1948).

_____. "Wohin Soll der Weg Gehen?" Deutsche
Volkszeitung (14 June 1945).

Alton, Thad P. "Economic Growth and Resource Allocation
in Eastern Europe." In Reorientation and Commercial Relations of the Economies of Eastern Europe,
pp. 251-98. Washington, D.C.: Government Printing
Office, 1974.

_____. "Economic Structure and Growth in Eastern
Europe," In Economic Developements in Countries of

Eastern Europe, pp. 41-67. Washington, D.C.: Government Printing Office, 1970.

"Aufruf der Kommunistischen Partei Deutschlands," Tägliche Rundschau (14 June 1945).

Baras, Victor. "Beria's Fall and Ulbricht's Survivial." Soviet Studies 27 (July 1975):381-95.

_____. "Stalin's German Policy after Stalin." Slavic Review (June 1978), pp. 259-67.

Baturin, N.A. "Trade of the Soviet Union with the German Democratic Republic." In Foreign Trade of the USSR with the Socialist Countries, pp. 110-29. New York: U.S. Joint Publications Research Service, 1959.

Bauer, Wilhelm. "Der allgemeine wirtschaftliche Charakter der Zonen." In Wirtschaftsprobleme der Besatzungszonen, pp. 5-22. Berlin: Duncker & Humblot, 1948.

Bender, Peter. "The Special Case of East Germany." Studies in Comparative Communism 2 (April 1969):14-34.

Bernstein, Barton J. "American Military Intervention in the Korean Civil War." In Major Problems in American Foreign Policy, Vol. II, 2nd edition, pp. 440-58. Edited by Thomas G. Paterson. Lexington, Mass.: D.C. Heath & Co., 1984.

Burks, R.V. "The Communist Politics of Eastern Europe." In Linkage Politics, pp. 275-302. Edited by James N. Rosenau. New York: The Free Press, 1969.

Byrnes, Robert F. "Russia in East Europe: Hegemony without Security." Foreign Affairs 49 (July 1971):682-97.

Childs, David. "The Ostpolitik and Domestic Politics in East Germany." In The Ostpolitik and Political Change in Germany, pp. 59-77. Edited by Roger Tilford. Lexington, Mass.: D.C. Heath & Co., 1975.

Chodow, L.G. "Ökonomische und politische Grundlagen der Zusammenarbeit zwischen der DDR und der UdSSR." In DDR-UdSSR: Aus zwei Jahrzehnten wissenschaftlicher Zusammenarbeit, pp. 80-83. Edited by I.S. Galkin.

East Berlin: Deutscher Verlag der Wissenschaften,
    1971.

Conrad, Bernt. "How definitive Is the Oder-Neisse
    Line?" The German Tribune (21 April 1985).

Contius, Wolf Günther. "Der 17. Juni in der Sowjet-
    presse." Osteuropa (August 1953), pp. 269-77.

Croan, Melvin. "Reality and Illusion in Soviet-German
    Relations." Survey (October 1962), pp. 12-28.

Croan, Melvin, and Friedrich, Carl J. "The East German
    Regime and Soviet Policy in Germany." Journal of
    Politics 20 (April 1958):44-63.

Drewitz, Heinz. "Die Wissenchaftlich-technische Revolu-
    tion und ihre Konsequenzen für die wissenschaft-
    lich-technische Zusammenarbeit der DDR und der
    UdSSR." In DDR-UdSSR: Aus zwei Jarhzehnten wissen-
    schaftlicher Zusammenarbeit, pp. 217-23. Edited
    by I.S. Galkin. East Berlin: Deutscher Verlag der
    Wissenschaften, 1971.

"Eastern Germany Since the Risings of June 1953." World
    Today (February 1954), pp. 58-69.

"Engels to Heinz Starkenburg." In Basic Writings on
    Politics and Philosophy: Karl Marx and Friedrich
    Engels, pp. 410-12. Edited by Lewis Feuer. Garden
    City, N.Y.: Doubleday & Co., 1959.

"Erklärung des Zentralsekretariats der SED zur jugo-
    slawischen Frage." Neues Deutschland (4   July
    1948).

Ernst, Maurice. "Postwar Economic Growth in Eastern
    Europe." In New Directions in the Soviet Economy,
    pp. 873-916. Washington, D.C.: Government Printing
    Office, 1966.

Fabritzek, U.G. "Die SED zwischen Moskau und Peking."
    Osteuropa (March 1973), pp. 185-92.

Fairbanks, Charles H., Jr. "National Cadres as a Force
    in the Soviet System: The Evidence of Beria's
    Career, 1949-53." In Soviet Nationality Policies
    and Practices, pp. 144-86. Edited by Jeremy R.
    Azrael. New York: Praeger, 1978.

Finley,   David D.   "A Political Perspective of the Eco-
     nomic   Relations in the Communist Camp." The West-
     ern Political Quarterly (June 1964), pp. 294-316.

Gerschenkron, Alexander. "Russia's Trade in the Postwar
     Years." American Academy of Political and Social
     Science Annals (May 1949), pp. 85-100.

Gilpin,   Robert.   "The Nature of Political Economy." In
     U.S. Power and the Multinational Corporation,
     pp. 20-43. New York: Basic Books, 1975.

Granick,   David. "The Pattern of Foreign Trade in East-
     ern Europe and Its Relations to Economic Develop-
     ment Policy." Quarterly Journal of Economics
     (August 1954), pp. 377-400.

Grosse,   Karl Friedrich.   "Sowjetische Deutschland-
     politik." Aussenpolitik 4 (July 1953):417-25.

"Grundsätze und Ziele der neuen Partei." Tägliche
     Rundschau (23 April 1946).

Hangen,   Welles. "New Perspectives Behind the Wall."
     Foreign Affairs (October 1966), pp. 135-47.

Hardt, John P. "East European Economic Development: Two
     Decades of Inter-relationships and Interactions
     with the Soviet Union." In Economic Developments
     in Countries of Eastern Europe, pp. 5-41. Washing-
     ton, D.C.: Government Printing Office, 1970.

"Harry Hopkins and Josef Stalin Discuss Lend-Lease and
     Poland, 1945." In Major Problems in American For-
     eign Policy, Vol. II, 2nd edition, pp. 289-95.
     Edited by Thomas G. Paterson. Lexington, Mass.:
     D.C. Heath & Co., 1984.

Hartmann, Frederick H. "Soviet Russia and the German
     Problem." The Yale Review (Summer 1954), pp. 510-
     24.

Haubold, Hans. "Zum Stand der Wirtschaftsbeziehungen
     zwischen der DDR und der UdSSR." In Zwei Jahr-
     zehnte deutsch-sowjetische Beziehungen, 1945-1965,
     pp. 145-55. Edited by A. Anderle. Berlin: Staats-
     verlag der DDR, 1965.

Heiland, Burkhard. "Die DDR: Der bedeutendste Aussen-
     handelspartner der Sowjetunion." Deutsche Aussen-

politik (August 1959), pp. 865-72.

Hirsch, Felix E. "The Crisis of East Germany." International Journal (Toronto) 9 (Winter 1954):8-15.

Holzman, Franklyn D. "More on Soviet Bloc Trade Discrimination." Soviet Studies (July 1965), pp. 44-
65.

_____. "Soviet Foreign Trade Pricing and the Question
of Discrimination." Review of Economics and Statistics (May 1962), pp. 134-48

Horvath, Janos. "Grant Elements in Intra-Bloc Aid Programs." The ASTE Bulletin (Fall 1971), pp. 1-15.

Jester, Robert S. "CEMA's Influence on Soviet Policies
in Eastern Europe." World Politics 14 (April
1962):505-19.

Kalweit, Werner. "Ökonomie--Kernstück der Festigung der
DDR." Einheit 5 (1970):619-27.

Kanzig, Helga, and Rolfs, Klaus. "Zur Zusammenarbeit
zwischen der DDR und der UdSSR, 1949-1974." Zeit-
schrift für Geschichtswissenschaft 22 (September
1974):933-49.

Keren, Michael. "The GDR's Economic Miracle!" Problems
of Communism (January-February 1976), pp. 85-92.

Köhler, Heinz. "East Germany's Terms of Trade," Kyklos
16 (1962):286-301.

Korbonski, Andrzej. "Political Aspects of Economic
Reforms in Eastern Europe." In Economic Development in the Soviet Union and Eastern Europe, Vol.
1, pp. 8-41. Edited by Zbigniew M. Fallenbuchl.
New York: Praeger, 1975.

Krisch, Henry. "Politics of the German Democratic
Republic," Studies in Comparative Communism 9
(Winter 1976):389-420.

Kroll, Hans. "Zur politischen Bedeutung des Vertrages
zwischen Moskau und Pankow." Europa Archiv 14
(1964):513-16.

Laeuen, Harold. "Berijas Deutschlandpolitik." Osteuropa (April 1964), pp. 257-59.

Leskov, Vlas. "The Administration of Foreign Trade, 1946-1949." In Soviet Economic Policy in Postwar Germany, pp. 61-77. Edited by Robert M. Slusser. New York: Research Program on the USSR, 1953.

Liebe, Hans. "Agrarstruktur und Ernährungspotential der Zonen." In Wirtschaftsprobleme der Besatzungs- zonen, pp. 22-35. Berlin: Duncker & Humblot, 1948.

Livingston, Robert G. "East Germany between Moscow and Bonn." Foreign Affairs, January 1972, pp. 297-309.

McCauley, Martin. "USSR-GDR: Thirty Years of Friend- ship." Soviet Analyst (11 October 1979), pp. 4-5.

Mair, John. "Four Power Control in Austria." Survey of International Affairs, Vol. 22, pp. 269-379. London: Oxford University Press, 1956.

"Manifest an das deutsche Volk." Neues Deutschland (23 April 1946).

"Männer und kräfte des Politbüros." PZ Archiv nos. 4,5,7, 1951.

Mansbach, Richard W. "Bilateralism and Multilateralism in the Soviet Bloc." International Organization 22 (Spring 1970):371-80.

Marer, Paul. "Soviet Economic Policy in Eastern Europe." In Reorientation and Commercial Relations of the Economies of Eastern Europe, pp. 135-63. Washington, D.C.: Government Printing Office, 1974.

Mastney, Vojtech. "The Cassandra in the Foreign Commis- sariat." Foreign Affairs (January 1976), pp. 366- 76.

Meissner, Boris. "Sowjetrussland und der Ostblock: Hegemonie oder Imperium?" Europa Archiv (10 May 1962), pp. 285-306.

_____. "Der Sturz Berijas." Osteuropa (August 1953), pp. 282-85.

Mendershausen, Horst. "Mutual Price Discrimination in Soviet Bloc Trade." The Review of Economics and Statistics (November 1962), pp. 493-96.

_____. "The Terms of Soviet-Satellite Trade: A Broad-
ened Analysis." The Review of Economics and Statistics (May 1960), pp. 152-63.

_____. "Terms of Trade Between the Soviet Union and
Smaller Communist Countries, 1955-1957." The Review of Economics and Statistics (May 1959), pp.
106-18.

Mosely, Philip E. "Dismemberment of Germany." Foreign
Affairs (April 1950), pp. 487-98.

_____. "The Occupation of Germany." Foreign Affairs
(July 1950), pp. 580-604.

Nettl, J.P. "German Reparations in the Soviet Empire."
Foreign Affairs (March 1951), pp. 300-7.

Neumann, Franz L. "Soviet Policy in Germany." American
Academy of Political and Social Science Annals
(May 1949), pp. 165-79.

Nevsky, Viacheslav. "Soviet Agricultural Policy in
Eastern Germany." In Soviet Economic Policy in
Postwar Germany, pp. 87-126. Edited by Robert M.
Slusser. New York: Research Program on the USSR,
1953.

Orlov, N. "Deutschland en einem geschichtlichen Wendepunkt." Tägliche Rundschau (1 May 1952).

Osten, Walter. "Die Deutschlandpolitik der Sowjetunion
in den Jahren 1952-53." Osteuropa (Stuttgart)
(January 1964), pp. 1-13.

Petrov, Vladimir. "Eastern Europe, a Battleground."
Orbis 15 (Summer 1971):697-707.

Pieck, Wilhelm. "Der demokratische Weg zur Macht."
Tägliche Rundschau (23 April 1946).

Rakowska-Harmstone, Teresa. "Socialist Internationalism
and Eastern Europe--A New Stage." Survey (Winter
1976), pp. 38-54.

Rakowski, Horst. "Zu einigen Aspekten des Freund-
schaftsvertrages und der Arbeitsweise der parität-
ischen Regierungskommission für ökonomische und
wissenschaftlich-technische Zusammenarbeit DDR-
UdSSR." In DDR-UdSSR: Aus zwei Jahrzehnten wissen-

schaftlicher Zusammenarbeit, pp. 223-29. Edited by
I.S. Galkin. East Berlin: Deutscher Verlag der
Wissenschaften, 1971.

Richert, Ernst, "Zwischen Eigenständigkeit und Dependenz." Deutschland Archiv (September 1974),
pp. 955-82.

Rudolph, Vladimir. "The Administrative Organization of
Soviet Control." In Soviet Economic Policy in
Postwar Germany, pp. 18-60. Edited by Robert M.
Slusser. New York: Research Program on the USSR,
1953.

Schenk, Fritz, and Lowenthal, Richard. "Soviet Goods
vs. Hard Goods." New Leader (5 January 1959),
pp. 6-8.

_____. "Behind the Economic Crisis of 1956." New
Leader (12 January 1959), pp. 16-8.

Schulz, Eberhard. "Die DDR als Element der sowjetischen
Westeuropa-Politik." Europa Archiv (25 December
1972), pp. 835-43.

Schulz, Hans-Dieter. "Moskaus wichtigster Partner: Die
Stellung der DDR im Ostblock." Europa Archiv (10
November 1964), pp. 785-94.

Schuster, Rudolf. "Die Scheinkonföderation als Nahziel
der sowjetischen Deutschlandpolitik." Europa
Archiv (20 June 1959), pp. 349-68.

Shell, Kurt L. "Totalitarianism in Retreat: The Example
of the DDR." World Politics (October 1965),
pp. 105-17.

Smith, Jean Edward. "The Red Prussiansism of the German
Democratic Republic." Political Science Quarterly
82 (September 1967):368-85.

Snell, Edwin M. "East European Economies Between the
Soviets and the Capitalists." In East European
Economies Post Helsinki, pp. 12-52. Washington,
D.C.: Government Printing Office, 1977.

_____. "Economic Efficiency in Eastern Europe." In
Economic Developments in Countries of Eastern
Europe, pp. 240-96. Washington, D.C.: Government
Printing Office, 1970.

Snell, Edwin M., and Harper, Marilyn. "Postwar Economic
    Growth in East Germany: A Comparison with West
    Germany." In Economic Developments in Countries of
    Eastern Europe, pp. 558-96. Washington, D.C.:
    Government Printing Office, 1970.

"Soviet Policy and the German Problem." World Today
    (July 1959), pp. 269-77.

Spittmann, Ilse. "East Germany: The Swinging Pendulum."
    Problems of Communism (July-August 1967), pp. 14-
    20.

Stent, Angela. "The USSR and Germany." Problems of
    Communism (September-October 1982), pp. 1-24.

Suranyi-Unger, Theo. "Staatliche und Private Auf-
    wendungen in Osteuropa." Osteuropa Wirtschaft 1
    (May 1956):115-23.

Tarle, E. "The Possible and the Impossible." New Times
    21 (21 May 1952):6-9.

Thalheim, Karl C. "Die sowjetische Besatzungszone
    Deutschlands." In Die Sowjetisierung Ost-Mittel-
    europa, pp. 333-71. Edited by Ernst Birke. Frank-
    furt am Main: Alfred Metzner Verlag, 1959.

Tulpanov, Sergei I. "Die Rolle der SMAD bei der Demo-
    kratisierung Deutschlands." Zeitschrift für
    Geschichtswissenschaft 2 (1967):240-52.

"Über die sozialdemokratische Ideologie der Gruppe
    Zaisser-Herrnstadt." Neues Deutschland (22 August
    1953).

Ulbricht, Walter. "Das Widererstehen des deutschen
    Imperialismus." Einheit (June 1951), pp. 602-23.

Vasjanin, Jurij L. "Die Entwicklung der ökonomische
    Zusammenarbeit zwischen der DDR und der UdSSR."
    Deutsche Aussenpolitik 18 (September-October
    1973):1073-88.

Wiles, P.J.D. "Economic War and the Soviet Type Econo-
    my." Osteuropa Wirtschaft (March 1965), pp. 27-42.

Winston, Victor. "The Soviet Satellites--Economic Lia-
    bility?" Problems of Communism (January-February
    1958), pp. 14-20.

Wolfe, Thomas W. "The Soviet Union's Strategic Stake in the GDR." World Today (August 1971), pp. 340-49.

Wszelaki, Jan. "Economic Developments in East-Central Europe, 1954-59." Orbis 4 (Winter 1961):422-51.

Wyschka, Gerhard. "Die Bedeutung der Aussenwirtschaftsbeziehungen der DDR mit den sozialistischen Ländern." Deutsche Aussenpolitik (October 1968), pp. 1185-93.

Yershov, Vassily. "Confiscation and Plunder by the Army of Occupation." In Soviet Economic Policy in Postwar Germany, pp. 1-14. Edited by Robert M. Slusser. New York: Research Program on the USSR, 1953.

Yerusalimsky, A. "The Bonn Compact and the Lessons of German History." New Times 23 (4 June 1952):6-10.

Zyzniewski, Stanley, J. "Economic Perspectives in Eastern Europe." Political Science Quarterly 75 (June 1960): 201-28.

_____. "Soviet Foreign Economic Policy." Political Science Quarterly 73 (June 1958):206-33.

Index

ABOUT THE AUTHOR

ANN L. PHILLIPS, a Visiting Lecturer of Government, Smith College, specializes in Soviet-East European relations.